Fantasies of Neglect

The Rutgers Series in Childhood Studies

The Rutgers Series in Childhood Studies is dedicated to increasing our understanding of children and childhoods, past and present, throughout the world. Children's voices and experiences are central. Authors come from a variety of fields, including anthropology, criminal justice, history, literature, psychology, religion, and sociology. The books in this series are intended for students, scholars, practitioners, and those who formulate policies that affect children's everyday lives and futures.

Edited by Myra Bluebond-Langner, Board of Governors Professor of Anthropology, Rutgers University and True Colours Chair in Palliative Care for Children and Young People, University College London, Institute of Child Health.

Advisory Board
Perri Klass, New York University
Jill Korbin, Case Western Reserve University
Bambi Schieffelin, New York University
Enid Schildkraut, American Museum of Natural History and Museum for African Art

Fantasies of Neglect

Imagining the Urban Child
in American Film and Fiction

PAMELA ROBERTSON WOJCIK

Rutgers University Press

New Brunswick, New Jersey, and London

Library of Congress Cataloging-in-Publication Data
Names: Wojcik, Pamela Robertson, 1964– author.
Title: Fantasies of neglect : imagining the urban child in American film and fiction / Pamela Robertson Wojcik.
Description: New Brunswick, New Jersey : Rutgers University Press, 2016. | Series: The Rutgers series in childhood studies | Includes bibliographical references and index.
Identifiers: LCCN 2016003240| ISBN 9780813564487 (hardcover : alk. paper) | ISBN 9780813564470 (pbk. : alk. paper) | ISBN 9780813564494 (e-book (web pdf)) | ISBN 9780813573625 (e-book (epub))
Subjects: LCSH: City children in motion pictures. | City and town life in motion pictures. | Motion pictures—United States—History—20th century. | American fiction—20th century—History and criticism. | City children in literature. | City and town life in literature.
Classification: LCC PN1995.9.C45 W58 2016 | DDC 813/.5093523—dc23
LC record available at https://lccn.loc.gov/2016003240

A British Cataloging-in-Publication record for this book is available from the British Library.

Visit our website: http://rutgerspress.rutgers.edu

Manufactured in the United States of America

This book is dedicated to Sam and Ned.
I hope I neglected you enough.

Contents

Acknowledgments

This book would not exist without the generous support of numerous people and institutions. The Institute for Scholarship in the Liberal Arts at the University of Notre Dame provided me with a summer stipend and subvention. I was able to present parts of the book at the "Cinema and the Legacies of Critical Theory International Conference in Memory of Miriam Hansen," the International Association of Media and History 2013 conference on Childhood and Media, the 2013 Society for Cinema and Media Studies conference, Northwestern University, the Chicago Film Seminar, and the "Fun with Dick and Jane: Gender and Childhood" conference at the University of Notre Dame. Portions of chapter 1 were published as "Vernacular Modernism as Child's Play," *New German Critique* 41, no. 2 122 (Summer 2014): 87–99. Portions of chapter 2 are in "Little Orphan Annie as Streetwalker," in *Representations of Childhood in Comics*, edited by Mark Heimermann and Brittany Tullis (Austin: University of Texas Press, 2016). Garth Jowett encouraged me to look at Paul Cressey's "Boys, Movies, and City Streets." Steve Elworth led me to key information about River House. Nathaniel Myers, Robinson Murphy, and Paula Massood each read portions and gave me advice. Karen Lury and Marah Gubar both provided inspiration through their own perceptive work on childhood and gave me detailed notes and guidance for shaping the final manuscript. Barbara Green and Jim Collins, my colleagues at the University of Notre Dame, deserve special mention. They each read the manuscript in full, as each chapter was drafted. This book would not have been possible without their generosity, insights, and advice. Special thanks to Leslie Mitchner, at Rutgers University Press, for her enthusiasm for the project, her acumen, and her perseverance. Finally, thanks to Rick Wojcik for giving me time and space to work, for supporting my twisted Shirley habit, and for carrying on the adventure of raising urban kids with me.

Fantasies of Neglect

Introduction

Mapping the Urban Child

"One day Lori said to himself, 'I want to see Times Square.'" So begins the 1963 children's book *How Little Lori Visited Times Square*. Written by Amos Vogel and illustrated by Maurice Sendak, *How Little Lori Visited Times Square* is a charming picture book in which Lori, a boy about six or eight years old, repeatedly tries and fails to get to Times Square by himself. Lori walks to Eighth Street; takes the wrong subway and goes to South Ferry; takes the wrong bus and arrives at 242nd Street; takes a taxi but, because he has no fare, gets kicked out; takes the elevated train to Queens, then a boat to Staten Island, a helicopter to Idlewild, a horse-and-wagon ride to Central Park, and a pony ride that only goes in a circle. He swims with sea lions at the zoo and rides an elevator to the top of Macy's, but he cannot get to Times Square. Finally, he is carried on a very, very slow turtle that promises to take him to Times Square. The narrator reveals, "And this was four months ago—and nobody has heard from them since."

Compare Lori's narrative to what happened in 2008 when journalist Lenore Skenazy published an article in the *New York Sun* entitled, "Why I Let My 9 Year Old Ride the Subway Alone." Skenazy explained that her son, Izzy, had been begging her to let him do just that and that she had finally relented. Giving him a subway map, a Metro Card, a $20 bill, and quarters for a pay phone (but not a cell phone), she unleashed him at

Bloomingdale's and allowed him to find his way home, taking the Lexington Avenue subway and then the Thirty-Fourth Street cross-town bus. Her article suggested that parenting had become overprotective and anxious, and she detailed the many shocked and negative reactions she got from parents, who could not imagine letting their child roam free in the city. Skenazy's article stirred a major controversy and led to a slew of follow-up articles—such as one in the *Toronto Globe and Mail* that asked whether sending your child alone on the subway constituted child abuse (Dube)—and numerous TV appearances, notably on NBC's *Today Show*, where Ann Curry asked in a teaser if she was a "really bad" mom and after which she was dubbed "America's Worst Mom." This experience led Skenazy to launch a blog and later write a book with the moniker *Free-Range Kids*.[1]

How Little Lori Visited Times Square portrays a child who is mobile and independent in an urban setting. Lori manages to make his way all over New York, even leaving Manhattan for Queens. Lori is lost but not endangered. He encounters adults, animals, and various modes of transport and traffic. He finds busy commercial districts, residential areas, parks, and water. When he comes across a familiar and familial site, his uncle's house in Queens, he chooses not to stop. His story ends with him lost, for four months. But rather than a cautionary tale, we are told in a bit of authorial editorializing that this is "a very funny book and you should not read while drinking orange juice, or you will spill it!" Skenazy's story is similarly one of a young boy moving freely through the city. Izzy, unlike Lori, manages his journey perfectly well. But instead of a constructive tale of a boy gaining independence and showing competence, Izzy's story is widely viewed as a story of maternal failure and abandonment. His taking the subway, and doing it safely, registers as potential child abuse.

Obviously, one story is a fiction meant to amuse, and the other is a nonfiction account of real-world events. But more than the difference in genre, the two stories mark changing views of the urban child. Between *How Little Lori Visited Times Square* and *Free-Range Kids* a lot has changed in terms of how we imagine the relationship between children and the city. Never an uncomplicated relationship, the idea of the child roaming the city, once a rather commonplace model, now seems extraordinary, almost unthinkable.

When Jane Jacobs wrote her famous 1961 book, *The Death and Life of Great American Cities*, she took for granted that the city was and should be a space filled with children. The presence of children was so common as to be viewed as something of a nuisance by city planners and pedestrians. The question was not whether children existed in the city but whether they should be allowed to play in the streets and on the sidewalks or be relegated to playgrounds and parks, both for their own safety and as a way to regulate their actions. The child was viewed as potentially "both at risk in [the] public sphere, and as a cause of trouble in public space" (Valentine 1). In this vein the playground movement started in Cambridge, Massachusetts, in the early twentieth century, as a way of correcting antisocial behavior or of training among urban children, especially working-class and immigrant children (Valentine 4). In contrast to that movement, and arguing for a model of urbanism defined by density, diversity, and use, Jacobs favored letting children play on sidewalks, under the watchful eyes of neighborhood adults, including not just mothers but male and female workers and passers-by. In this way, she believed, children would be both safe and assimilated into manners and proper behavior. Playgrounds, she argued, were too isolating and likely to lead children into trouble.

Jacobs describes a world familiar to most of us mainly from early twentieth-century films and novels—kids playing stickball and hopscotch on the sidewalk, sitting on stoops, going to the candy store, throwing balls across the street, tormenting shopkeepers, mixing it up with other kids, and chasing fire trucks down the block. The historical presence of children in city streets, however, is real and documented, not just something that exists in fictions. To get an idea of how densely populated by children city streets once were, consider these figures: in 1911 the Juvenile Protection Association in Chicago counted the number of children playing on city streets and sidewalks. One three-block stretch on Halsted Street between Taylor Street and Twelfth—the neighborhood where Jane Addams and Ellen Gates Starr located Hull House—had 418 kids playing in the afternoon and 744 at night (Hoben 458). According to the same statistics, on a seven-block stretch they found 2,299 children playing in the afternoon and then 3,687 in the evening.

This image of a city block filled with children contrasts sharply with our twenty-first-century milieu, and it was transforming even as Jacobs wrote. As early as 1967, Albert Eide Parr noted that, because of increased traffic, the child's mobility and "daily orbit" had been sharply curtailed (4). As Helen Penn remarks, "One of the most significant changes in the urban landscape over the last century has been the disappearance of children" (180). It is not the case that there are not kids living in cities; rather, they do not inhabit public city space in the same way as before. In the modern-day scenario the increased regulation of children's lives, under what has come to be called "helicopter parenting,"[2] has led to what Gill Valentine refers to as a "retreat from the street" (72). A number of factors, including the expansion of the suburbs, widening car ownership, increased traffic, and increased (if false) perceptions of stranger danger have led parents to circumscribe children's activities more tightly, permitting children to roam less freely and instead be driven from place to place (Hillman, Adams, and Whitelegg; Valentine). In addition to rising obesity rates among children, this highly circumscribed life has led to what has been described as the "islanding" of children's activities, in regulated zones and places, such as playgrounds, care centers, children's gyms, schools, craft centers, museums, and similar venues (Zeiher, "Shaping Daily Life" 66). Driven in cars from spot to spot, "children have . . . disappeared from public view" (Penn 180) and from the public sphere (Zeiher, "Children's Islands" 143). As opposed to when Jacobs wrote, now, "being out on the streets *per se* labels children as coming from poor and uncaring families" (Penn 181).

Children's lack of mobility and absence from urban streets has a few different consequences. First, because they lack freedom to move about in public space, contemporary children have less spatial knowledge than previous generations and a dislocated sense of space, based on car trips rather than walking (Valentine 74). Furthermore, the less knowledge of place they have, the less opportunity they have for certain kinds of identity formation. As Pia Christensen suggests, "children's coming to understand themselves takes place through their experience, memories, and use of the house, street, neighborhood, village, and city at large" (15). A more circumscribed spatial experience precludes certain kinds of knowledge and experience, such as how to handle an encounter with a stranger, when to cross the street safely, or how to maneuver a bike through traffic. Children are more protected from risk and thus more fearful. In addition, by virtue of being kept off city streets, children are judged less capable and thus seemingly more in need of tight regulation. Valentine argues that at the heart of concerns about children's safety in public space is a "belief that children are not competent to negotiate space alone" (55). Crucially, children's absence from public space transforms the character of that space. Insofar as public space is meant to be open and available, and a site of encounter among various, even undesirable, people, the loss of children in public means that children are no longer exposed to encounters with a range of people, and many adults are not necessarily encountering children (Valentine 97; Parr 4). For Valentine, public space is no longer public, insofar as it excludes and marginalizes young people. Concomitantly, she argues, young people are not viewed as legitimate members of the public (97).

It is tempting to read *How Little Lori Visited Times Square* and *Free-Range Kids* as a "then" and "now," a story from some long-gone period of a more free urban childhood and an account from our contemporary model of constrained childhood. And that is partly true. But if we look at present-day representations, something like Lori's urban mobility still exists, if only on the level of representation. A child today could read *The Invention of Hugo Cabret*, Brian Selznick's marvelous 2007 graphic novel, which was adapted into the film *Hugo* by Martin Scorsese in 2011, about an orphan boy secretly living in a Paris train station and maintaining the clocks. Likewise, Selznick's ambitious 2011 graphic novel, *Wonderstruck*, tracks two separate stories set fifty years apart. In parallel stories, Rose, a deaf girl in the 1920s, and Ben, a deaf boy in the 1970s, each run away and travel to the American Museum of Natural History in New York seeking a lost parent. *When You Reach Me* (2010), by Rebecca Stead, traces the adventures of two kids, Miranda and Sal, on Manhattan's Upper West Side in the late 1970s. The enormously popular *Magic Tree House* series of books by Mary Pope Osborne—fifty-three books and counting, since 1992—trades on the premise that two suburban Pennsylvania kids can travel through time and space to solve mysteries for Merlin the Magician and his sister, Morgan Le Fay. Recent films aimed at kids with an urban setting include Disney's *The Princess and the Frog* (Ron Clements and John Musker 2009), in which young Tiana navigates Jazz Age New Orleans; *Hotel for Dogs* (Thor Freudenthal 2009), in which three orphaned kids in foster care secretly take over an abandoned New York City hotel and turn it into a hotel for abandoned dogs; and *Little Manhattan* (Mark Levin 2005), in which a pair of fifth graders travel around the Upper West Side and even into another borough, on their own.

Texts aimed at adults also continue to tout the image of the urban child. In addition to *Hugo*, consider *Extremely Loud and Incredibly Close*. In both Jonathan Safran Foer's 2005 novel and its 2011 film adaptation (Stephen Daldry) the child protagonist, Oskar, wanders New York City largely by himself, ringing the doorbells of people named Black, whom he mistakenly believes hold the key to understanding his father's life prior to his death on 9/11. In Cathleen Schine's *Fin & Lady: A Novel* (2013) Fin, an eleven-year-old boy, is orphaned and then uprooted from a farm in Connecticut to live with his free-spirited half-sister in New York's Upper East Side and then Greenwich Village in the 1960s.

The majority of these texts are set in the past and thus potentially represent a lost way of life infused with nostalgia. In a sense, scenes of children's urban life are as remote from many kids' contemporary experience as is Laura Ingalls Wilder's *Little House on the Prairie* (1935). None, however, mark the difference between "then" and "now" through commentary. Instead, they naturalize children's mobility in urban space as a given. Furthermore, the reader or viewer may be less concerned with the "then" of the representation—the book or film's setting—than with the "now" of reading. These texts are experienced in conjunction with one another, and they exist in the "now." In addition, these texts exist alongside classic children's texts and films with urban settings that are still being read and viewed today, such as *How Little Lori Visited Times Square*, Sydney Taylor's *All of a Kind Family* (1951), Kay Thompson's *Eloise* (1955), Ezra Jack Keats's *Snowy Day* (1962), Eleanor Estes's *The Alley* (1964), Louise Fitzhugh's *Harriet the Spy* (1964), and its film adaptation (Bronwen Hughes 1996), or E. L. Konigsburg's whimsical 1967 children's book, *From the Mixed-Up Files of Mrs. Basil E. Frankweiler*, along with famous musical film adaptations such as *Oliver!* (Carol Reed 1968), *Annie* (John Huston 1982; Will Gluck 2014), and *Mary Poppins* (Robert Stevenson 1964). Some of these, originally set in their moment of production, have become historical artifacts, removed in time from the period of reception but nonetheless experienced in the "now."

Instead of a strict chronologic relationship, therefore, in which we think of a "then" and "now" in which kids did "then" and do not "now" exist in urban settings, these texts invite us to consider the *image* of the urban child as existing diachronically, across a span of time, with changes related to the historical context of production and reception. While the historical conditions of children's mobility in the city have changed dramatically, these texts point to an enduring *fantasy* of mobility.

To be sure, we can think of the urban child as a residual aspect of the culture. In *Marxism and Literature* Raymond Williams argues that at any given moment culture consists not only of the dominant but also of residual effects of seemingly outmoded, but nonetheless active, aspects of the culture and, at the same time, emergent elements that offer a substantial alternative to the dominant. Thus, we can consider representations of the urban child as carrying a residual urbanism against the dominant suburbanization and "islanding" of children. But, where the residual culture can seem outmoded (think VHS, cassette tapes), and dated, part of a "then," it can also be revitalized and become emergent or newly dominant (think men's hats, vinyl records, the mustache, food localism). The figure of the urban child seems to present a counter to or critique of the current state of childhood, to represent a "then" that is desired and desirable in the "now," and perhaps into the future.

Rather than mere nostalgia, these representations of urban childhoods can be taken as producing an abiding imaginary of the urban child. Whether representing the present or the past, they are always already constructing what John Gillis refers to as a "mythical landscape of childhood." As Gillis suggests, mythical landscapes can continue to exist when literal landscapes have been transformed:

> Mythical geography consists of the mental maps that orient us in the world where physical landmarks and signposts are often obscure or absent. The mythical landscapes of childhood constitute a kind of parallel universe, one that bears a similarity to physical geography but has the virtue of being invulnerable to both temporal and spatial changes that are constantly transforming the real world. The mythical landscapes of childhood reassure adults that things are what they wish them to be. It is a geography to live *by* as opposed to a geography to live *in*. It does not exist on maps but is present in literature, in art and photography, and is alive in popular culture. (317)

Existing at the level of representation and discourse, the mythical landscape of urban childhood is no *less* real now, for being absent from real life; nor was it *more* real when it more closely mirrored (some) children's lives in, say, the 1960s or the 1930s. These representations both reflect and produce the urban and the child, as intertwined ideas and ideals. They present a philosophy of, or reflection on, urbanism and the child. Looking to these representations, we can think about the values ascribed to urban childhood, what has been lost as children have left urban space and what can be regained or reimagined.

Rural vs. Urban

Stereotypically, the ideal childhood landscape was historically imagined as rural, "piping down the valleys wild, rather than roaming the city streets" (Ward 5). In *The Country and the City* Raymond Williams submits, "We have seen how often an idea of the country is an idea of childhood: not only the local memories, or the ideally shared communal memory, but the feel of childhood: of delighted absorption in our own world, from which, eventually, in the course of growing up, we are distanced and separated so that it and the world become things we observe. In Wordsworth and Clare, and in many other writers, this structure of feeling is powerfully expressed, and we have seen how often it is then converted into illusory ideas of the rural past" (297). This rural imaginary becomes a romantic ideal. Rousseau, in particular, fostered the romantic "cult of rusticity" (Gubar, *Artful Dodgers* 12) and set up a strict moral opposition between country and city. Rather than education, Rousseau recommended letting the child roam free in the countryside, "far from the black morals of cities which are covered with a veneer seductive and contagious for children" (Rousseau 95). In this spirit Charles Loring Brace founded the New York Children's Aid Society in 1853 to provide lodging for homeless children but shifted his efforts to "placing out" urban children with farm families, for adoption or foster care, running "orphan trains" to the American Midwest and West until 1929 (Ashby 39, 103, and passim).

Much children's literature contributes to the cult of rusticity. Owain Jones notes the preponderance of rural settings in classics of children's literature such as A. A. Milne's *Winnie the Pooh* (1928), Beatrix Potter stories such as *The Tale of Peter Rabbit* (1902), Kenneth Grahame's *The Wind in the Willows* (1908), and Johanna Spyri's *Heidi* (1880) ("Little Figures" 161). As I have suggested, however, an urban imaginary exists *alongside* the rustic imaginary and represents a curiously marginalized dominant in children's literature and film, as well as in representations of children generally. As Colin Ward notes, if, in the past, popular culture tended to postulate a pastoral childhood, by now "we have lived long enough in an urban world for a nostalgic myth of urban life to have been nourished by literature and reminiscence" (5). In *The Country and the City* Raymond Williams concurs. After acknowledging the "structure of feeling" attached to an "illusory rural past," he notes, "What is interesting now is that we have had enough stories and memories of urban childhoods to perceive the same pattern. The old urban working-class community; the delights of corner-shops, gas lamps, horsecabs, trams, piestalls: all gone, it seems in successive generations. These urban ways and objects seem to have, in the literature, the same real emotional substance as the brooks, commons, hedges, cottages, festivals of the rural scene" (297). Thus, an imaginary urbanism and urban landscape can now, in late modernity, provide a similar structure of feeling and shared sense of the past to conjure an imaginary individual or national childhood.

Supporting this view, consider the opening of Betty Smith's 1943 novel, *A Tree Grows in Brooklyn,* in which her protagonist, eleven-year-old Francie Nolan, contemplates her neighborhood:

> Serene was a word you could put to Brooklyn, New York. Especially in the summer of 1912. . . . Looking at the shafted sun, Francie had that same fine feeling that came when she recalled the poem they recited in school.
>
> *This is the forest primeval. The murmuring pines and hemlocks,*
> *Bearded with moss, and in garments green, indistinct in the twilight,*
> *Stand like Druids of eld.* (1)

The poem, "Evangeline: A Tale of Arcadie," by Henry Wadsworth Longfellow, from 1847, marks the disappearance of rural ways: "Waste are those pleasant farms, and the farmers forever departed!" But Francie's recollection of the poem ignores Longfellow's implicit suggestion that urbanization collides with nature. She elides the sense of loss by displacing the "mournful tradition still sung by the pines of the forest" to an urban landscape. Looking at the tenement district of Williamsburg in Brooklyn, Francie does not see the urban as distinct from "the forests primeval" but finds a similar serenity there. She locates a "Tree of Heaven" in the weedlike tree that grows "in boarded up lots and out of neglected rubbish heaps and . . . out of cement" (Smith 6). She thus locates the pastoral in the city. And, for her reader, the spaces Francie inhabits—the rag man's garage, the penny candy store, the five and dime, tenements—summon an imagined shared urban past and innocence (despite the harsh realities her story depicts). We might thus call the imaginary of the urban child an urban pastoral, or what Ward calls an "urban myth of paradise lost" (5), in which public urban spaces are transformed through children's activities into personal geographies and child-oriented maps of the city.

The urban imaginary exists in both optimistic representations of urban children, such as many of the books and films I listed above, and in negative characterizations of the urban, such as that of Rousseau, who castigates the city's "black morals." In *Les Misérables* Victor Hugo writes that "to paint the child is to paint the city" (chap. 12), the one illuminates the other. "Images of street children," especially, as Karen Sanchez-Eppler notes, "proved a popular means of representing and humanizing all that was troubling but attractive about urban spaces" (42). Notably, when the urban is portrayed adversely, the figure of the urban child is central. As Jones notes, "Images of inner city crisis often contain children and images of childhood crisis are nearly always set in an urban context" ("Little Figures" 165). In many discourses the child is victimized by the city, and the child's victimization must be understood as the upshot of the urban.

These two different imaginaries, or mythical landscapes, the rural and the urban, both play into competing but interrelated conceptions of childhood. On the one hand, since the late nineteenth century, children have been viewed as innocent, helpless, and in need of protection from danger and corruption. On the other, and at the same time, children have been viewed as adults in the making, inherently wild and in need of control (Gubar, *Artful Dodgers* 155; Valentine 2; Penn 183). As Dimitris Eleftheriotis notes, "Romanticized for its anarchic freedom, innocence and ability to see the world with fresh eyes, childhood is at the same time the object of the most incessant discursive and institutional attempts to contain and control it" (328). The romantics, for example, conceive of the child as "a race apart," associated with the primitive, needing to be kept apart from the adult world, contemporary culture and public sphere (schools, state, even family) (Gubar, *Artful Dodgers* 4). George Boas refers to this as the "cult of childhood" and suggests that the emphasis on untaught wisdom and intuition not only aligns the child with the primitive but also beats a retreat from the Enlightenment emphasis on reason (21). The cult of rusticity thus places childhood on the side of the primitive, and as innocent, but imagines that the child can be corrupted. To preserve innocence, one must regulate and control it.

Despite the fact that the notion of childhood innocence has been complicated in lots of ways—and always exists in tandem with the possibility of corruption and inevitable experience—the paradigm continues to dominate discussions of childhood. This conception of childhood innocence colors much criticism of children's film and literature. For instance,

Kathy Merlock Jackson claims that "prior to World War II, filmic portrayals of children were characterized by unerring innocence" (8), even as she discusses films like Charlie Chaplin's *The Kid* (1921), in which the child throws rocks at windows, fights in the street, has familiarity with the law, runs away from an orphanage, and more. At a certain level it is hard to conceive of a truly innocent child. For Kathryn Bond Stockton innocence is a queer concept: "The very moves to free the child from density—to make it distant from adulthood—have only made it stranger, more fundamentally foreign, to adults. Innocence is queerer than we ever thought it could be" (5).

The idea of the urban child can work within an innocence paradigm, and there are hosts of orphans and waifs in need of protection within the urban imaginary. However, the notion of childhood innocence conflicts with aspects of the urban child, who is social and knowing, if not corrupt. As Stockton argues, "Experience is still hard to square with innocence, making depictions of streetwise children, who are often neither white nor middle class, hard to square with 'children'" (32). The urban ideal works to situate the child within an experiential model of modernity. If "the countryside itself is seen as innocent and therefore other to modernity" (Jones, "Little Figures" 165), urbanization coincides with modernity and involves not just industrial production, a market economy, and massification but also a more alienated, transitory, and contingent model of existence. Urbanization thus displaces the child from conventional models of home, tied to family. As Hilde Heynen has argued, "A metaphorical 'homelessness' indeed is often considered the hallmark of modernity" (2). Displaced from conventional notions of home and family, the urban child is subject to social forces and available to contact and encounter with the world of adults and the public. The urban child is still tied to ideologies of family, but those ideologies are buffered by fantasies of familial failure.[3]

Therefore, as Stockton suggests, the image of the urban child does not match the stereotypical image of the child—whether that image is set in a rural past or, nowadays, a suburban present. The urban child, no matter how statistically common, registers as nonnormative, particularly in the United States. In this sense, as Sanchez-Eppler argues in relation to street kids, the urban child produces the middle-class normative child as its antithesis (44). The normative child, as Stockton explains, is rendered innocent: "For the child to be born as a cultural idea, adulthood must be seen as a wholly different state, as something the child initially did not possess and therefore must acquire in the place of innocence" (40). Urban and urbanized children are not fallen innocents but imagined as never innocent. If the imagined normative child grows *up*, from a position of innocence to experience, from youth to adulthood, the nonnormative child does not grow up. He or she grows *sideways* in Stockton's conception, moving laterally in proximity to adulthood.

In efforts to account for the nonnormative urban child, "one solution to this problem," Stockton claims, "is to endow these children with abuse" (32). Viewed as subject to abuse, the urban child is rendered innocent and in need of protection. Thus, the imaginary of the urban child is often conjoined with a fantasy of neglect. The urban child is seen as somehow inherently denied, lacking, or otherwise neglected because the urban environment is seen as somehow insufficient for or dangerous to children.

The Fantasy of Neglect

This book considers the abiding imaginary of the mobile urban child via the fantasy of neglect. What I am calling the fantasy of neglect consists of two conjoined fantasies. There is, on the one hand, the fantasy that the urban child is a figure of neglect and, on the other, the fantasy for the child of being neglected, or let alone. Both senses of neglect hinge on the child's spatial mobility. On the one hand, the child appears to be unmoored, unsupervised, and unprotected, as in the case of Skenazy's son, Izzy. On the other hand, the notion of neglect points to the positive thrill and possible risk of the child's freedom, independence, and movement, as with *How Little Lori Visited Times Square*. These conjoined fantasies bring together a host of ideas about the urban, children, space, parenting, neglect, poverty, reform, and more; and they shift over time.

My understanding of a fantasy of neglect is not meant to promote child abuse but to get at the power and necessity for neglect in our conception of childhood, including how childhood is rendered in literature and film.[4] The fantasy of neglect is not unique to the urban child. Indeed, neglect underpins many, if not most, of our representations of children.[5] *Home Alone* (Chris Columbus 1990), obviously, situates neglect in a suburban setting. But neglect and urbanism are more commonly sutured together than other placements; and the urban child is rendered nonnormative, as well as neglected, whereas suburban or rural children are more commonly tied to ideals of family and home. I am particularly interested in the way fantasies of neglect play out in an urban context and what philosophy of urbanism underpins representations of children and, conversely, what ideas and ideals of childhood come to the fore in the urban context.

According to the U.S. Department of Health and Human Services, in a document from 1993, neglect can be defined broadly as "a condition in which a caretaker responsible for the child, either deliberately or by extraordinary inattentiveness, permits the child to experience avoidable present suffering and/or fails to provide one or more of the ingredients generally deemed essential for developing a person's physical, intellectual, and emotional capabilities" (Gaudin 4). Of course, this definition begs the question of what might be essential for a person's development, and the government allows that conceptions of neglect vary according to community standards, which tend to differ according to income, neighborhood, ethnicity, and so on. As Matthews, Limb, and Taylor remind us, there is no single childhood but multiple variations, layered by such contingencies as place, parental caretaking practices, socioeconomic and sociopsychological factors, and the agency of children themselves (76). Neglect is not singular, either, but dependent on many of the same factors.

In its discussion of neglect, the U.S. Department of Health and Human Services cites the *Study of National Incidence and Prevalence of Child Abuse and Neglect* from 1988. This study differentiates among four kinds of neglect: (1) physical neglect, including not only physical abuse but also failure to provide health care and inattention to household hazards; (2) educational neglect, such as allowing truancy or failing to register a child for school; (3) failed supervision, such as a child left unsupervised or away from home without a parent knowing his or her whereabouts; and (4) emotional neglect, which ranges from encouraging drug abuse on the part of the child to a "marked inattention to the child's needs for affection, emotional support, attention, or competence" (Gaudin 6). While physical and educational forms of abuse certainly play a role in many fantasies of neglect, failed supervision and emotional neglect are the most common and are often intertwined in the urban childhood imaginary.

Ideas about what constitutes neglect change over time and reflect and refract other social issues. Ashby argues that concerns about endangered and needy children come to the fore at moments of social stress (2–3). In the late nineteenth century, he says, attention to children and neglect related to anxieties over increased urbanization and the growing squalor of burgeoning cities, including issues such as overpopulation, tenements, and slums. In the late twentieth century, matters related to endangered children served as a wedge for such issues as women's liberation, the collapse of the family, and the role and size of government in relation to programs like Aid to Families with Dependent Children (AFDC).[6]

Neglect is not even always seen as negative. Certain models of parenting advise a kind of negligence as good parenting. In his popular 1928 book, *The Psychological Care of Infant and Child*, John Watson views the showing of affection as producing "invalidism" and "nest instincts," that is, running to mom. Watson fantasizes in his book about separating children from their parents to be brought up more "scientifically," and he promotes a model of neglect: "The child is to be left alone" (Beekman 150). Similarly, Dr. Arnold Gesell's 1930 book, *The Guidance of Mental Growth in Infant and Child*, argues that "healthy attitudes of action" in the child entail "self-reliance . . . a steady process of detachment, first from the apron strings, later from the home itself" (Beekman 157–158).

The fantasy of neglect takes a few different forms. In the late nineteenth century and the early twentieth, philanthropic and reformist views dominate. In this vein Jacob Riis, in his famous analysis of early twentieth-century tenement living, *How the Other Half Lives*, paints a picture of ethnic slum children on the Lower East Side, peddling, begging, abandoned by overcrowded truant homes, and neglected by their family and community. In overcrowded tenements, he claims, nobody pays attention to the children or knows where they are: "Home to them is an empty name. . . . The streets . . . are their domain" (140). This view dominates certain characterizations of poor urban children from the nineteenth century forward to today.[7]

Urban planners adopt a related but slightly different approach. For many of them the city is inherently bad for the child. The mid-twentieth-century push to suburbia depended on this depiction of the city. In this mode the city is viewed as dangerous, owing to traffic and criminality, and not providing enough green space or safe play areas, and suburban living is considered more appropriate for raising children. To the degree that children are envisioned as viable occupants of the city, they are frequently regarded as unruly or potentially negative forces in need of control. Even as she promotes the idea of children playing in the streets and sidewalks, Jane Jacobs suggests that children need constant surveillance, not by a parent per se but by self-policing "watchers" in the neighborhood who will step in when a child is in danger or acting badly.

Contemporary twenty-first-century urban planning doesn't insist on the push to suburbia but regards the city as needing to be remolded to accommodate children. Contemporary urban planners and geographers aim to create safe and developmentally sound spaces for children. These are often supervised playgrounds and designated play and activity areas, such as Imagination Playground in the South Street Seaport area of New York, described on its website as "a breakthrough playspace concept designed to encourage child-directed, unstructured free play."[8] Concomitantly, nowadays parents are advised that it requires special training to be a city child and a city parent; parenting manuals promote not just togetherness but also surveillance and micromanagement. Witness numerous books about urban parenting and raising city kids, like Adam Gopnik's *Paris to the Moon* (2000) and *Through the Children's Gate* (2006), which chart Gopnik's wanderings around Paris and New York with his children, as if being a parent in those places is an adventure akin to touring challenging or exotic foreign locales. Parenting guides like *New York Magazine*'s special issue "Survival Guide" for urban parents from April 1997, *City Baby New York: The Ultimate Guides for Parents from Pregnancy to Preschool* (2005) and *City Kid New York: The Ultimate Guide for New York City Parents with Kids Age 4–12* (2010) suggest that city parenting is different in kind from suburban or rural parenting and include information on safety, schools, activities, party spaces, fashion, and kid-friendly restaurants.

At the same time, against these negative or problematic views of the city, another image emerges in memoirs of urban childhoods, children's books, and films. As Ward puts it in his landmark book from 1978, *The Child in the City*, the city child presents a paradox: while reformers, urban planners, and social workers portray the urban child as poor, unhappy, and deprived, photographs of the kids—and I would argue books and films about children—show city kids expressing joy, resourcefulness, and the ability to colonize urban space for their own purposes. In his analysis of early twentieth-century urban children David Nasaw similarly notes that, while reformers "painted their picture of urban youth in the most dismal tones," kids' own narratives presented "fun, the excitement of urban life" (ix). The children of the city, he says, "grew up without adequate air, light, and space to play and grow," yet "the children of the city did not wither and die in the urban air, but were able to carve out social space of their own" (vii). These narratives offer an idea of what it means to be a city kid and also a different vantage on the urban. They posit an ideal of authenticity—toughness, know-how, street smarts, pluck, fun, resourcefulness, and freedom—but they also infuse the urban with a spirit of play, improvisation, and masquerade.

Most representations of urban children play off the tension between the negative and positive connotations of neglect and hinge on some form of parental supervisory or emotional neglect. Narratives are filled with images of single mothers, single fathers, orphanages, and foster homes, in the context of poverty; or they represent married and often wealthy parents who are nonetheless rendered neglectful, either through inadequacy, divorce, or inattention. (Hugo describes one such child: "He was one of those children most deserving of pity, among all, one of those who have mother and father, and who are orphans nonetheless" [chap. 13].) Rather than exceptional, or simply pathologized, however, I would argue that these images and representations of urban neglect form a collective memory of childhood and a childhood imaginary. Some texts emphasize the negative, some emphasize the positive, and some render ambivalence, showing how both negative and positive connotations coexist. In early twentieth-century texts, neglect will be understood largely in terms of social conditions—poverty, homelessness, divorce—that push the child to the streets; but by midcentury neglect will be understood more in psychological terms, as denying the child the keys to happiness. The social and psychological figurations of neglect will intersect somewhat, but the understanding of what counts as parental neglect, especially, will be transformed from a sense that parents provide material support and necessities to a sense of the parent as responsible for providing the child with the tools for his or her psychological well-being.

Fantasies of Neglect in the Golden Age

As I have suggested, the fantasy of neglect and the imaginary of the urban child go hand in hand and exist over a broad span of time. This book focuses on the figure of the urban child in American film and literature of the twentieth and early twenty-first centuries. But it is worth looking to literary precedents from the nineteenth century Golden Age of children's literature to establish some rubrics. In particular, I highlight Charles Dickens and J. M. Barrie as modeling the two sides of the fantasy of neglect.

Arguing against the notion that Golden Age authors borrowed whole-sale from the romantics and simply invoked an ideal of innocence or child-of-nature paradigm, Marah Gubar claims that the Golden Age saw children as "socially saturated beings, profoundly shaped by the culture, manners, and morals of their time" (*Artful Dodgers* 9). The urban child, in this sense, "is caught up in the constraints of the culture he inhabits—just as older people are—and yet not inevitably victimized as a result of this contact with adults and their world" (Gubar, *Artful Dodgers* i).

Dickens, more than any other writer, laments the condition of the urban child and pictures the urban child as primarily poor, a humanitarian issue, and a potential threat to society. According to Gubar, the two dominant strategies in Dickens are (1) to "emphasize the incompetence of children: their pathetic unfitness for the demands being made on them, their inability to survive in an uncaring, materialistic world" or (2) to acknowledge the skills acquired by children but to view those skills negatively as "dreadful precocity," or the child turned adult by circumstance (*Artful Dodgers* 152).[9]

Here we can think of *Oliver Twist* (1867) as exemplary. In this novel Oliver represents the innocent child who is victimized by uncaring modern institutions and seems adrift and incompetent in the urban environment. In part Oliver is a displaced child of nature. Recuperating in Mrs. Maylie's country home, "Oliver, whose days had been spent among squalid crowds, and in the midst of noise and brawling, seemed to enter a new existence there" (Dickens 238). Oliver discovers nature and is healed by it. In this, Dickens seems to offer a Rousseauian celebration of nature as primal and purifying:

> Men who have lived in crowded, pent up streets, through lives of toil, and who have never wished for change; men, to whom custom has indeed been second nature, and who have come almost to love every brick and stone that formed the narrow boundaries of their daily walks; even they . . . have been known to yearn for at last one short glimpse of Nature's face; and carried far from the scenes of their old pains and pleasures, have seemed to pass at once into a new state of being . . . a vague and half formed consciousness of having held such feelings long before, in some remote and distant time, which calls up thoughts of distant times to come, and bends down pride and worldliness beneath it. (Dickens 238)

Rusticity, here, provides a counter to the urban and to the squalor, pride, and worldliness associated with it.

But Oliver is not allowed to live in nature or exist outside the forces of modernity. Orphaned and alone, he is sent to the city, where he must live in terrible conditions at the parish workhouse. Abused by the beadle, Mr. Bumble, and the workhouse board, then by the funeral director to whom he is apprenticed, he runs away. Meeting Jack Dawkins, nicknamed the Artful Dodger, he is brought to the East End of London to meet Fagin, a criminal who runs a ring of boy thieves. Together, Fagin and another criminal, Bill Sikes, try aggressively to corrupt him (his corruption being key to his stepbrother's scheme to steal his fortune). Oliver resists being fully corrupted, his natural innocence serving as protection. Any criminality attributed to him is excused in the book by his youth, the fact that he "may never have known a mother's love, or the comfort of a home; that ill-usage and blows, or the want of bread, may have driven him to herd with men who have forced him to guilt" (Dickens 217). In this sense Oliver is a helpless victim. He is also helpless or incompetent to battle the evil forces himself. He spends much of the novel physically incapacitated—recovering from a fainting fit at one benefactor's and from a gunshot after a failed robbery attempt at another's—and he must rely on the help and knowledge of strangers to be restored to his rightful place as heir to a small fortune.

Dickens contrasts Oliver with the Artful Dodger, who is not a victim but a threat.[10] Already corrupted and hardened, the Dodger is "altogether as roistering and swaggering a young gentleman as ever stood four foot six" (56). An orphan, like Oliver, the Dodger thrives in the corrupt urban environment and serves as Fagin's best thief. The corrupt Dodger is no longer childlike: "He was a snub-nosed, flat-browed, common-faced boy enough; and as dirty a juvenile as one would wish to see; but he had about him all the airs and manners of a man" (Dickens 55). The other boys who work for Fagin, likewise, are found "smoking long clay pipes, and drinking spirits with the air of middle-aged men" (Dickens 59). As Gubar discusses, Dickens views "precocity as a horrifying offense against the true nature of childhood . . . a pastoral purity opposed to the industrialization and commercialization of contemporary society" (*Artful Dodgers* 9). Dodger's precocity warps his childhood and leads to his punishment in jail, whereas Oliver's "pastoral purity" is visible to outsiders who rescue him and restore his family name and wealth.

In contrast to Dickens, consider J. M Barrie's Peter Pan narratives: the play *Peter Pan, or the Boy Who Would Not Grow Up* (1904); the novelization of the play, *Peter and Wendy* (1911); and the short novella *Peter Pan in Kensington Gardens*, which originally appeared as an interlude in a longer adult novel, *The Little White Bird* (1902). Taken together, they participate in the positive fantasy of neglect, the child's desire to be left alone and free. Like Dickens's, Barrie's texts are structured around neglect. In both *Peter Pan, or the Boy Who Would Not Grow Up* and *Peter and Wendy*, the Darling children—Wendy, John, and Michael—suffer the neglect of parents who are too distracted and, in the case of the father, too concerned with money to properly care for them. First, they are given a Newfoundland dog, Nana, for a nurse, to save money, "as they were poor, owing to the amount of milk the children drank" (Barrie 7). Then, when the "nurse" is treated as a dog and locked up for the night while the parents are out, the children are seduced by Peter Pan, who leads them to a land of adventure in Neverland. In Neverland Wendy becomes the attentive "mother" to a slew of Lost Boys, all of whom are victims of neglect, having fallen "out of their perambulators when the nurse is looking the other way" (Barrie 29) and left unclaimed for seven days. Peter, too, is a figure of neglect. As we learn in *Peter Pan in Kensington Gardens*, all children begin their lives as birds but eventually forget their bird-selves and lose their ability to fly. Peter, however, "forgot" his human limitations and at seven days old deliberately flies out his window to the treetops in Kensington Gardens. There, he lives as a "Betwixt-and-Between" (Barrie 172), neither bird nor boy, for many years. When ready to return home, he discovers that his mother has borne another son and barred the window, presumably to keep the new child from flying away but, in Peter's eyes, as a means of keeping him out.

Unlike in Dickens, however, where the child is disempowered or corrupted by neglect, in the Barrie texts, neglect allows the children to be mobile and free, figuratively to fly away to a land of adventure and play. As an exotic island setting, Neverland provides something of a counter to the urban, but the children's ability to access it depends on the porousness and permeability of their urban home, its setting in a densely populated and easily accessible area. And, as Barrie makes clear, Neverland is an imaginative construct that children carry with them, an imagined island where they play rather than a literal location. In Neverland the children engage in battles with the villain Captain Hook, fight pirates, befriend "redskins," observe mermaids, learn about fairies, and discover new and exciting flora and fauna.

The children in the Peter Pan tales are extremely competent. They are able to trick and kill Hook and fourteen other pirates, and they rescue themselves from danger using things at hand, such as a lost kite or a bird's nest. At home in London the children rely on their mother to tell them stories. In Neverland Wendy becomes the storyteller, and all of the children improvise, pretend, and masquerade, sometimes for fun and sometimes better to defend themselves against the enemy. For example, Wendy plays mother and Peter father to the Lost Boys. They all eat pretend meals and build pretend homes. Peter imitates the ticking of the clock in the crocodile's stomach to scare Captain Hook and replicates Hook's voice to deceive the pirates, and all the boys masquerade as pirates. Neverland serves at once as a rehearsal for adult life, as Wendy tries on the role of mother, and as a delay of it, as Wendy, in the play, flies away just as she is told she will have to leave the nursery. It not only allows the child to "never grow up" but also provides a respite from the structure and ordinariness of home. When Peter first flies back to his mother in *Peter Pan in Kensington Gardens*, for instance, he decides to leave again because he cannot imagine wearing clothes again, wants to sail his boat again, and wants to tell his story to the birds. Back in Kensington Gardens, he has a number of farewell feasts, "his last sail, and his very last sail, and his last sail of all, and so on" (Barrie 198), thus opting for fun over family (or clothing).

Other than Peter—who cannot grow up or return home because he stayed away too long—the children suffer no ill consequences. The Darlings return to their expectant parents and Nana. They bring the Lost Boys home to become adopted into their family. Wendy is able to fly back and forth between London and Neverland for many years, to help with spring cleaning. Then, when she is too old, her children begin their own Neverland adventures.

In both the Dickens and Barrie texts, whether the urban experience is rendered negatively or positively, the children are seen as mobile figures in an urban landscape, knowledgeable about city streets, available to encounter and contact. In Dickens's *Oliver Twist*, children dominate certain city streets: "The street was very narrow and muddy, and the air was impregnated with filthy odors. There were a good many small shops; but the only stock in trade appeared to be heaps of children, who, even at that time of night, were crawling in and out of doors, or screaming from inside"

(58). While the sight of urban children here functions as a shorthand for squalor—a motif we will see frequently in film—the narrative also hinges on children's mobility across urban space. For example, Oliver walks seventy miles to London, accompanied by the Artful Dodger only for the last leg of the trip. Along the way he begs for food and money at cottage doors, at inns and farms, and from passengers on passing coaches. In a different vein Dodger and his fellow thief, Bates, saunter through the streets of London, knowingly observing people to determine who can and cannot be robbed, and then, after a robbery, run quickly, without being seen or caught, back to Fagin's. Sikes's young girlfriend, Nancy, makes her way to the police station to check on Oliver, next tricks bystanders to help her abduct Oliver off the street, and later contrives a secret meeting on London Bridge at midnight with one of Oliver's benefactors. In *Peter Pan* Peter teaches the Darlings to fly, and they fly all over London and beyond before heading to Neverland. In *Peter Pan in Kensington Gardens* the birdlike Peter flies over Saint Paul's to the Crystal Palace and Regent's Park. Another child, Maimie, escapes her nurse and lingers in the Gardens after nightfall, to join Peter and the fairies.

Children and Urban Space

These texts, and the figure of the urban child generally, provide a different way to think about the spatiality of childhood. Critics' conceptions of children's space often ignore both reality and representation to situate children in interior spaces. Thus, Ian Wojcik-Andrews claims that children's films are "often set on, in and around small or enclosed spaces" (181), and Claudia Mitchell and Jacqueline Reid-Walsh limit their analysis of physical children's spaces to the child's bedroom. Linking women and children, Lissa Paul argues that

> the forms of physical . . . entrapment that feminist critics have been revealing in women's literature match the images of entrapment in children's literature. . . . Children, like women, are lumped together as helpless and dependent; creatures to be kept away from the scene of the action, and who otherwise ought not to be seen and heard. . . . Because women and children generally have to stay at home without affairs of state to worry about, their stories tend to focus on the contents of their traps, the minute and mundane

features of everyday life around which their lives revolve: household effects, food, clothing, sewing, interior decorating. (150–151)

Even as she acknowledges that children "are not yet closed in by the rules of adulthood," Paul willfully ignores all the ways in which children are shown to be actors in the public sphere, not relegated to interior space or domestic settings. Discussing *Harriet the Spy*, for instance, Paul does not focus on Harriet's remarkable ability to traverse urban space by herself, or the time she and her friends spend walking to and from school or playing in the park, but on the domestic scenes she witnesses when spying (scenes that require her to leave her own home, move from neighborhood to neighborhood, and secretly access *other people's* domestic space).

I would argue that few if any representations of children are set exclusively in the child's bedroom or in enclosed spaces. For example, suburban narratives, like *E.T.: The Extraterrestrial* (Steven Spielberg 1982) or *Super 8* (J. J. Abrams 2011) show kids moving freely through suburban areas, visiting abandoned spaces, woods, train tracks, and remote neighborhoods. These films alternate scenes of enclosure in the family home with scenes of mobility outdoors. Rural narratives, too, tend to be outdoor narratives. As Jones argues, discourses around country childhoods emphasize outdoor play, "spatial freedom, and freedom from adult surveillance" ("Little Figures" 162).

Representations of the urban child do not relegate the child to his or her bedroom or enclosed spaces but instead set much of the action in the street. Perfectly stitching together the fantasy of neglect and the importance of the street for the urban child, Hugo writes: "The child never felt so well as when he was in the street. The pavements were less hard to him than his mother's heart" (chap. 13). In 1911 Hoben observed that "the street becomes an extension of the home. It is alike the parlor and the playground of the poor" (451). As Matthews suggests, the street stands in for a range of public artificial outdoor spaces including alleys, shopping areas, parking lots, vacant lots, and more. For Matthews the street figures as a liminal space, a place of separation from adults and a domain of transition (102), or a "thirdspace," "set between the freedom and autonomy of adulthood and the constraints and dependency of infancy" (Matthews, Limb, and Taylor 65). It is "a space that is deeply invested with cultural values that forms part of the spatiality of *growing up*" (Matthews 103). While reformers long tried to dislodge kids from city streets, kids in the early twentieth century often opted for the unstructured life on city streets over more highly structured play spaces in playgrounds and parks (Jacobs 110; Nasaw 36).

As Michel de Certeau suggests, the city can be seen from different perspectives, by looking from above, as at a map or grid, or from the ground, by walking. While the view from above produces a legible view for the voyeur, the view from below is lived and experienced, rather than viewed from a distance. The possible paths taken through the city are myriad and yet singular: they are both spatial practices and speech acts. Walking, pedestrians appropriate space and give it shape; the walk from point A to point B, and beyond, implies and produces relations among spaces and between people and spaces (Certeau 91–98).

Nasaw claims, "The children of the city . . . grew up with street maps etched in their brains" (33). But the map children know and live by differs from conventional or official maps of the city. Rather than a space leading from point A to point B, the street in the childhood imaginary becomes a play space, a space for games, and a space hidden from adults. As Jones notes, "Frequently adults and children are seen using and seeing the same spaces but putting different interpretations on them" ("Little Figures" 172). Put simply, children map the city differently than adults do. In a lovely passage about growing up in Pittsburgh in the 1950s, Annie Dillard writes:

> I walked. My mother had given me the street as soon as I could say our telephone number. I walked and memorized the neighborhood. I made a mental map and located myself upon it. At night in bed I rehearsed the small world's scheme and set challenges: Find the store using backyards only. Imagine a route from the school to my friend's house. I mastered chunks of town in one direction only; I ignored the other direction, toward the Catholic Church. . . . Walking was my project before reading. The text I read was the town; the book I made up was a map. (43, 46)

In Dillard's mental map the city is where she comes to know herself. She locates herself within it. It is a space carved out by games and the imagination and entails routes not used or acknowledged by adults: backyards only, toward friends, and away from church. For Vivian Gornick, similarly, in her book *The Odd Woman and the City*, the streets are crucial to her world making and sense of self: "We used the streets the way children growing up in the country use fields and rivers, mountains and caves: to place ourselves on the map of the world" (12).

FIGURE 1. This 1961 photo, titled "Wishing Makes It So," shows kids colonizing space for their own purposes, in this case, turning a playground into a swimming pool. UPI photo.

In an essay about adult memories of urban childhood, Alvin Lukashok and Kevin Lynch find that the child's view of the city is determined largely by play. In their findings the child is "sensitive to the floor"—the ground surface (asphalt, brick, cobblestone, gravel, dirt, etc.)—"because it is the prime condition of his main activity—play" (143; see also Lynch). Children relate to trees and foliage more than buildings (thus finding nature in the urban rather than in opposition to it). Children prefer to play in spaces that are not structured, such as alleys, vacant lots, places to dig, places with broken bottles or rocks, bushes, and garages—"anywhere but the playground" (Lukashok and Lynch 145).

These memories confirm Jones's argument that children's spaces are defined by disorder, or "anti-order," a preference for "derelict and abandoned spaces . . . where the 'normal' adult ordering has not taken place" (Jones, "Little Figures" 173–174): "Within the *derelictions* which sometimes befall the adult orders (social, material, symbolic, disciplinary) which largely pattern the world (e.g., the city or the house), children can find and make their own orders (material, symbolic, disciplinary) in ways which mean the world (or a bit of it) becomes a geography for (their) otherness" (Jones, "'True Geography'" 204).

Children find disordered spaces and also have a disordered understanding of space, at least in comparison to adult understandings. The street in the childhood imaginary does not set the same boundaries as it does for adults, who view certain blocks and streets as borders or boundaries between safe and unsafe communities or as political districts. Rather, the child recognizes different boundaries, unseen to adult eyes or through adult practices. At the same time, they are aware of differences between neighborhoods, often marked through signifiers of class or wealth (nicer homes, single-family homes, bigger yards, more clean streets and alleys).[11]

According to Lukashok and Lynch, children do not grasp the city as a whole, nor do they adhere to the neighborhood designations of planners or government. Instead, they have a small and sharply limited sense of neighborhood, often restricted to their block. Nasaw concurs: "The block was the basic unit of organization for city kids. Play groups and gangs were organized exclusively by geography" (32). In her discussion of neighborhoods, Jacobs distinguishes between districts and street neighborhoods. Whereas Greenwich Village may be a district, a medium-sized area within a city that mediates "between the politically powerless, street neighborhoods, and the inherently powerful city as a whole" (121), street neighborhoods are small streets or groups of streets within which people can live, run errands, work, and play. Blocks, as opposed to districts or larger street neighborhoods, serve as a means of grouping residents into playgroups and provide a sense of smallness within the large city.

Of course, while kids' understanding of the city is determined by geography—the block the kid lives on—geography is often determined by factors such as race, class, and nationality. Thus, different kids "know" the city differently. In a short essay in which he describes the ghetto child's unfamiliarity with some nicer sections of the city, and of buildings like skyscrapers, Robert Coles observes that the ghetto child "contains a sense of the world that is heavily defined by the particular physical environment of the ghetto—its sounds and smells, the sights if offers, the kind of elbow room its buildings provide, or quite literally the leeway its streets and alleys fail to provide" (49–50). In this view neighborhood and housing don't just shape but also limit one's experience of the city.

Children in films and fiction routinely cross from sanctioned child spaces such as the apartment or sidewalk to adult spaces, such as the bar, the racetrack, the speakeasy; they engage in relationships with myriad adults who are not their parents, including negative influences, such as the predatory Fagins and molesters of the cultural imagination, and kindly strangers who enable a family romance; and they constitute diverse communities that collapse momentarily, and only for children, racial boundaries; they join other kids, becoming a collective at some times, a mob at others. Often, the child engages in dangerous or illegal activity—such as stealing, spying, and truancy. Frequently, the child faces risk and danger, from other kids, and from adults and authorities such as the police, who are always present in the mise-en-scène of urban childhoods.

Bypassing adult ways of inhabiting the city, children produce their own city and their own philosophy of urbanism, a philosophy that transforms familiar spaces into spaces for play and adventure. While most accounts of the urban do not consider the ways in which children inhabit or indeed produce the urban, Henri Lefebvre opens up a way to consider how children's use of the city, even more perhaps than any other users, produces the urban as "permanent disequilibrium, seat of the dissolution of normalities and constraints, the moment of play and the unpredictable" (*Right to the City* 129), spaces of encounter and contact. For Lefebvre, representational space—lived space as experienced by users and inhabitants, and also as described by artists, philosophers, and writers— stems from childhood: "When compared with the abstract space of the experts (architects, urbanists, planners), the space of the everyday activities of users is a concrete one, which is to say, subjective. As a space of 'subjects' rather than of calculations, as a representational space, it has an origin, and that origin is childhood, with its hardships, its achievements, and its lacks" (*The Production of Space* 362). Childhood, here defined as hardship and lack, moves space away from abstraction to use and toward subjectivity. If the "experts" know space abstractly, the child lives space; and lived space, understood as a sign system, bears the marks of his maturation and failure to mature.

Examining the figure of the urban child in film and literature moves us from abstract space—what Certeau describes as a strategic view and Jacobs, like Lefebvre, calls an abstraction—to a tactical view, or use of the city, to social space. These texts give us a sense of spatial mobility that affords childhood a sense of freedom. They are animated by the conception of a child's map, the desire to traverse unusual spots, or take unique routes, or adopt a unique vantage amid adult activities.

In his examination of representations of children's urban mobility, Eric L. Tribunella argues for the idea of the child flâneur, noting that both Walter Benjamin and Charles Baudelaire associate the flâneur with the child, viewing the activity of the flâneur as a recovery of childhood curiosity and wonder. Arguing that children's literature "recovers" childhood, through texts written by adult authors "who speak through the child," Tribunella suggests that "placing the child in the city and often imbuing the protagonist of urban fiction with both a crucial gaze and a sense of wonder, children's literature both confirms the possibility of the child flâneur and makes use of this figure to contend with the ramifications of modernity" (67). In this sense the urban child can be seen as a key figure in representing and understanding the city and reflecting upon the experience of modernity.

The Urban Child and Cinema

Representations of the urban child's social space are not, I contend, merely reflections of childhood or nostalgic images we return to as adults. They are a small but key trope in cinema that is central to our collective imagination of space and of our identities. "To practice space," Certeau writes, "is this to repeat the joyful and silent experience of childhood: it is, in a place, *to be other and to move toward the other*" (110). As Jones remarks, "Otherness . . . does not just mean simple separation and unknowability. It is a more subtle idea of the knowable and unknowable, the familiar and the strange, the close and the distant being co-present in adult-child relations. . . . Otherness . . . is essential to what children are. It should be essential to ideas of childhood, too" ("'True Geography'" 197). "To be other and to move toward the other" is to be child and adult, at one and the same time—growing sideways, as Stockton would have it—in a return to childhood through spatial practice.

This dynamic of being the other and moving toward the other defines not only spatial practice but also the cinema. As psychoanalytic theory suggests, cinema invites us to see simultaneously our self and not our self, to experience identification and distance, at the same time. This sense of simultaneous identification and distance is most strongly marked, perhaps, when we, as adults, watch children onscreen. As Vicky Lebeau notes, "Part of the novelty of the cinematograph is its capacity to bring the end of a man's life into renewed and mobile contact with its beginning," the uncanny effect of the child image, which supports "the possibility of seeing oneself as young and old *at the same time*" (33). As Jacqueline Rose reminds us in her gloss on Freud, childhood is not merely a stage of life but diachronic: "It persists as something which we endlessly rework in our attempt to build an image of our own history" (12). Defining the *infans* as "at once a moment in the emergence of psychic life and a state of mind and being that never goes away" (84), Lebeau suggests that the image of the child and the cinema share an idiom, "as each come[s] to carry the delights as well as the terrors of an elsewhere, of a way of being otherwise" (84). In this sense both the image of the child and the cinema transport us to another place and time, an elsewhere, "bordering on an otherness within, a space and time that we have all known without knowing it" (84).

If, as Lebeau suggests, cinema and childhood are "two distinct but converging institutions of modern cultural life" (20), is it any accident that so many cinematic movements, at the moment of their emergence, turn to the image of the child? Eleftheriotis recognizes this link between cinematic origins and childhood, locating childhood as a key metaphor of early cinema. In part, Eleftheriotis, with Lebeau, identifies early cinema as an imaginary signifier, a model of spectacle and attractions as Tom Gunning describes it, that is prior to the symbolic and, thus, like cinema's childhood. In addition, Eleftheriotis sees in our memories and imaginings of early cinema a fantasy of a shared childhood, a common origin. Furthermore, and most important for my argument, he views cinephilia as deeply associated with images of childhood, in narratives that "appeal to the child that every adult has once been" (Eleftheriotis 326).

The urban child, in particular, holds a special place in the origins of cinema and cinematic movements. Consider such key figures in silent cinema as the Girl in *Broken Blossoms* (D. W. Griffith 1919) or the boy in Chaplin's *The Kid*. The urban child is central to the French New Wave in films such as *The Red Balloon* (Albert Lamorisse 1956) and in François Truffaut's oeuvre, in particular, with such films as *Les Mistons* (1957), *The 400 Blows* (1959), and *Small Change* (1976). The urban child is equally prominent in Italian neorealism and especially in Vittorio De Sica's films, such as *The Children Are Watching Us* (1944), *Shoeshine* (1946), *Bicycle Thieves* (1948), and *Heart and Soul* (1948).

Not only the child but also the street holds a special status in cinema and cinema theories. Siegfried Kracauer, whose work emphasizes cinema's role in both reflecting and revealing reality, argues that films "evoke a reality more inclusive than the one they actually picture," and he describes this reality as "life," or more specifically the "flow of life," which he regards as open-ended (71). "The flow of life," like children's spaces, is constantly in flux and disorderly. It can be seen, Kracauer argues, in representations of the quotidian, the everyday life that nonetheless reveals aspects of reality that we would not see without cinema. The quotidian and cinema's revealing function are equated, in Kracauer's writings, with the street: "The street in the extended sense of the word is not only the arena of fleeting impressions and chance encounters but a place where the flow of life is bound to assert itself" (72). According to Kracauer, the transient flux of "real life phenomena"—something close to what Lefebvre calls the urban—is what affects the film spectator "most strongly." Such phenomena "stimulate his senses and provide him with stuff for dreaming" (170). Kracauer, though, like others, argues that in dreaming the spectator achieves an illusory mastery, or imaginary omnipotence, equated with childhood. Noting that the "spectator's dreams revive those of his childhood days which have sunk into his unconscious," Kracauer notes that "the moviegoer again becomes a child in the sense that he magically rules the world by dint of dreams which overgrow stubborn reality" (171). In Kracauer's analysis, then, cinema and childhood not only converge with each other but also with the urban. Both the child represented and the childlike spectator achieves a fantasy mastery over the world, or, as Jones says, "a bit of it" ("'True Geography'" 204).

The fantasy of mastery depends on neglect, being left alone—to imagine, to dream, to rule the world, to create disorder and new orders. In envisioning the child's spatial mobility and independence in the streets, cinema enacts, over and over, the fort/da game of separation from the mother, a separation that *requires* the parent's absence, that requires, in other words, neglect. In Sigmund Freud's description of the fort/da game played by his grandson (13–15) there are two variants to the game. In one, the boy throws small toys out of his crib exclaiming with delight at their absence. In the other, he throws a small wooden reel, then, after enjoying its absence, reels it back in. These games of disappearance (*fort*, or gone) and return (*da*, there) enable the boy, on the one hand, to experience the delight of absence, of the "gone," while, in the second variant, they also facilitate his mastery. According to Freud, this game helps the boy manage his anxiety about his mother's absences, by creating a virtual symbolic mother who would be first gone, then there. It is a symbolic game that nonetheless teaches the boy to conceptualize his mother's absence and understand that she still exists, by making her present or re-present in memory and through play. In film, neglect represents an important fantasy of and for the child. As viewers, we see the child as simultaneously experiencing the mother's absence or neglect, managing his or her anxiety and achieving mastery over special space and objects, but we also see the child—our self and our other—as gone, elsewhere, on the street and in the cinematic imagination, but with the promise of return.

On the one hand, the fort/da game serves to domesticate trauma. But, as Miriam Hansen reminds us in her gloss on Walter Benjamin's reading of Freud, the game "also means enjoying one's victories over and over again, with total intensity" (Benjamin, qtd. in Hansen, *Cinema and Experience* 194). Cinema functions like the fort/da game in enacting repetition. Hansen explains that "Benjamin regarded film as the medium of repetition par excellence on account of its technological structure" (*Cinema and Experience* 195) including mechanical reproduction and exhibition practices. Moreover, cinema provides what Benjamin calls "room for play [*Spiel-Raum*], an intermediary zone not yet fully determined in which things oscillate among different meanings, functions and possible directions . . . an open-ended, dynamic temporality, an interval for chance, imagination and agency" (Hansen, *Cinema and Experience* 192). The mobility afforded by cinema—its ability to imagine and traverse space—is brought to the fore in films about the urban child, whose use of space enables viewers to "comprehend and reconceive their environment in the mode of play" (Hansen, *Cinema and Experience* 193).

Play, according to Hansen, is a key strategy for negotiating the effects of modernity. As Hansen describes, Benjamin views film as importantly reconfiguring urban space in modernity. Film, on the one hand, makes us see "commonplace milieus" in new ways—similar to what Kracauer describes as rendering the familiar strange—and, on the other, shows us "a vast and unsuspected field of action"—or room-for-play (Benjamin, *SW* 127; *Work* 48–49)—that explodes the "prison-world" of our familiar surroundings "so that we can now set off calmly on journeys of adventure among its far-flung debris" (Benjamin, *SW* 117; *Work* 37). In Hansen's characterization film "at once unveils and refracts the everyday, thus making it available for play—for a mimetic appropriation and reconfiguring of its ruined fragments" ("Room-for-Play" 27). Through film, according to Benjamin, "the individual suddenly sees his scope for play, his field of action immeasurably expanded" (Benjamin, *SW* 124). The space is unfamiliar:

"He does not yet know his way around this space" (Benjamin, *SW* 124). Not knowing the space breaks the spectator free from everyday familiarity and opens the spectator up to adventurous reconfigurations and reimaginings. As Zhang Zhen notes, the concept of play "captures Benjamin's fascination with the figure of the child and the implications of children's playful and performative 'mimetic faculty' with which they explore new objects in the world and boundaries of their bodies" (13). This link to childhood is largely read allegorically in relation to adult film spectatorship. Having "all these spaces at our disposal," we are, in Kracauer's words, "*like* children" (Kracauer, qtd. in Hansen, *Cinema and Experience* 19; emphasis mine).

While the figure of the child is usually thought to be "a figure rather than a specific demographic" (Zhang 14), the image of the child in cinema provides a relay for and metonym of the spectator's childlike experience of space in cinema. The image of the child in diegetic space parallels and dynamizes the spectator's experience of cinematic space. Cinema's defamiliarization of space and production of "room for play" parallels the spatial practice of children, whose views and uses of the city are largely determined by play (Lukashok and Lynch). Like cinema, the child "explodes the prison world of familiar surroundings," preferring spaces defined by disorder, derelict spaces, and untidy corners or colonizing spaces intended for other uses (Jones, "Little Figures" 173–174). In films about children cinematic space and children's space are stitched together within the mise-en-scène that transforms familiar spaces into spaces for play and adventure.

Mapping the Book

In focusing on the urban child, I am seeking to excavate a dominant trope of cinema that has been nonetheless neglected. Star studies approach such child stars as Shirley Temple as palimpsests for commodity culture, whiteness, girlhood, and other issues but not especially in relation to urbanism. While certain cinematic urban children have been analyzed—as, for example, autobiographical stand-ins for the auteur, in the case of Truffaut's Antoine Doinel—most critical work on children tends to focus on different models of risk or aberration. Lebeau, for example, organizes her chapters around tropes of childhood sexuality and death, while Karen Lury focuses on children in genres such as Japanese horror films, in which children are ghostlike presences, or war films, in which they navigate the terrors of war through fantasy and fairytale structures; and she, like Lebeau, considers the sexuality of white female children in film as well as the relationship between children and animals, in terms of performance. My interest in the urban child may intersect with some of these areas and certainly deals with risk. But I am more interested in the quotidian taken-for-grantedness of the urban child, her status as a figure of modernity and urbanism, and her mobility and relative freedom in urban spaces, a freedom produced through what seem to be particularly urban and modern models of neglect.

The following chapters examine the fantasy of neglect about the urban child across the twentieth and early twenty-first centuries, looking primarily at film but also some literature. Although, the image of the urban child is crucial to the imaginary of cinema and literature as a whole, I limit my focus to American texts. This is partly to rein in the scope of the project but also to focus attention on how American urbanism and American childhoods are jointly imagined. Ideologies of childhood, parenting, and neglect, as well as ideas about the urban, differ across national boundaries as well as across historical periods. I limit the films I discuss to films with child actors in live-action films, not films in which adults such as Lillian Gish portray children, or films in which animated nonhuman characters, such as the fish in *Finding Nemo* (Andrew Stanton and Lee Unkrich 2003), stand in for children, because I think they mobilize the sense of risk and adventure more fully than more fantastic renderings. This is not to say that Disney's *The Princess and the Frog* or other films that portray animated urban children couldn't tell us something about the imagination of the urban and neglect. This book is not intended to be an overview or catalogue of every urban child in film, but it explores certain tropes and tendencies in film using exemplary texts. The reader will, I hope, be able to think of, and perhaps write about, other texts that fit the bill.

In analyzing representations of the urban child, I include both texts aimed at adults and texts aimed at children. In part this is because both adult-oriented and child-oriented texts participate in larger discourses about the urban child. I am seeking to unpack this discourse, not to provide a reception study or reader response theory. Further, it is difficult to extricate children's film or children's literature from adult film and literature. With much film and literature it is difficult to distinguish with any certainty between children and adults as intended audience. Prior to the mid-1960s' introduction of a ratings system for film, all films were regarded as more or less available to a general audience. To be sure, there were children's matinees, but films at those matinees were not defined generically, and they included a wide range of films that were potentially of interest to adults, such as westerns, serials, monster movies, and comedies. Even after the rise of G-rated films and children's film as a genre, audiences are mixed. Parents take kids to kid movies, and kids see films that may or may not be designated children's films, whether in the cinema, or at home on TV, or through digital technologies. Similarly, children's books are read by adults, whether the adult reads to a child or, as is frequently the case with young adult literature like *Harry Potter* novels, *The Hunger Games* trilogy, or comics, the adult may choose to read books seemingly aimed at children by and for themselves.[12] Concomitantly, though perhaps less frequently, at least some kids read texts aimed at adults, such as newspapers and magazines, as well as texts like graphic novels, whose intended audience is broad.

In terms of genre the category of children's film or children's literature is hard to sort. In part, as Rose suggests, the production and consumption of children's literature is overwhelmingly adult. Adults write, edit, sell, buy, and often read children's literature and children's film. Thus, Rose views the category of children's literature—and I would suggest, by extension, children's film—an impossibility. Similarly, Wojcik-Andrews complicates the category of children's film, noting that there are films aimed at children, films about children and childhood that may or may not be aimed at children or even rated to allow their viewing, and films children watch that are neither aimed at them nor about children or childhood (Wojcik-Andrews 1–19).[13]

Perry Nodelman recognizes children's literature as a distinct genre but, at the same time, acknowledges that children's literature is never solely for or about children. Beyond acknowledging the adult role in producing and consuming these texts, Nodelman suggests that children's literature is internally filtered through a "hidden adult" perspective. According to Nodelman, children's texts are focalized through child or childlike protagonists (animals, certain adults), but they are not generally first-person narratives. Rather, they are spoken by a third-person narrator whose narration often presents a double point of view: one childlike view and one adult view, which registers a conflict between childlike and adult perceptions and values (77). Because of this doubled narration, Nodelman claims that children's books "disperse innocence in the process of celebrating it" (79): "What texts of children's literature might be understood to sublimate or keep present but left unsaid is a variety of forms of knowledge—sexual, cultural, historical—theoretically only available to adults. . . . The unconscious of a text of children's literature is the adult consciousness that makes its childlikeness meaningful and comprehendible" (206). Therefore, even in texts with a clear audience and form directed at children, one can detect an adult perspective and voice. Though restricted to children's literature, Nodelman's argument also applies to film, which is similarly double-voiced.

Even if there is a genre of children's film or literature, I am not claiming that there is a genre of the urban child. Instead, I am locating the urban child as a figure who appears across a range of genres and categories in film and literature, including adult-oriented novels, child-oriented fiction, comic strips, texts written in first-person narration and third-person narration, girl-centered or boy-centered texts, film adaptions, and genres of film such as drama, comedy, melodrama, film noir, musicals, and historical fiction.

Rather than an audience or genre study, then, this book examines the figure of the urban child in a few particular historical moments. I have chosen a historical approach, rather than one that traces certain tropes, such as the role of the cinema as childhood space, because I believe that showing historical shifts in the discourse around the urban child will have more explanatory power. I will attend to gender throughout, examining not only the ways that girls and boys are shown as differently mobile and differently at risk but also views about motherhood and fatherhood, which are at the forefront of many of these texts.

In considering representations of the urban child, there will be, on the one hand, certain themes and tropes that recur across a wide range of texts. These relate to the child's knowingness, toughness, know-how, street smarts, pluck, resourcefulness and spirit of play, improvisation, and masquerade, as well as his or her mobility and ability to colonize space. At the same time, as notions of the urban and definitions of childhood change over time, the image of the urban child will change, too. Rather than a singular urban child, there will be the urban child defined by poverty, and the urban child defined by wealth, the female urban child and the male, the black urban child and the white; there will be urban children who operate within collectives and ones who go it alone, urban children with parents and those without. These urban children will exist in the imaginary, but that imaginary will be produced and consumed within different historical and ideological contexts and will feed different ideas and ideals of childhood and of the city. Across this book, then, my goal will be to consider the function as well as the image of the urban child and how different fantasies of neglect interact with different fantasies of childhood and the city.

1

Boys, Movies, and City Streets; or, The Dead End Kids as Modernists

Many of the most stereotypical images of urban childhood neglect have their point of origin and dominance in Depression era Hollywood. During the Depression orphans, waifs, and street urchins dominate the screen. Not coincidentally, the Depression was the era of the child star. Figures such as Shirley Temple, Jackie Cooper, Freddie Bartholomew, Dickie Moore, Virginia Weidler, Deanna Durbin, Judy Garland, Mickey Rooney, Jane Withers, and the ensemble actors of the Jones Family, Dead End Kids, and Our Gang films series saturated the screen. Beyond movies, comics and radio showcased the kids of *Little Orphan Annie* and *Gasoline Alley*. The presence of child stars and child-centered texts was not entirely new. Nineteenth-century theatergoers witnessed the ascent of child star Elsie Leslie, who played Little Lord Fauntleroy at age seven, and the silent film era featured adult actresses such as Mary Pickford and Lillian Gish in numerous child-like roles, as well as child stars such as Jackie Coogan, Chaplin's sidekick in *The Kid* (Charlie Chaplin 1921). But the proliferation and dominance of child stars and child images in the Depression was extraordinary, and those child stars often featured in narratives of neglect and poverty.

Some have argued that the rise of children in film was a response to the Motion Picture Production Code's clamping down on violence and sexuality in films (J. Hampton). Certainly, child-centered films circulate in a context of concern about media influence. But to posit that child-centered films were presented in the 1930s as better influences for children ignores the role already played by children in silent cinema and does not explain the appeal of children to audiences or the complexity of their representations. Moreover, the child films investigated here were not marketed as children's films: in the 1930s no such ratings system existed. Children watched a wide range of films, including gangster pictures, romance, melodrama, screwball comedies, as well as, potentially, child-centered films (Brown 2). More likely to target children were serials, westerns, and adventure stories. Surprisingly, perhaps, Universal horror films of the 1930s were especially appealing to children (Brown 15). Accordingly, child-focused films should be considered adult or family fare: their target audience and fan base seem to have been adults as much as children. Indeed, Noel Brown argues that, while child-star films were successful, there is no evidence that juvenile audiences were the spectators. Thus, the images of childhood neglect must appeal to adult fantasies and fears of childhood as much as provide sources of identification for children.

Rather than a strategic sop to censors, some critics have argued that child films provided a "palliative" counter to the miseries of the Great Depression (Brown 17; Eckert). If, however, these films provided an escape, they did so in complicated ways. The notion that these films provide an escape may be related more to the spectator's feelings of sentimentality or utopian affect when watching them than to the content of the narratives.

In part, these Hollywood child films function much like the musicals and other forms Richard Dyer analyzes in his essay "Entertainment and Utopia." Dyer takes seriously the usual dismissal of entertainment as "escape" and "wish-fulfilment" to suggest that entertainment responds to real needs in society, by offering forms of nonspecific utopianism ("what utopia would feel like rather than how it would be organized" [20]). He argues that in order to make spectators feel better, entertainment doesn't just offer us visions of a better world (pretty people, nice cars, lavish sets) but also, and more importantly, provides the illusion that it solves problems. But entertainment delimits the needs and desires of society even as it addresses them because it offers solutions to only some needs and problems, and that enables us to ignore others. These problems are, in Dyer's account, the generic problems of people in capitalist societies rather than more specific issues. They work at the level of affect. So exhaustion, related to the condition of living and working under capitalism, is resolved filmically through scenes that convey energy (tap dancing, for example). A sense of scarcity is countered by scenes of abundance (expensive sets, images of wealth, lots of extras). Emotional intensity (such as torch songs) counter feelings of dreariness; images of community offset feelings of alienation; and transparency (characters speaking or singing their feelings directly) neutralizes the effects of being manipulated and lied to. Like the "solutions" of capitalism—buying more products—these texts create problems internally and then resolve them within the film, deflecting the real concerns that might have brought one to the movie theater seeking escape in the first place, providing a false and temporary respite only.

In child films of the 1930s the feelings of utopia are produced, for example, through energetic musical performances in the case of Shirley Temple and Jane Withers; heartfelt expressions of sentiment in the case of Temple, Withers, and Jackie Cooper; scenes of community in Our Gang and the Dead End Kids; intensity in moments of crisis; a child's tears; and so on. Abundance figures occasionally—as the urban child encounters wealth. Still, these films do not completely direct attention away from real-world concerns. Rather than deflect or ignore the traumatic effects of the Depression in a purely escapist mode, images of childhood in the 1930s serve to acknowledge and work through many of the anxieties of the Depression. In line with Dyer's argument, however, direct topical references to the Depression or the New Deal are rare (Temple's film *Just around the Corner* [Irving Cummings 1938] is an exception that will engage the New Deal directly). Instead, the issues of the Depression and of the status of children are refracted into more long-term lingering issues of modernity accentuated by the Depression, including urbanization, industrialization, overcrowding, massification, immigration, changing social mores, and family structures.

Instead of reading these films as a direct response to the strictures of the Production Code or to assume that they present images of childhood innocence that will cheer audiences, we need to think of the "palliative" effects of child-centered films and their relation to the Depression in more complex terms. The rise of the child in American film needs to be examined in the context of a number of intersecting trends and issues in American culture that galvanize images of childhood neglect for adult audiences. The

Depression engendered many contradictory discourses around children. In the 1930s the displacement of children from home, loss of parents, and loss of income created a sense of crisis around childhood, with fears about child homelessness, runaways, truancy, and risk all potentially leading to child endangerment and the loss of innocence (Mintz 235–248). Parental abandonment and desertions also raised questions about the value of the child and family, as more and more children were placed in custody or left to fend for themselves (Mintz 237). At the same time, as Viviana Zelizer explains, from the late nineteenth century through the 1930s, perceptions of childhood shifted, from viewing children as economically worthwhile participants in public and family life to being economically "worthless" but emotionally "priceless." This transition was uneven, however: nineteenth-century working-class children were still expected to contribute wages and household assistance even as middle-class children began to be viewed differently; and the Depression restored the need for "useful" children across a wide range of families.

This tension between viewing the child as "priceless" and as economically useful continues throughout the 1930s. In line with views of the child as priceless, or intended to be outside the realm of economic usefulness, child labor laws were under debate from 1904, with Progressive activists, such as the National Child Labor Committee and National Consumers League, working to pressure Congress to enact laws protecting children. Children's working conditions in mills and factories were publicized using the photographs of Lewis Hine and other means to shape public opinion.[1] Not until 1938, however, did President Franklin Delano Roosevelt sign the Fair Labor Standards Act, which placed limits on child labor, excluding agricultural work. Thus, while children were ever more ideologically positioned outside the labor force, they were legally available or, in many cases, subject to it.

In terms of child stars, in particular, the California Child Actors Bill, also known as the Coogan Act or Coogan Bill, was passed in 1934 to protect the earnings of child actors. The law was named for the very successful child star Jackie Coogan, who earned approximately $4 million in his youth but discovered, when he was twenty-three years old, that his mother and stepfather had spent almost all the money he had earned. After suing his parents, Coogan recovered less than $126,000 of the $250,000 left of his fortune. The Coogan case not only set in motion laws that still stand today—requiring set aside amounts from children's earnings, schooltime, and limited workdays—but also exposed the problematic relation between children and work and the child's use value within the family. Coogan's mother claimed, "No promises were ever made to give Jackie anything. Every dollar a kid earns before he is 21 belongs to his parents. Jackie will not get a cent of his earnings" ("Strange Case"; Zierold 7–45).

The child star, and images of youth, thus worked to reassert the pricelessness and innocence of childhood at a time when the status of the child—his or her worth and his or her innocence—were up for grabs. The child star, of course, embodied contradictorily both the image of the priceless child and the image of extreme wealth and success under capitalism, as a figure whose labor was simultaneously celebrated and obscured. Many other critics have examined the figure of the child star in relation to economics and labor. Charles Eckert, for example, analyzes the way Shirley Temple's star text obscures not only her labor but the labor of all the other film production personnel around her at the same time that she plays characters who engage issues of the Depression by modeling charity and concern for the working class. Rob King analyzes Jackie Coogan, arguing that Coogan's portrayals of poor dependent children were easily commoditized and absorbed into consumer culture—turned into costumes and dolls. My interest here is less in the labor of the child star herself than the ways in which the filmic representations of children engage issues of labor and economics and similarly highlight the density of the child's innocence and pricelessness.

Most viewers and commentators today assume nostalgically that the child-star era was an age of innocence. But children in Depression era texts are very often orphaned or displaced or even homeless; they are often depicted as trapped in poverty or as falling out of the middle or upper class into poverty; often, they are workers, or petty criminals, subject to the economy, not existing outside it. Films focused on children in this period situate the child in an urban milieu structured by economic status and often outside traditional family structures. As I suggested in my introduction, the urban child is always already compromised in terms of innocence, and many of the texts from this period assert innocence, if at all, only in the face of the child's experience and knowingness. The urban child, similarly, unnerves precisely because, in the context of a culture of "pricelessness," she registers as out of place, too adult, not innocent. There is sweetness and sentiment in these films, to be sure, and moral virtue, but never lack of knowledge or complete insulation from harsh realities.

Because they raise the specter of so many issues associated with urbanization and modernity, neglected-child films of the 1930s can be read in terms of what Miriam Hansen has termed "vernacular modernism." As opposed to modernist aesthetics, the concept of vernacular modernism will "encompass cultural practices that both articulated and mediated the experience of modernity" ("Mass Production" 333).[2] In her figuration classical Hollywood cinema can be "imagined as a cultural practice on a par with the experience of modernity, as an industry-produced, mass-based, vernacular modernism" (Hansen, "Mass Production" 337). Rather than a mere reflection *of* modernity, vernacular modernism must, in some way, reflect *upon* modernity. Hansen writes: "The question was, and continues to be, how particular film practices can be productively understood as *responding*—and making sensually graspable our responses—to the set of technological, economic, social and perceptual transformations associated with the term modernity" (Hansen, "Tracking Cinema" 608). This reflexivity differs from the self-reflexive style often associated with modernism; indeed, vernacular modernism encompasses "plenty of films that transmute conflicts and contradictions arising from modernity into conventional narrative and compositional forms" (Hansen, "Tracking Cinema" 613). Vernacular modernism thus differs from what Liesl Olsen has identified as the modernist penchant for representing and describing the ordinary, insofar as Olsen's argument still balances the ordinary as *subject* against modernism as *style*.

In the late nineteenth and early twentieth centuries, as the image of the child focalized anxieties over increased urbanization, and the growing squalor of industrialized cities, including overpopulation, tenements, and slums, the urban child in cinema could function as a palimpsest showing the effects of modernity. In particular, 1930s child-focused films depict what David Pike, in his consideration of subterranean spaces in nineteenth-century literature, has characterized as "a burgeoning modernity perceived personally—through the lived space of the child—rather than solely as representation, as modernism" (872). The contradictions of modernity are played out through the figure of the child in these films by balancing, on the one hand, a kind of social miserabilism, or woeful sociological gaze, and, on the other, a sense of mobility, spatial freedom, and play. While showing kids as subject to economic and social forces, and as figures of neglect, these texts also show kids as independent, resourceful, and playful—able to navigate urban life with amazing pluck and skill.

Acting Urban

To consider how the urban child functions as a vehicle for vernacular modernism, we need to define the parameters of the urban in the child-centered narratives of this period.

Part of my argument in this book is that not only definitions of the child but also ideas and ideals of the urban change historically, and in tandem. Additionally, at any given time multiple and contradictory urbanisms might coexist. Films are selective and ideological in their vision: they produce different ideals and images of the city and variable philosophies of the urban. Therefore, for example, 1930s RKO musicals starring Fred Astaire and Ginger Rogers depict urbanism in terms of an urbane, sophisticated, global cosmopolitanism—a world of resorts, white telephones, fancy hotels, and nightclubs, all animated and romanticized through spontaneous and erotic dances. Their cities are wealthy, white, and devoid of children. By contrast, the urbanism of Depression era child films tend to focus on lower-class neighborhoods, street life, different ethnicities and occasionally mixed-race groups, and the encounter among children and between children and adults. For moviegoers, potentially seeing an Astaire-Rogers musical in the same week as a film featuring Jackie Cooper as a tough newsboy, these visions of the city might be each as real or as fantastic as the other but hard to imagine conjoined.

Urbanism is more than setting. Being an urban child is not simply a matter of being placed in a city setting. Rubes and hicks can come to the city; it does not make them urban. The urban child, by contrast, is *of* the city. Thus, in considering the paradigm of the urban child in the 1930s, we need to consider what actions an urban setting generates and, equally, how the child's performance produces the urban.

In what follows, I will consider the performance of urbanism in the films starring the Dead End Kids, the ensemble of actors who gained stardom on the stage in Sidney Kingsley's sensational play *Dead End* (1935). My analysis is limited to some of their earliest films in the 1930s, before they become the Little Tough Guys, the teenage East Side Kids, or the grown Bowery Boys in films that continue through the 1950s. In the late 1930s the Dead End Kids are still convincingly kids, seemingly as young as nine and not older than thirteen. Furthermore, these early films differ from later incarnations. As Amanda Klein has argued in her book on film cycles, the initial cycle of Dead End Kids films was topical, addressing the plight of urban youth via a Progressive emphasis on social justice (62). Within a very short span of time, however, rather than "referents of real people suffering in a real world," the Dead End Kids began to signify themselves as types or "'facsimiles' of their former selves" (Klein 80). Accordingly, as the Dead End Kids splintered into Little Tough Guys, East Side Kids, and the Bowery Boys, their films turned toward comedy and comedic suspense films, similar to Abbott and Costello monster films. These later films do not place the boys as clearly in an urban environment and do not address concerns about neglect or urbanization.

While considering their performance of urbanism, I will also signal ways in which their films render modernity from a child's perspective. I will be taking the Dead End Kids as paradigmatic for, at least, representations of urban boys, but I will acknowledge some differences from other representations of urban boys. To be sure, the actors Billy Halop, Leo Gorcey, Huntz Hall, Gabe Dell, Bernard Punsley, and Bobby Jordan themselves "act urban" in order to embody the Dead End Kids. While Leo Gorcey fell into acting and played more or less himself for twenty years, most of the other kids trained at the Professional Children's School and/or had some schooling and experience as child actors in radio and onstage before being cast in the play *Dead End*. Rather than focus on the actors who formed the Dead End Kids, however, I consider the characters they play as themselves performing the urban, or, to be precise, I consider the way in which the actors show urbanism as a mode of everyday performance for the characters and do not consider the particular method the actors used.[3]

In the Dead End Kids films, as in many other 1930s child-focused films, the performance of urbanism is intertwined with the performance of class, gender, and race. The urban children in these films are generally white, ethnic, lower-class children living on the Lower East Side or other ghettos.[4] Boys dominate depictions of the urban tenement child in these films. The Dead End Kids will add an African American character as the series continues (largely for comedic effect), but they initially exist in a white world populated by Greek, Italian, Irish, and Jewish immigrant working-class families. Most often, in the Dead End Kids films, women are relegated to maternal or sisterly roles, though one girl teams with the boys in *Angels Wash Their Faces* (Ray Enright 1939). Parents are absent and neglectful. For most of the boys, parents are offscreen—a mother yelling for her son to come home, or a boy's casual description of his father drunkenly beating the boy's mother (in *Dead End* [William Wyler 1937]). Generally, the main boy protagonist lives only with his older sister, who cares for him and tries to protect him from street life. Other siblings are absent and never mentioned. The boys are generally associated with low-level criminality. The films usually involve run-ins with the police and other institutions of government, including school and the mayor's office. Those institutions are imagined to be corrupt. The boys sometimes triumph over some form of corruption or evil but are not reformed or significantly altered in their manners, behavior, or attitude. The films are comedic overall but allow some romance—usually for a Kid's sister—and some melodramatic moments.

In everyday performance, as onstage, such things as clothing, sex, age, race, size and looks, posture, speech, facial expressions, bodily gestures, and the like indicate social status. In the Dead End Kids films the characters are costumed to suggest poverty. They mostly wear torn, dirty, ill-fitting pants, sweatshirts, and T-shirts; and they do not change their clothes much in the course of a film, except occasionally to put on a clean suit in moments when they are expected to rise in social status, such as when they are released from reform school in *Crime School* (Lewis Seiler 1938) or become an honorary mayor and his cabinet in *Angels Wash Their Faces*. Their speech pattern signifies their lower-class status. Their accent both marks their regional location in New York's Lower East Side and carries traces of their class—lots of *d'em*s and *d'ose*s. They use slang expressions and malapropisms rather than correct English. Their postures are simultaneously slouchy and antagonistic—they slump on stoops, perch on top of tables, walk aggressively, and move quickly from a state of repose to a fighting stance. There are slight variations across the ensemble in terms of aggressivity, with Gorcey's and Halop's characters the quickest to fight, but all the kids are shown as ready to engage in violent behavior. They do not follow rules of society in terms of manners or law. They are frequently seen spitting, shoving people, committing petty crimes, colonizing spaces, and antagonizing both grown-ups and other kids.

Crucially, the Dead End Kids operate as a gang. They collectively antagonize neighbors, shopkeepers, and other kids. Occasionally the boys remind each other of how to behave, and they adhere to a strictly coded law of the streets that demands loyalty to the group and no "squealing." In the play and film *Dead End*, for example, Tommy (Halop) attempts to carve "the mark of the squealer" onto the forehead of his friend Spit (Gorcey) when he discovers that Spit has named him to police. The gang also operates by a system of exclusion that denies membership to girls, effeminate boys, and others. *Dead End* will show membership as a privilege accorded the new kid on the block, Milty (Punsley), only after he has passed a series of tests, including being "cockalized," which consists of his being thrown to the ground, his pants pulled down, dirt rubbed onto his genitals, and then spit upon (Turner 220; Kingsley 1.31).

Setting the Urban Stage

While the setting of the Dead End Kids films moves among the street, the kids' hideout in an abandoned building, one or two tenement rooms, and, generally, a jail, courtroom, or reform school, the primary setting is the Lower East Side or, more precisely, the block, shown as a community with its own rules and boundaries. Erving Goffman differentiates between the front region, where the performance takes place, and the back region, where the performer can let down his mask. (Think of the distinction for waiters between the seating area and the kitchen.) In the Dead End Kids films no such difference exists. The Kids behave the same regardless of the setting, whether in their private homes or on the street. The lack of distinction between front and back region is also due to the porousness of space in the urban area depicted. Urban domestic settings are inherently porous, as they combine public and private space. In these films, moreover, private matters are always public. Streets are strewn with laundry, characters shout to each other from windows and across streets, people chase fire trucks to scenes of fire and crime, police enter tenement apartments at will, and gossip and news travel quickly. There is no sense of private or hidden space in which the actor can prepare or drop his mask.

At the same time, the Lower East Side is treated in these films as itself a back region for upper Manhattan, situating that space as a local variant of the urban that runs counter to more glamorous modernist fantasies of the city. In her description of Shanghai silent film as exemplary of vernacular modernism, Hansen notes that many of the films produce fantastic modernist spaces, with art deco glamour, but juxtapose those settings with "less glamorous spaces of urban living: overcrowded housing, dingy cabins and apartments, factories, offices, bustling and unsafe streets" ("Fallen Women" 14). In her discussion of Japanese films she notes the importance of images that Kracauer would align with "blind spots of the mind," things revealed

FIGURE 2. In *Angels with Dirty Faces* laundry and crowded streets evoke the Lower East Side.

through cinema that would otherwise be overlooked, including refuse (Kracauer 54): "Objects that push the film's aesthetic toward the 'formless': images of trash, detritus, rubble, waste—literally, the abject" (Hansen, "Tracking Cinema" 605). Hansen argues that American films of the Depression introduce such images in order to clean them up. In contrast, I would suggest that in these films those images are mobilized as, on the one hand, a counter to the veneer of modernism and, on the other, as spaces of localism and play. They are not refigured or reformed in the films but maintained as a local, in the vernacular sense—defined through class, ethnicity, and historical circumstance.

In these films the Lower East Side is sometimes explicitly pitted against front-stage Manhattan, in shots that juxtapose the two regions. In *Crime School*, for example, the opening shot of the film shows the depopulated image of the New York City skyline, signaling the front region of the city, its most perfect image. But a speedy horizontal wipe right quickly removes that image and replaces it with one of the Lower East Side. This shot contrasts the more abstract image of New York with an image of the local, marked as lower class. We see crowded streets with laundry hanging out windows, street vendors, cars and pushcarts side by side, and children playing everywhere—on the sidewalk, in the street, and on fire escapes.

Angels with Dirty Faces (Michael Curtiz 1938) does not explicitly juxtapose the Lower East Side with glamorous New York but showcases the neighborhood as its own universe, separate from the rest of the city. It provides an anthropological view in a circular pan that shows the familiar image of laundry—a key signifier of backstage activity, here performed on the front stage, as it were—covering the front of every building, with women hanging out windows beating rugs. We see horse-drawn carriages and pushcarts but no cars (this scene serves as a flashback to the childhood of characters who are adults in the diegesis almost twenty years later—a newspaper headline reports that Warren Harding has been nominated for the presidency). Children crowd together on the street, squat on sidewalks, and hang on fire escapes, and girls dance in the street, to the music of an organ grinder.[5]

In both the play and film *Dead End* the juxtaposition of "front" and "back" regions dominates the mise-en-scène. The boys hang out at the end of the street, the eponymous "dead end," where the tenement district and East River abut the back entrance to a new high-rise building, the East River Terrace Apartments. Residents of the high-rise must use the back entrance because of an elevator problem, and they are exposed to the slum boys, who use the dock as a hangout and swimming hole. This juxtaposition emulates the historical placement of River House, built on East Fifty-third Street at Sutton Place in 1931. Sutton Place had been an industrial enclave with coal, lumber- and brickyards, breweries, cigar manufacturers, coffin factories, and slaughterhouses. Gentrification began in the early twentieth century, and the area became fashionable in the 1930s. But development halted during the Depression, and the area still had many tenements and traces of industry. River House, a twenty-six-story cooperative apartment building, afforded residents a private dock and floating pier where they could anchor their yachts (Sanders, *Celluloid Skyline* 220–221). Thus, the play and film mirror historical reality in creating a juxtaposition of classes in jarring distinction.

The film *Dead End* underscores the difference between the two sides of New York it depicts in its opening shots. First, Samuel Goldwyn's name covers the screen, establishing this as a prestige picture. Then a rapid zoom shows a sign reading "Dead End." Credits follow, not including any of the boys' names (as this film serves to introduce them to movie audiences). A title explains the process of gentrification and juxtaposition of high-rise luxury and tenements. Behind it we see the skyline. The camera then tilts downward, from the lofty height of the skyscrapers down into the tenement district, "as if to mimic the perspective of the rich tenants who gaze down into the ghetto from the safe vantage point of their opulent apartments" (Klein 64). The image gets darker and darker as it descends, then the camera pans left through the tenement blocks. As in the other films, visual shorthand establishes the region: laundry hanging to dry, tenants sleeping on fire escapes, and garbage cans. A beat cop walks past a milkman, and then we follow the cop's progress down the street until he passes the doorman of the East River Terrace Apartments scrubbing the front, then pokes a man sleeping on a bench and forces him to move on. Unlike other films, the streets here are largely empty because of the early hour.

Other child-centered films of the period similarly demarcate the difference between the generic setting of the city and the "back region." In the Monogram Pictures film *Boy of the Streets* (William Nigh 1937), starring Jackie Cooper, for example, opening credits appear over a montage of images, signaling a move from a modernist conception of the city to the vernacular. First, we see the Monogram logo—a black-and-white art deco futuristic drawing of a skyline with tunnels floating in the sky to connect buildings. An airplane and a blimp cross paths in the sky; then a fast-moving train pulls the art deco letters for MONOGRAM diagonally downward and left across the screen, and another pulls PICTURES diagonally upward to the right. From the logo we cut to the film's title (with Cooper's name prominently above the line) and an aerial pan of the skyline behind. This dissolves into a shot of the East River, with the skyline in the distant background, then cuts to the familiar image of a ghetto street, presumably in the Lower East Side—with pushcarts, cars, and pedestrians jumbled together in the street and crowded sidewalks. Cut-ins show more kids on sidewalks as the credits conclude, and the film cuts to a nighttime scene in which kids ride bicycles, boxcars, and scooters down the street wearing Halloween masks. Another Cooper film, *Streets of New York* (William Nigh 1939), moves more simply from a still image of the skyline at night followed by an overhead still shot of traffic on a city boulevard, then a still image of train tracks, then a still of more crowded and narrow city streets filled with trucks, and finally the familiar image of an ethnic neighborhood filled with pedestrians, until cutting to a nighttime scene of boys at a newsstand hawking newspapers on Christmas Eve.

These "back region" images in these child films situate the action in both a time and place. In E. Relph's terms the Lower East Side in these films is defined as a community and by a sense of "placeness" (35). The "placeness" of this region is defined by its imageability—the repetition of certain visual tropes (e.g., laundry, girls dancing in the streets, pushcarts)—and by the sense of its being an enclave—enclosed and with boundaries. In showing this back region, the films provide spectators with a sense of what Relph calls "vicarious insideness" (50), access to an experience of place. This differs from "incidental outsideness," in "which places are experienced as little more than background or setting for activities and are quite incidental to those activities" (Relph 52). In Relph's characterization the placeness of a place is not dependent on its veracity—it need not be a "real" place. The Dead End Kids films, like the majority of Warner Bros. films in the 1930s, were shot on the studio backlot.[6] Yet the sense of place, and insideness, persists.

To consider how placeness works in the Dead End Kids films, contrast them to the Our Gang series of short films. While the Dead End Kids films situate us clearly in the Lower East Side, using visual shorthand and contrasting the neighborhood to other images of New York, the locations for the Our Gang films are very hard to decipher. Presumably, the films are set in Los Angeles and, to a degree, reflect Los Angeles's relatively undeveloped appearance in the 1930s. They were mostly shot in the Hal Roach studios but occasionally used one Los Angeles location shot for an exterior or street corner. Wherever they were shot, the films show amorphous spaces that are not clearly marked as being urban, suburban, or rural.

In each Our Gang film there is an almost postmodern assemblage of spaces that are efficacious for the narrative but lacking in any sense of place. In "Fly My Kite" (Robert McGowan 1931), for instance, the action starts in a cozy living room where the mixed-race, mixed-sex gang plays with Grandma (Margaret Mann), a kindly old lady who reads pulp fiction to them, boxes with them, and does cartwheels to warm up. An exterior shot shows what appears to be a single-family home, largely isolated from any other buildings, looking more rural than urban or suburban. But, when Grandma's no-good son-in-law arrives to tell her he is kicking her out, we see an internal doorbell, suggesting that this is an apartment building. Outside, the gang plays in an empty lot, strewn with garbage, signaling urban space again. But its distance from any buildings makes it equally available to be read as a rural field. In "Honky Donkey" (Gus Meins 1934) a rich kid (Wally Albright) and his chauffeur (Don Barclay) drop his mother off to shop at a fancy department store on a busy city street. At the kid's insistence the driver takes him to "alleys, dirty ones," so he can find kids to play with. He finds the gang in an alley, playing a game in which they have rigged a merry-go-round with a mule driving the machinery. Kicked out of the alley by the owner of the land and with nowhere else to play, they go to the rich kid's house, a mansion that is framed in such a way as to make unclear its location and its proximity or lack thereof to other buildings. In "Hook and Ladder" (Robert McGowan 1932) the kids set up a make-shift firehouse in a barn so they can be volunteer firemen. There, they have beds laid out upstairs, clothing, and a Rube Goldberg alarm system run by a cat and a dog. How or why they have access to a barn is never stated, let alone how they got a dozen beds in there. When the fire alarm rings, they travel by horse and buggy and with a second goat-driven cart through what appears to be a small town, with low-rise storefronts, then arrive at a ware-house (filled with dynamite, of course). "The First Round-Up" (Gus Meins 1934) takes the boys from an enclosed yard, up a two-mile hill, to a creek for a camping trip.

Settings for the Our Gang films are gag driven. Whatever space the story requires magically appears. Similarly, whatever props the kids need for their schemes is always at hand. In "Hook and Ladder," for example, they have fireman hats, slickers, a horse-drawn carriage, axes, and fire hose. In "The First Round-Up," when Spanky McFarland and Scotty Beckett find out that the older kids are going camping, they come back with full backpacks and gear. The kids in these films are provided for, not neglected—they have parents, teachers, friendly neighbors, and helpful policemen. Rather than a clearly defined urban setting, or an image of neglect, we get something like Mayberry—a small town populated by kooky adults and playful kids. Because Our Gang films do not clearly place the kids in an urban setting, they do not clearly engage modernity. Instead, the films tend to skew more toward a timeless image of childhood innocence than the Dead End Kids films or those with Jackie Cooper.

If setting follows action in the Our Gang shorts, in *Dead End*, by con-trast, setting motivates the action and produces a sense of vicarious inside-ness for the film viewer. The Dead End Kids hang outside the high-rise building, intimidate the wealthy residents who live there, and antagonize the doorman. In particular, they berate and eventually attack the child whom Jeffrey Turner, borrowing from Leslie Fiedler, characterizes as the

FIGURE 3. In *Dead End* the Dead End Kids harass wealthy Philip, the boy from the high-rise, showing the proximity of tenement kids to luxury.

"Good Good Boy," Philip (Charles Peck), an effete, sheltered wealthy child (Turner 218). When the boy's beating is discovered, one of the boys, Tommy, knifes Philip's father after he threatens to have him arrested. In another subplot the adult male Dave (Joel McCrea), from the tenements, romances wealthy Kay (Wendy Barrie), who lives as a kept woman in the high-rise, while his would-be girlfriend Drina (Sylvia Sidney) suffers in silence as she struggles to keep her brother Tommy safe and participates in a strike at work. This place motivates and shapes the narrative, delimits characters' options, and mobilizes a host of anxieties about modernity, from the perspective of both the displaced poor and the gentrifying rich. It presents urbanization via tropes of immigration, massification, and overcrowding, as well as in terms of gentrification and the potential erasure of localism and diversity.

Dead End shows this place as enclosed. Partly owing to the film's origins as a stage play, characters enter the neighborhood from outside, but outside the neighborhood is never shown onscreen (thus maintaining its theatrical feel). Gangster Baby Face Martin (Humphrey Bogart), a former kid on the block, returns to see his mother (Marjorie Main) and former girlfriend Francey (Claire Trevor). Francey has moved out herself and become a prostitute but is lured back to the block to see Martin. Dave shoots Martin down in the alley so that he exits in a body bag. Characters in this neighborhood dream of escape. Kay plans to leave on a yacht with her lover, unless Dave can get a job with enough income to keep her. Dave dreams of becoming an architect, but he wants to stay and work within the neighborhood, to improve it. Drina dreams of taking Tommy away to a better neighborhood, but Dave reminds her that she may never get far enough away to keep him from trouble. When characters exit the neighborhood—when Dave has a job interview downtown, or Francey leaves after being shunned by Martin, or Drina goes to join the strike—their actions remain offscreen so that we, as viewers, experience a claustrophobic vicarious insideness.

Because the neighborhood is, in effect, closed, the encounters available to the boys are limited to people who enter the neighborhood. In each film there are, on the one hand, kindhearted and moral people who try to influence the boys and, on the other, corrupt forces that lure them into trouble. In *Angels Wash Their Faces* Ronald Reagan plays a well-meaning district attorney who attempts to help reform school parolee Gabe Ryan (Frankie Thomas), mainly to appeal to his sister Joy (Ann Sheridan). But when Gabe is framed by a local gangster for a deadly act of arson, it is the boys, not the D.A., who save him—by bullying the gangster, tying him and his accomplice to a post, and threatening them with violence until they confess. In *Crime School* the new warden of the reform school, Mark Braden (Humphrey Bogart), ousts the corrupt villains who run the institution, again, because he favors Sue Warren (Gale Page), whose brother (Halop) is incarcerated.

In Jackie Cooper films, similarly, we see a tug-of-war between good and bad influences, all localized within the neighborhood. In *Boy of the Streets*, disappointed when he learns that his father is not the high-minded civic leader he has imagined but instead an unemployed "stooge," Cooper's character, Chuck Brennan, is lured into crime by local hotshot gangster Blackie Davis (Matty Fain). Only when Davis shoots the local beat cop, a kindly Irishman who helps Brennan and his friends, does Brennan turn against Davis. Ultimately, though, his only option to escape the influence of Davis and rise to a better position than his father's, and his only means out of the neighborhood, is to join the navy.

In the context of debates about media influence on kids, these films often show the bad influence as the more attractive. In *Angels with Dirty Faces* the priest, Jerry (Pat O'Brien), and the good girl Laury Ferguson (Ann Sheridan) are both neighborhood kids who seek to make a difference. But it is James Cagney's Rocky Sullivan who fascinates the boys. In *Dead End* Dave and Drina try to protect Tommy, but it is Bogart's Baby Face Martin who teaches him to use a knife and gives approval to his gang's attacks on Philip and Milty. Admittedly, in each film the criminal gets his "due"— Cagney's Rocky Sullivan famously puts on an extravagant masquerade of cowardice on death row to lessen the boys' admiration for him—but neither film allows the boy an escape or provides much hope that his life will be different after the gangster dies.

Play and Urbanism

The film image of children using public spaces as an arena for play and recreation—and not segregated in set-aside play areas like playgrounds or parks—becomes shorthand for lower-class life. These images mark a kind of social miserabilism, signaling overcrowding and a reformist concern about kids not having adequate space to play, but they also show urban space as dynamic, contingent, and available for play and encounter.[7] Kids colonize space and use it for their own purposes, mixing with adults and breaking down barriers between play space and work space, private life and public life. Here, as Kracauer suggests, the street offers "the senselessly tempting jumble of reeling life . . . adventure and untasted possibility" (Kracauer trans. in Hansen, *Cinema and Experience* 11).

The setting in the Dead End Kids films is marked by poverty and, for some characters, despair. But for the boys these spaces are places of play and amusement. The Dead End Kids transform the street, which is cast as a space of potential misery, into a play space. In *Angels with Dirty Faces*, for example, one scene shows Bim (Leo Gorcey), Swing (Bobby Jordan), and Patsy (Gabe Dell) walking through a crowded Lower East Side neighborhood. In the space of a single block they swipe a flask off one pushcart and a tomato off another, swap packs of stolen cigarettes, try to "conk" a police officer on the head by throwing the stolen tomato in the air over their heads, casually commandeer a baby carriage, with a baby in it, then shove the carriage back down the sidewalk when its parents complain, mocking

FIGURE 4. The Dead End Kids have a streetside tea party in *Angels Wash Their Faces*.

the father's ethnic accent as they do so, all before joining the rest of their gang on a stoop before they attempt to spontaneously and opportunistically rob Rocky Sullivan (Cagney).

In *Angels Wash Their Faces*, when Gabe Ryan moves into their neighborhood, the Dead End Kids—in this film, Billy (Billy Halop), Sleepy (Bernard Punsley), Lee (Leo Gorcey), Huntz (Huntz Hall), Luigi (Gabe Dell), and Bernie (Bobby Jordan)—notice his moving cart. Billy stops in his tracks and says, "Hey, look-it! Immigrants!" As they make their way down the block to examine the "immigrants," Lee casually swipes a parasol off a pushcart and does a balancing act along the curb. They steal a plate off another cart and play keep-away with it until it smashes. They run. They then spontaneously commandeer items off the Ryans' moving truck. As they array themselves in chairs in the street, they speak in fake posh accents: "What, no cha-zee longe?" Lee says (mispronouncing *chaise lounge*). "These persons must be riffraff." A dissolve marks the passage of time and shows that the boys have set up an imaginary tea party in the street, using the Ryans' dishes. They adopt female ethnic personae with accents, postures, and manners of those women, in effect playing their own mothers. Bernie announces, "Ladies, tea is ready." Billy addresses Luigi using an unpronounceable Italian-sounding name. Luigi responds by speaking in an Italian accent about "her" son, Tony, and calls Billy Mrs. O'Grady. Billy, with an adopted Irish accent addresses Lee as Mrs. Finnegan. Lee, in turn, responds in a feminine voice, then says "We Finnegans are real tea men."[8] As in the scene from *Angels with Dirty Faces*, they improvise, use everyday objects as props, and enact a performance that is simultaneously play and theatricalized menace. They enact class, ethnic, and gender masquerades, exploding ideas of authenticity.

Play situates the Dead End Kids in opposition to labor, thus marking their innocence at the same time that their play shows their urban toughness. In negotiating space, and asserting their control over events, things, and people in the street, the Dead End Kids' play also absorbs and transforms the effects of overcrowding, immigration, and assimilation. Rather than traumatized subjects of modernity, they are shown as spontaneous, improvisational, able to make do with objects at hand, and able to command space. They can assimilate different identities—mothers, shopkeepers, Italians, Irish—without losing their own identities. The ideal cinematic subject that Kracauer describes as "things normally unseen" (46–57), the familiar objects of everyday life, become animated in these scenes as playthings, mobilized for staged scenes. In this sense the Dead End Kids function as objective correlatives for the cinema itself, which, in Kracauer's terms, "has to completely break apart the natural contexts of our lives" through the "continual transformation of the external world, the crazy displacement of its objects" (trans. Hansen, *Cinema and Experience* 12) to show us reality in new ways.

Boys and City Streets

From a twenty-first-century perspective the Dead End Kids might seem like exaggerated cartoons of youth. But for a 1930s audience they could provide a titillating sensational spectacle of poverty, class, and gender. As Turner says in relation to Kingsley's play, "Representing the poor as an evening of theatrical spectacle provided privileged, white New Yorkers an unusual but popular evening of entertainment" (223).

No matter how seemingly exaggerated, the depiction of the Dead End Kids resonates with other depictions of modern urban boys. The image of boys' street life in the Dead End Kids movies corresponds remarkably well not only with other child-centered films but also with analyses of urban boys by activists and social scientists, from the late nineteenth century forward, none of which view boys as innocents and all of which consider urban boys to be a social problem, even a menace. These include writings by Charles Loring Brace, father of the orphan trains that relocated an estimated 250,000 orphaned, abandoned, or homeless children to rural areas between 1853 and 1929. In his late nineteenth-century analysis of street boys Brace says that in comparison to wealthy New Yorkers, they bear something of the "same relation which Indians bear to the civilized western settlers" (61). He defines these homeless youth as a "fighting, swearing, stealing and gambling set" (62) but says that the boys also have a code of honor and a deep sense of fun. Viewing proletariat New York as a hotbed of crime, Brace ascribes this development to the weakening of marriage ties, overcrowding, and intemperance.

In a similar vein William Byron Forbush argues in *The Boy Problem* (originally printed in 1901, with four editions by 1913) that boys naturally migrate to gang formations and that gangs determine a boy's ethics: "The way the gang-ethics evolve is through the mob spirit—that blind, conscienceless movement of men . . . a sort of least common denominator of the ethics of the constitution of individuals" (22). Allen Hoben, one of the speakers at the Chicago Child Welfare Exhibit in 1911, concurs that gangs lead to mob rule: "The street gang will be found in every neighborhood, running free through the streets and alleys, the boys together encouraged to do without hesitancy things that they would otherwise not contemplate" (457). Because, however, Forbush views the gang instinct as necessary—as how individuals become socialized and saved from "narrowness of mind, selfishness and self-conceit" (63)—he recommends ways in which adults can promote a positive gang instinct in boys (through clubs, churches, school sports, and so on).

A 1904 analysis of boys in London depicts three types of boys: one, for whom "home life has never existed," a second, for whom "home life hangs low in the balance," and a third, who regards home as "the center of his activities" (Urwick 88–90). This scale of neglect places the first boy among the street boys, while the second is more or less similar to the kids in the Dead End Kids films, "accustomed to look for the greater part of his amusements in the street" (Urwick 88). The third is not a figure of neglect. For the first and second types home is a place largely of dread, frustration, and boredom. The streets, or "merely that fragment of the town with which his roamings have made him familiar," present the first boy with "novel surprises and objects of alluring interests" and are a place where the "most uniform law discoverable is the absence of all uniformity" (Urwick 91). For the second, the street "remains a thing of joy and resistless fascination" (Urwick 94). In this context the study proclaims that "children are savages," all the more so for being neglected: "In truth when one reflects upon the number of 'homes that are no homes' in London, the wonder is not that the children who fall into crime are so many, but that they are so few" (Urwick 140–141).

More specifically in a 1930s American context, we can compare the Dead End Kids to the description of the boys' community in the unpublished Payne Fund study *Boys, Movies, and City Streets*, by Paul G. Cressey. The elaborate Payne Fund Studies in the early 1930s produced fourteen books by social scientists examining the effects of movies on children's emotions, sleep, attitudes, and conduct, as well as considering the place of movies in children's lives (Jowett, Jarvie, and Fuller 57). Overall, the Payne Fund texts presented a rather complex view of children's relations to the movies. They suggested that the movies had a "definite impact on children's emotions, attitudes and knowledge base" (Jowett, Jarvie, and Fuller 91). But the Payne Fund Studies also acknowledged that influence did not exist in a vacuum but was "modified by the viewer's age, gender, social background, and a host of other factors" and that while some films shocked or titillated, others presented moral ideals and a vision of a better society (Jowett, Jarvie, and Fuller 91). Nonetheless, Henry J. Forman, a freelance writer hired to produce a summary of the studies, put forth only negative results in an antimovie polemic, *Our Movie Made Children* (1934), which became a best seller and influenced public opinion (Jowett, Jarvie, and Fuller 9; Sammond 62–73). The more nuanced academic claims of the studies, summarized by the research director W. W. Charters under the title *Motion Pictures and Youth* (1933), were less widely circulated and less influential.

Among the fourteen proposed volumes of the Payne Fund Studies, all but one, Cressey's *Boys, Movies, and City Streets*, were published. Garth Jowett, Ian Jarvie, and Kathryn Fuller explain in some detail why this volume of the Payne Fund Studies was never published, mainly related to crises in Cressey's personal life. Many of its findings, however, made their way into both Forman's bowdlerization of the studies and Charters's more academic report on the studies and circulated widely (Jowett, Jarvie, and Fuller 9). What survives of Cressey's manuscript has been published under the title "The Community—A Social Setting for the Motion Picture." It shows Cressey's efforts to understand the social environment of delinquent boys and consider movies not in terms of a one-way street of influence but as part of a larger network of contacts and encounters.[9]

Cressey's study is set in the fictional neighborhood of Intervale, a pseudonym for East Harlem, a neighborhood much like that of the Dead End Kids. In fact, the text opens with a description of the neighborhood that could almost be a shot breakdown of the beginning of a Dead End Kids film:

> The street, the sidewalks swarm with people. Pushcarts range along the curb; the proprietors hawking their wares to all passersby. . . . People elbow each other for passage along the sidewalk while others pause to bargain loudly with the pushcart peddlers. The shrill notes of a hurdy-gurdy are heard down the street and from somewhere overhead in the solid block of dingy six floor tenements comes the strident noise of a radio out of control. A street car clangs its way along among the pushcart peddlers and their customers, and a moment later an elevated train roars by overhead. The traffic lights change and from another direction a heavy truck lumbers along spreading the dust and dirt of the street in its wake. The boys in the side-street at their game of ball give way before it, but in the ensuing traffic are able in some way to continue their play . . . even though at the risk of life and limb. Such is the street world with its hazards to which many of the underprivileged boys of America's largest cities are exposed. (Cressey 133)

The boys are situated in a busy urban neighborhood, subject to overcrowding, noise, pushy salesmen, and the dangers of traffic.[10] For Cressey these scenes of street life indicate hazard and an impoverished lifestyle. He acknowledges that this neighborhood is an "interstitial region in the layout of the city" (Cressey 158), or what I have been calling a back region. "The city," he writes, "has been only vaguely aware of this great stir of activity. . . . This region of life is in a real sense an *underworld*" (Cressey 158).

Describing the neighborhood as having the "highest rate of male juvenile delinquency in any natural area with a dominant white population"

(135), Cressey ascribes many of the area's problems to its being "a 'first generation settlement' for immigrants and their families" (135). He claims that problems arise from the clash of cultures, "contradictory mores" and the conflict between Old World values and "New World" children (Cressey 135–136). The adults do not relate to each other, Cressey argues, because they cleave to national identities. But the kids override those concerns: "Because of population congestion they may have *thousands* of possible playmates from whom to choose, [and] children find in the social world of the streets an emancipation from the narrower nationalistic standards of their parents" (137; emphasis mine). In this light children negotiate issues related to immigration through play and through the forced encounters of urbanism.

As in The Dead End Kids films, and along with Brace and Forbush, Cressey finds that the juvenile community consists of groups, not individuals. Cressey adopts medicalized language to detail what he views as a form of social pathology. The gangs provide a "social incubator" and lead to "social contagion" (Cressey 155). This contagion spreads partly from boy to boy, as gangs lure new kids into crime and other unsavory behaviors. But, as in the Dead End Kids, contagion is also spread by adults. "The boy is exposed to the chance associations and experiences which may be his lot," Cressey says. The boy is out of the house, on the street, but he is in an enclosed environment. His influences are limited to contacts within that environment. Parents, in Cressey's view, are neglectful; they "do not have the means or opportunity for supervising their children's play" (154). Therefore, "virtually the only people of affluence seen in the community, to whom the youth can look for his stimulus to ambition, are the bootlegger, the racketeer, and the politician" (Cressey 154). Linking gangsters and politicians, as equally corrupt, Cressey views the community of Intervale as a nearly hopeless hatch that will reproduce itself over and over (or, like the Dead End Kids films, perhaps, as a cycle that requires that characters and plots repeat over and over again).

The gangs in Cressey's study all have a "'hangout'—sometimes a corner cigar store, a candy store, a restaurant or 'private social club'—the speakeasy, the 'fence,' the taxi dance-hall and the houses of prostitution" (139). These spaces, hardly sanctioned child spaces, are the petri dishes of Cressey's "social incubator." Here, he says, the "worst associations are established and . . . many crimes are planned" (140).

Boys, Sex, and Movies

Although Cressey's study dovetails with many aspects of the Dead End Kids and other urban-boy films of the 1930s, his report diverges from the depiction of the Dead End Kids in two key ways. The first major difference is that the boys in Intervale are sex obsessed and sexually experienced. Cressey details boys having sex with girls, including intercourse and mutual masturbation, and also boys having sex with boys, including sodomy, fellatio, and mutual masturbation (143). Most shockingly, the boys report a routine practice of having what was "known in the vernacular as the 'line-up'" (Cressey 143), and what would now be characterized as a gang-bang, or rape of a girl involving more than one man.

Clearly, this emphasis on childhood sexuality could not be included in the Dead End Kids films. The Motion Picture Production Code of 1930 explicitly prohibited any inference of sexual perversion, images of children's sex organs, scenes of rape or attempted rape, and the deliberate seduction of girls. Many filmmakers found ways around the Code, of course, but it would have been harder to get away with sexual scenes in child films (though we will see that female sexuality is teased in films starring girls). While the Dead End Kids films trouble notions of childhood innocence in many ways, they avoid any explicit mention of the boys' sexual interest or experience. The Dead End Kids films elide boy-girl relations almost entirely. The romance subplot of the films is always between adults, usually the sister of a Dead End Kid and a do-gooder. This erasure of boyhood sexuality insulates the Dead End Kids so that they can be read as childish and not as gangsters, boys not men. But there are hints of sexual aggression in the brutal "cockalizing" of *Dead End*, a lesser but no less shocking form of the sexual acts and acts of sexual aggression Cressey describes.

The other major elision of the Dead End Kids films in comparison to the Intervale study relates to the movies. According to Cressey, "second only to time spent in the home, in the school, and on the street" (presumably equal firsts) "is the time the boy spends in the movies" (166). Most of the boys in the study went to the movies once or twice a week, though virtually none claimed the movies as a hobby (Cressey 138). The movies, Cressey believes, were not the most desired activity of the boys but afforded an accessible space. In the same way that bad influences enter boys' lives because they are on the street and in adult spaces, Cressey argues, the boys are drawn to commercial entertainment as a substitute for "wholesome play" (138). The boys do not seek out specific movies by traveling to particular cinemas but attend the cinemas in their neighborhood, which are cheaper and more accessible. The space of the theater serves numerous functions besides providing entertainment. These include serving as a babysitter for mothers who "check" their kids while they go shopping, as an alibi for gangs who arrive en masse, as a warm space where families can go to save on heating, and more (Cressey 171). For the boys, the movies are often a space of sexual assignation and pickups—both heterosexual, in which boys approach girls, sit with them, and begin petting; and homosexual, in which the boys are approached by older men and are paid for fellatio (Cressey 172–177). Still, the boys remember movie plots, movie stars, and particular scenes from movies well, favoring not only gangster movies like *Little Caesar* (Mervyn LeRoy 1931), *The Public Enemy* (William Wellman 1931), and *Scarface* (Howard Hawks and Richard Rosson 1932), which make gangsters attractive to the boys, but also didactic films like *Are These Our Children?* (Wesley Ruggles 1931), which provides the boys with a cautionary tale of a boy fallen into crime (Cressey 197–199).

Oddly and strikingly, the space of the cinema is missing from the Dead End Kids films of the late 1930s. And this absence is largely typical of child films of the period. The movies are not pictured in the Jackie Cooper films, or those of Shirley Temple, or even most Our Gang films. Some Jane Withers films reference the movie industry—mentioning stars, for example—but do not visit sets or show people making or attending movies. By contrast, live entertainment, based on a vaudeville aesthetic, appears in many of these films, especially those with Temple, Withers, and Our Gang; and, there, the children are performers not spectators. Movies figure tangentially in the vaudeville performances: Temple, Withers, and Our Gang all engage in parodies of contemporary film stars and genres. Radio figures similarly, at least in Temple's films. Yet in relation to films that portray circumstances of poverty, the seeming contradiction of poor kids having money for movies—a contradiction Cressey notes—might be too complicated. More than that, though, the absence of movies in Dead End Kids films negates the influence of the movies in these boys' lives. In portraying urban boys' street life as unconnected to the movies, Hollywood avoids taking the blame for their behavior. If Cressey and other Payne Fund Studies find even some link between delinquency and the movies, that influence is absent here.

This absence reveals a cheat in the Dead End Kids version of vernacular modernism. Although the films address many aspects of modernity, including urbanism, overcrowding, tenement culture, and immigration, they ignore commercial mass entertainment and consumerism. Instead, concerns that extend back to the Victorian era and into the Progressive Age are highlighted. These residual effects are brought to the fore, and dominant and emergent forms of modernity, such as mass media, are hidden from view (Williams, *Marxism and Literature*). This creates a displaced sense of time slightly out of synch with the contemporary. Despite, then, the emphasis on place and placeness, the Dead End Kids are somewhat removed from reality and located in a more mythological landscape of childhood. They produce a form of vernacular modernism that partakes of the vernacular as quotidian and local. It exists in, but does not reflect, popular mass-mediated culture.

What work, then, do Dead End Kids films perform? To be sure, they reflect on and provide a working through of the effects of some aspects of modernity. And they do so by showcasing cinema's ability to mobilize space and produce room for play. But from the perspective of the twenty-first century can we still say that these films provide a matrix for our anxieties and fantasies about the urban? Is the spectator's experience of the Dead End Kids today one of negotiated trauma or nostalgia? Put another way, after we unpack the ways in which the Dead End Kids reflected on modernity in the 1930s, what difference does it make *now*, given that what counts as modernity has shifted?

Taking up Miriam Hansen's invitation to investigate cinema history in order to discover "different futures whose potentialities may be buried in the past" (*Cinema and Experience* xvii), in the case of the Dead End Kids we have a now-strange, because historically distant, vantage on modernity and childhood. Insofar as kids' real-life mobility contracts, and children disappear from city streets, representations of the urban child serve not only as a nostalgic reminder of the past but also as a prompt for the future, to rediscover and revive the child in urban space. These representations of the urban child's social space are not, then, merely reflections of childhood or nostalgic images we return to as adults. In defamiliarizing the city, and showing it from a child's perspective, these texts reveal the "room for play" in both the cinema and the city.

2

Shirley Temple
as Streetwalker

Girls, Streets, and
Encounters with Men

If child films of the 1930s can be taken as a form of vernacular modernism, working through the traumatic effects of modernity via narratives of urbanization, overcrowding, immigration, poverty, and changes in the status of family, child films also partake of the tendency to gender the experience of modernity. Thirties texts that focused on girls differ markedly from texts focused on boys. These texts tend to read the girl's experience of the urban and of modernity as different in kind from that of the boy's. In part, this difference replays familiar tropes of female sexuality and risk in city streets; however, these texts also ascribe to girls a surprising mobility and ability to navigate space and the effects of modernity, and they produce a version of the urban as a space of transformative contact and fortuitous encounter.

The difference between boy and girl narratives in the 1930s partly reaffirms differences in the ways boys and girls are described in sociological literature of the period. In Progressive studies of urban youth, such as those discussed in the previous chapter, a strong distinction is made between boys and girls. In *Studies of Boy Life in Our Cities* (Urwick) girls are relegated to a single chapter, "The Girl in the Background" (233–254). Whereas boys in that volume are described as "savages" (Urwick 140), girls are aligned with "purity, temperance, righteousness, and peace" (Urwick 233). But the girl is prevented from developing into "the *best* in womanhood" (Urwick 234) by her environment, which leads her to seek pleasure and excitement. In this reading, girls are styled creatures of "charm" (Urwick 234) and "susceptibility" (Urwick 238), their power and their endangerment both tied to their sexuality, and they are "more liable than boys to surrender their best selves to the degrading influences of their environment" (Urwick 239). In this analysis the girl is victim—degraded by her environment—but also an agent who uses her sexuality and charm to gain advantage: "Girls 'run after boys' because it amuses them to do so; because the pursuit offers unlimited excitement; because they are conscious of certain powers and are anxious to exercise them fully" (Urwick 242).

In Charles Loring Brace's writings, too, the urban girl is marked as a more pathetic victim of the urban environment than the boy:

> A girl street-rover is to my mind the most painful figure in all the unfortunate crowd of a large city. With a boy, "Arab of the streets," one always has the consolation that, despite his ragged clothes and bed in a box or hay-barge, he often has a rather good time of it, and enjoys many of the delicious pleasures of a child's roving life. . . . With a girl vagrant, it is different. She feels homelessness and friendless[ness] more; she has more of the feminine dependence on affection. . . . Then the strange and mysterious subject of sexual vice comes in. It has often seemed to me one of the most dark arrangements of this singular world that a female child of the poor should be permitted to start on its immortal career with almost every influence about it degrading. . . . There is no reality in the sentimental assertion that the sexual sins of the lad are as degrading as those of the girl. (71)

Here, as above, the girl is more susceptible to influence than the boy; she feels her neglect and lack more deeply than the boy; she is subject to the streets, influenced by them, not a figure of agency or fun. Her status in the streets is defined almost entirely through her role as sexual object. She is driven "toward the preservation of purity," and therefore "her fall is deeper" (Brace 71). At the same time that the girl is a creature of influence, however, she also learns to masquerade as, and then become, a creature of desire: "She soon learns to offer for sale that which is in its nature beyond all price, and to feign the most sacred affections. . . . She no longer merely follows blindly and excessively an instinct; she perverts a passion and sells herself" (Brace 72).

In the Payne Fund Studies there is no equivalent girl version of *Boys, Movies, and City Streets*. Girls do not appear to be involved in the gangs or play of boys but are "in the background" when Cressey discusses the boys' sexual activity. Girls appear in Cressey's study as rape victims in the description of the "line-up" (143) and as partners or objects of desire in the boys' assignations, pickups, and petting. The trade press summary of the Payne Fund Studies, *Our Movie Made Children*, similarly, does not include any material about the lives of girls, but it does focus on girls as spectators for "sex pictures" (melodramas, women's films, romantic comedies, and other genres in which romance is central) in a chapter titled "Sex-Delinquency and Crime." Forman's summary of the Payne Fund findings claims a strong influence of movies on girls, who are defined as sexual delinquents. By contrast, in the chapter "Movie Made Criminals" boys are defined as delinquents mainly through stealing and violence. When boys' sexual acts are described, they are situated within narratives of victimizing girls—using movies for getting aroused before raping a girl, or getting a woman aroused by taking her to the pictures. At the same time, the girls are portrayed as victims of their own (movie-induced) desire. Movies, in this summary study, "set up cravings" in girls "which seemingly they cannot combat" (Forman 216).

Each of these studies assumes the terms of, and colludes with, definitions of a modern "girl problem," parallel to but not equivalent to the "boy problem." The "girl problem" from the Victorian age to the Progressive era and into the 1930s was defined as "rejecting Victorian standards of girlhood virtue to lay claim to sexual desire, erotic expression, and social autonomy" (Alexander 12). The girl was viewed, on the one hand, as naturally pure but susceptible to influence and, on the other, as too independent and too desirous.

This sense of girls as a problem emerges at the same time that definitions of girlhood themselves are changing. As Sally Mitchell argues, the word *girl* only becomes "dramatically visible" in about 1880 (6). Then, it does not indicate chronological age but a "state of mind" that blurs the category of girl, adolescent, and woman (much as the renewed concept of girls does today). In Mitchell's account, between the years 1880 and 1915 a new category of girlhood arises, a "new girl" who exists in a "provisional free space" between being a child at home and assuming wholly adult responsibilities (3). Defined as an interstitial space between the child's home and the married woman's home, the space of the "new girl" is defined by independence and freedom (Mitchell 4). This category of the "new girl" exists largely in the imaginary: she is a figure produced in books, magazines, and clothing styles aimed at girl consumers and is promulgated through clubs, sports, schools, and girls' own writing. Most girls, of whatever class, do not have access to this freedom. Working-class girls might start working as early as age twelve whereas a middle-class girl might remain under her parents' supervision until her mid-twenties or later (Mitchell 7). But, Mitchell argues, both classes of girls "knew (and perhaps dreamed) about some of its freedoms," primarily through their reading of popular "new girl" fiction (4).

The "new girl" is not, by and large, sexualized. Instead, her freedom enables her to participate in sports, gain professional training, masquerade as a boy, and have adventures. By the 1930s, however, because of changes in rules about school and labor, the category of girl had been divided from that of the adolescent and the woman (Mitchell 173). Mitchell notes the "creeping sexualization" and "regendering" of young women (182) and the concomitant juvenation of school girls (180). Only as girls become segmented as a population and as older girls become more sexualized do romance narratives come to the foreground. Prior to that, the "new girl" narratives Mitchell analyzes are largely escapist fare, aimed at promoting feelings of empowerment in girls.

The "girl problem" of the Victorian and Progressive eras would likely have applied to the more broad conception of girls Mitchell defines under the rubric of the "new girl," a conception that blurs the lines between schoolgirls and teens. Against Mitchell's sense that sexuality only creeps into the girls' realm at around the time of the First World War, the discourse on the "girl problem" sexualizes girls of all ages strongly. Mitchell suggests that the 1930s draw a line between school-age girls and more advanced girls. In Depression era films, however, girls are still defined both as schoolgirls and, in quite a distinct manner, as erotically available adults. Thus, the film *Girls on Probation* (William McGann 1938) focuses on twenty-something sexualized "girls" and asks in the trailer, "Were These Girls Born to Be Bad? Are They the Marked Woman of Tomorrow? Reform or Ruin? Which Lies Ahead for America's Daughters?"

At the same time that the term *girl* still applies to a broad span of chronological age in 1930s cinema, younger girls are, as Mitchell suggests, represented as more youthful and less obviously sexual.[1] Even so, representations of school-age girls transmit fears of the "girl problem," if only to deflect the reality of girls' sexuality; they demonstrate innocence by teasing it, and demarcate young girls from young women by blurring temporarily and parodically the difference. Texts of the 1930s yoke together seemingly contradictory narratives of the fallen woman and the "new girl." They show girls being unmoored from home—orphaned or displaced—and then finding themselves on streets where they encounter men. Their encounters, however, do not lead to "degradation" or victimization. Instead, they emphasize the girl's mobility and freedom and ascribe to her significant agency to transform and improve not only her situation but also that of the men. In this way, in contradistinction to the boys' narratives I analyzed in the last chapter, these films offer a vision of the urban as largely benign and of girlhood as powerful.

Shirley Temple as Streetwalker

Consider three scenes from Shirley Temple films:

1. In the Shirley Temple vehicle *Bright Eyes* (David Butler 1934) we are first introduced to Temple's character, Shirley Blake, hitchhiking. She walks down a quiet street that does not immediately register as an urban street, but is in Los Angeles, wearing a leather aviator jacket and cap. A large noisy truck stops, and the driver, wearing a newsboy cap, offers her a ride. She refuses, saying she needs a "faster car." Then a second man stops. He drives a shiny convertible and wears a fedora. Shirley accepts his ride.

2. In *The Little Princess* (Walter Lang 1939) Temple's Sara Crewe leaves the exclusive seminary where she *had been* a student but *now* must work as a scullery maid—having been rendered poor by her father's death—to roam the streets of nineteenth-century London and find her father, who is presumed to be dead. Wrapped in a black shawl, she first meets a stranger, a veteran of the war, and asks him about her father. He cannot help her, but he directs her to the hospital where she encounters another man whom she happens to know,

a soldier who was formerly employed at her school. He takes her inside the all-male Veterans Hospital.

3. *Stowaway* (William A. Seiter 1936) shows Temple in Shanghai. Abandoned in a small boat on a wharf by the no-good gambling caretaker who is supposed to get her away from the bandit attacks that have killed her missionary parents, Temple's character, Ching-Ching, dressed in traditional Chinese garb, takes a walk—through obvious back projection—seeking food for herself and her dog. She wanders the wharf, past large and small boats and numerous Chinese workers, then exits to the street, where she passes along sidewalks crowded with pedestrians, past numerous stores and sidewalk retailers, until she stops to admire the lines of a white convertible. Her eye is drawn offscreen to the left, where, through the crowd, she observes a white man, Tommy Randall (Robert Young), owner of the convertible, trying to buy a dragon's head souvenir. Amused, Ching-Ching sidles up to him and offers to help translate. Speaking fluent Mandarin, she asks the cost and negotiates a better price. Then she and the stranger spontaneously take each other's hands and walk away laughing. "You know, you look so young," Tommy remarks, "but you talk so old." He invites Ching-Ching to lunch, and they ride off in his car.

In these three scenes Temple freely and confidently roams the streets. These scenes show her pluck and fortitude, as well as her charm. In each scene she easily and happily encounters a man who aids her. Each scene begins with her walking the streets alone and ends with what is, in effect, a pickup. In each scene Temple is both literally and figuratively a streetwalker. She plainly walks city streets, and she metaphorically invokes the image of the streetwalker. As numerous critics and theorists have argued, the figure of the woman on the street was a figure of suspicion in early modernity. Masculine figures such as "the dandy, the flâneur, the hero, the stranger" could roam freely, whereas women "could not stroll alone in the city" (Wolff 41). As Sharon Marcus puts it, "Men freely stroll the boulevards, mingling with the crowd and collecting impressions, but women enter the streets only at the risk of being taken for streetwalkers" (1). Temple's mobility here is surprising both for her being a child and for her being free from associations with prostitution because she is child. Nonetheless, these scenes of risk, encounter, and pairing with a man connote streetwalking, even if they do not follow through on the sexual denotations.

FIGURE 5. Shirley Temple roams the streets of Shanghai in *Stowaway*.

In each scene Temple seems, as Kristin Hatch says, "too knowing for such a young girl" ("Discipline and Pleasure" 127). (She looks so young but talks so old, as Robert Young observes in *Stowaway*.) Hatch notes that images like this—and myriad others among Shirley Temple films—can be read from a contemporary perspective through discourses of pedophilia and child endangerment, as images of inappropriate contact and affection between the young female star and her older male costars. Hatch, however, rehistoricizes the narratives of the "little seductress" to suggest that the child-loving narrative and male fandom of Shirley Temple were not pedophiliac but served a disciplinary function as fantasies of male rehabilitation. Loving Shirley Temple tames men and brings out their compassion and restraint, much as the figure of the child in temperance narratives cures the drunkard. Gaylyn Studlar argues that Temple's films assured viewers that "masculinity could be made devoutly paternal and irrevocably domesticated at a time when the ties between men and their families were particularly fragile" (63). In both Hatch's and Studlar's accounts, Temple's image and characters indirectly address a crisis in masculinity brought on by the

Depression. Hatch writes, "The spectacle of male child loving proved to be particularly appealing during the Depression, a period when the survival of the nation seemed to depend upon the compassion and restraint of its men" and when the "social disruptions of the 1930s" were attributed to "a failure of the patriarchy" ("Discipline and Pleasure" 134, 135).[2]

Without discounting either Hatch's or Studlar's important correctives to reading Temple through contemporary pedophiliac discourse, I want to slightly revise their readings to suggest not only that Temple reforms and rehabilitates men but that she does so specifically by raising the specter of the fallen woman. It is not simply the case that Temple is pictured as inno-cent; rather, the question of her innocence is teased over and over in scenes that point to the possibility of sexual knowingness in order to disown it.

Not only does Temple walk the streets, but in many films she is assigned an exchange value that monetizes her "priceless" charm. In *Little Miss Marker* (Alexander Hall 1934) the bookie Sorrowful Jones (Adolphe Men-jou) agrees to take the child as a marker for her father's bet, stating, "Little doll like that is worth twenty bucks any way you look at it." But how are we meant to "look at it"? In what sense and what world is a child worth twenty bucks? And for what? In *Now and Forever* (Henry Hathaway 1934) her father, Jerry Day (Gary Cooper), seriously considers an offer of $75,000 to let daughter Penny (Temple) stay with her dead mother's family rather than with him. In *Dimples* (William A. Seiter 1936) the child agrees to live with the wealthy dowager Mrs. Caroline Drew (Helen Westley) in order to get money to cover her grandfather's debts. These moments not only belie the fantasy of priceless love but indicate an awareness of the hairline distinction between the innocent child and the prostitute in the context of the Depression.

Rather than take Temple to be exceptional—in her precocity, her cute-ness, her potential eroticization—my reading aims to situate her in her historical moment and to consider the ways in which her star image is more archetypal than wholly unique. In particular, I situate Temple within potentially contradictory discourses about urban girlhood in the period related to sexuality and risk, on the one hand, and girls' mobility and free-dom, on the other. I link her to other representations of urban girlhood in the period, including the comic strip *Little Orphan Annie*, the films of child-star Jane Withers, and Judy Garland's Dorothy in *The Wizard of Oz* (Victor Fleming 1939). These texts, in different ways, each parodically invoke the figure of the streetwalker by showing girls who roam city streets and have frequent "pickup" encounters with men. While the fallen woman functions as a paradigmatic trope of modernity for the nineteenth century, these texts update the figure to produce a more contemporary variant of a spatially mobile and powerful girl.

It may seem odd to think of Temple as an urban star. Her films vary widely in their locale, and she is as often situated on a plantation (*The Little Colonel* [David Butler 1935], *The Littlest Rebel* [David Butler 1935]) or in a rural setting (*Heidi* [Allan Dwan 1937], *Rebecca of Sunnybrook Farm* [Allan Dwan 1938], *Susannah of the Mounties* [William A. Seiter 1939]) as an urban one. Moreover, according to Kathryn Fuller-Seeley, in box-office terms Temple did only "middling" business in large urban picture palaces but was strongly favored by independent small-town exhibitors who viewed her films as family fare, in opposition to films they viewed as too adult or bawdy (46, 48, 52–53). Thus, in certain ways Temple's appeal would seem to be more small-town than urban, more innocent than knowing or sophisticated. At the same time, however, Fuller-Seeley notes that Temple's films often had mature themes, with subplots involving gangsters, and that her films often figure her as a miniature adult more than as a child. I am suggesting, furthermore, that Temple merits being viewed in an urban context, not merely because she stars in films set in an urban context but also, and more importantly, because the Temple character registers as innocent only through an invocation of experience, sophistication, and knowingness. Even when she is rural, she is never a hick but always precocious and commanding.

Temple's Burlesque of the Fallen Woman

As many have noted, reviews of the time acknowledged Shirley Temple's sexualization. Graham Greene, famously, was sued for libel over his assessment of Temple's erotically charged performance. Greene's 1936 review of *Captain January* (David Butler 1936) characterizes the film as "depraved" and locates in Temple a "coquetry quite as mature as Miss [Claudette] Colbert's" and "an oddly precocious body as voluptuous in grey flannel trousers as Miss Dietrich's" (128). Greene attributes to Temple a kind of sexual knowingness. In a review of *Wee Willie Winkie* (John Ford 1937) a year later, he writes: "Watch the way she measures a man with agile studio eyes, with dimpled depravity" (234). Viewing Temple as too knowing for a child, Greene claims that "infancy is her disguise, her appeal is more secret and adult" (233). He considers hers an inauthentic "mask of childhood, a childhood skin-deep" (Greene 234). He argues that her films disown her sexuality through narrative devices that proclaim her purity: "Her admirers—middle-aged men and clergymen—respond to her dubious coquetry, to the sight of her well-shaped and desirable little body, packed with enormous vitality, only because the safety curtain of story and dialogue drops between their intelligence and their desire" (Greene 234).

Gilbert Seldes, less naysaying than Greene (and, unlike Greene, not sued for libel over his remarks), compares Temple to Mae West, arguing that Temple produces a "growl of satisfaction" from the men in the audience, whose "roar of approval is not for what is sweet, but for what is mocking and hearty and contemptuous." He attributes to Temple an "air of command, the certainty that thereafter you would never look at another woman again which you find in every movement of Mae West across the screen" (Seldes 86). Seldes delights in precisely what Greene denigrates—Temple's knowingness, her awareness of herself, and her confidence, not her innocence.

In these readings Temple's performance is no different in kind from that of sexually aware women. She is compared to Claudette Colbert, Marlene Dietrich, and Mae West. Because she is a child, however, we are meant to interpret her actions, and those of the men who admire her, as innocent. Temple invokes the specter of the fallen woman parodically. I mean *parody* in the sense Linda Hutcheon posits when she describes parody as a denaturalizing critique that imitates through repetition but with a difference (6). Parody, in this sense, need not necessarily be comedic. Parody, according to Hutcheon, might imitate the conventions of a text or trope ironically, thereby subverting the intended meaning.

The *Baby Burlesks* (Jack Hays and Charles Lamont 1932–1933) series of short films, in which Temple stars as a very young child, provide a model and forerunner to the kind of sexual parody I am describing here. The series as a whole shows kids, probably aged four to five, in diapers, for which they are much too old. The diapers are meant to lower their age and render them babies, innocents. At the same time, the narratives place the "babies" in adult scenarios. In the first of the *Baby Burlesks*, *Runt Page* (1932), a parody of *The Front Page* (play: Ben Hecht and Charles MacArthur 1928; film: Lewis Milestone 1931), the disjunction between child bodies and adult situations is emphasized by a gimmick of dubbing adult voices in for the

FIGURE 6. Shirley Temple parodies Marlene Dietrich's performance from *Blonde Venus* in *Kiddin' Hollywood*.

child actors. In the other shorts the disjunction occurs through the sophisticated scenarios (and the kids speak their own lines). In *Kiddin' Hollywood* (1933),[3] for example, Temple plays aspiring actress and bathing beauty contest winner Morelegs Sweettrick, a clear allusion to Marlene Dietrich, known for her legs. Hired as a cleaning lady, not an actress, Sweettrick gets her break when the female star, Freta Snobbo (Gloria Ann Mack), a clear Garbo parody, proves too temperamental for the director. Sweettrick emphatically wiggles her way across the soundstage and proffers "What about me?" Dressed in an imitation of Dietrich's sexy costume from *Blonde Venus* (Josef von Sternberg 1931)—a sequined bodysuit and sequined arrow through her curls—Sweettrick enters the stage, as Dietrich's theme music, "Falling in Love Again (Can't Help It)" (Friedrich Hollaender 1930) plays nondiegetically. Sweettrick sings "We Just Couldn't Say Goodbye" (Harry Woods 1932) and prompts a series of boys' reaction shots that are as clear an instance of the male gaze as any in film.[4] When costar Frightwig von Stumblebum (Arthur Maskery), an Erich von Stroheim substitute, joins

Sweettrick before the camera, he bends her back for a kiss that goes on for so long the director checks his watch. Finally, however, her character in the film-within-a-film rejects him to stay with her husband and child.

The *Baby Burlesks* have precursors on the nineteenth-century stage. As Marah Gubar notes, the 1879 all-child version of Gilbert and Sullivan's *H.M.S. Pinafore, The Children's Pinafore*, was "part of a long tradition of all-child productions that enjoyed great popular and critical success on both sides of the Atlantic as early as the 1840s" ("Who Watched" 410). For Gubar these all-child productions do not reassert childhood innocence or affirm the categorical difference between children and adults, as some have argued, but, instead, signal what she calls a "category crisis" ("Who Watched" 411). Building on Marjorie Garber's analysis of transvestism, Gubar claims that "age transvestism" in shows with children performing adult roles "destabilized the idea that a strict line divided child from adult, innocence from experience" ("Who Watched" 411). The *Baby Burlesks*, similarly, evince a category crisis, between adult and child, knowingness and innocence. Rather than play the children as naive and unaware of the roles they play, the *Baby Burlesks* simultaneously mobilize mature subjects and performance modes *and* images of infancy to produce liminal subjects, not a binary opposition.

The *Baby Burlesks* parody sexually provocative contemporary stars, films, and mores. In a similar but less obvious manner Temple, in her urban feature films, parodies the figure of the fallen woman, subversively echoing and paralleling the trope of the fall while nonetheless avowing her innocence. In doing so, she simultaneously denaturalizes the figure of the fallen woman and the innocent child.

While Temple demonstrates aspects of the "seductress" across her films, her urban films imply a knowingness that seems particular to her status as an urban child. This is foregrounded in *Young People* (Allan Dwan 1940). After her mother dies, Temple's character, Wendy, is adopted, unbeknownst to her, by two vaudevillians billed as the Ballantines (Jack Oakie and Charlotte Greenwood). The Ballantines care for her but have never given her a proper home; instead, they have been "strangers" in every town. They decide to retire to the country to be "normal" (sleeping in beds, not trains; cooking dinner). In the small country town they are viewed suspiciously by the townspeople who do not trust their big-city ways. Wendy, an old vaudevillian herself, tries to fit in with the school kids by putting on a show. She stages a performance of the song "Young People" (Harry

Warren and Mack Gordon 1940). The lyrics assert the children's wish to be perceived as mature: "We're not little babies anymore, No! / We don't play with dollies on the floor, Nah!" Rather than children, they identify as what would now be called tweens:

> We're not old, yet, we're just in-between.
> We're nine and we're ten, well, that's almost sixteen.
>
> .   .   .   .
>
> Stop that baby talk, that umsey-wumsey mush.
> The days of bibs and teddy bears and kiddie cars are gone,
> For time ta-ta-ta-ta marches on.

These lyrics—sung alternately by boys and girls, individuals and groups—assert not only the tween sets' distance from infancy but also their sexual maturity. Only nine or ten years old, they perceive themselves as almost sixteen, not as kids but as young ladies and their boyfriends, who "know ev'rything there is to know":

> When we're in the parlor and the lights are low,
> Don't bribe us with a nickel, we'll refuse to go.
> Sisters, better tell your romantic gents
> We have a minimum number charge of fifty cents.

More than just sexual knowledge, the singers assert their urbane sophistication:

> We hate to hear a fairy tale before we go to bed.
> We'd rather have you telling us what Walter Winchell said.
> We know our table manners, when to use a knife and fork,
> And we know that the Stork is a nightclub in New York.

Along with the lyrics, the kids' costumes signal their wished-for adult status. They wear a mishmash of ill-fitting clothing—long dresses with feather hats, beads, furs, and dangling earrings for the girls, and suits with suspenders and bowler hats or top hats for the boys. Wendy, the star and director of the number, wears a kimono, with a flower in her hair, rather like a geisha. At some level the kids' performance could reinforce their innocence—like the diapers in the *Baby Burlesks*—showing how far from adulthood they are. But the parents' reaction suggests that the performance instead compromises their innocence. When the orchestration jazzes up, and the kids start dancing a conga, the parents react with rage, yanking their children off the stage and complaining of their "disgraceful exhibition." Out of place in the small town, and amid small-town values, Wendy (who reads *Variety*!) is viewed as endangering the morals of other children. Her show business acumen and charm are unveiled as overly sophisticated and are associated with her urban ways. This film exposes, in a sense, what lurks in Temple's other films: a strong sense that her status as a professional performer makes her sophisticated and knowing and renders her innocence a masquerade.

Shirley Temple's urban narratives not only indirectly address a crisis of masculinity in the Depression, as Hatch and Studlar argue, but also provide what Miriam Hansen calls "a sensory-reflexive horizon for the experience of modernization and modernity," or, in other words, makes visible the "fantasies, uncertainties, and anxieties" associated with modernity ("Fallen Women" 10, 14). In Hansen's account women, especially fallen women, "function as metonymies, if not allegories, of urban modernity" and "metaphors of a civilization in crisis" ("Fallen Women" 15). As Studlar notes, Temple's films are often set in the nineteenth century but clearly resonate with concerns of the Depression, such as "displacement from home, loss of family livelihood, and the death of parents" (61). In combining the figure of the fallen woman, if only metaphorically, with the image of the child, Temple conjures the potential risk for the child in the city, of course; yet her youth also allows for multiple readings and mobilizes a range of anxieties related to urban living and modernity. In particular, Temple reorients the potentially jarring contingency and indeterminacy of modernity into a positive realm of possibility and encounter, and she navigates uncertainties about immigration, poverty, and feminism through narratives of adoption and marriage.

The Crash as Fall

In her real life young Shirley Temple is the product of extreme helicopter parenting. One report from the set of *Dimples* says that "her mother never gets more than thirty yards away from Shirley all day and all night. She teaches her her lines, helps dress the child in her costumes, sits by while Shirley gets her school lessons and stays near the camera or the director while Shirley is shooting" (Shaffer). Norman Zierold, in a very positive description of Temple's mother, Gertrude, writes that "there is hardly a case on record of a child star more completely under the thumb of her mother" (81). In his account Temple's need for her mother led the studio to pay her to remain on set every minute her daughter was there (Zierold 82). Despite this degree of attentiveness in real life, however, in her films Temple is a figure of neglect who exhibits a high degree of autonomy and independent mobility.

Temple's films repeatedly enact a fall, in which she is unmoored from home and family. In part, this ties Temple to the deep tradition of orphan narratives that runs through British and American literature and film (C. Nelson, *Little Strangers* 4; Griswold, *Classic American Children's Story* 241–242; J. S. Sanders). At the same time, it marks a particular anxiety about the status of family in the Depression. Divorce declined during the Depression because fewer people could afford it, but, as Steven Mintz points out, "desertions soared. By 1940 more than 1.5 million married women lived apart from their husbands," and there was a 50 percent increase in the number of children placed in custodial institutions during the first two years of the Depression (237). Additionally, the number of homeless children rose dramatically (Ashby 108).

Figuratively, Temple's status as orphaned and dependent child, unmoored from home, also triggers associations with immigration, and issues of assimilation and class emerge. The Temple character is sometimes explicitly an immigrant. In *Stowaway* she travels illegally, hidden in a car trunk, then in a ship's cabin, from Shanghai to America. In *Now and Forever* she moves from America to Europe. In *The Little Princess* she immigrates to London from India. Crucially, she is a global figure who moves freely across national boundaries. Because of her lack of home, she is similar to Georg Simmel's modern stranger: "the stranger . . . not in the sense often touched upon in the past, as the wanderer who comes today and goes tomorrow, but rather as the person who comes today and stays tomorrow," one who is not a "soil owner" in the literal or figurative sense, who does not belong to the dominant group, and who is fundamentally mobile and free (402–403).

Temple's fall, which echoes the stock market crash that brought on the Depression, is familial and economic but enacted spatially. In *The Little*

FIGURE 7. In *Just around the Corner* Shirley Temple moves from the penthouse to an underground apartment, signaling her change in status.

Princess, when her father is thought dead, her bills unpaid, she is moved from her spacious private room to a tiny attic room. Additionally, where before she only traveled the city in a carriage, after her fall she walks, traversing the city to seek her father, frequently entering the largely male arena of the veterans hospital. Poor, Temple's Sara Crewe is open to new encounters, including one with the Indian manservant Ram Dass (Cesar Romero), whom she meets across the airshaft separating their buildings. In *Just around the Corner* (Irving Cummings 1938) her fall occurs when her single father loses his position as an architect who designs skyscrapers. Temple, as Penny, is moved away from her private school and back to the exclusive Riverview hotel where her father lives, but whereas previously they had occupied the penthouse, now they live in the basement, beneath street grates that reveal people walking above. This shift in status also moves her out of the private play area inside the hotel and into the alley nearby, which is filled with tough street urchins—a clear nod to *Dead End* and its East River Terrace apartments. This juxtaposition, of extreme wealth and working-class culture, and Penny's movement from one to the other, spatially enacts her plight.

Some Temple films allegorize the stock market crash by literalizing the motif of crashing. In *Poor Little Rich Girl* (Irving Cummings 1936), for instance, Temple's nurse is killed in a car crash while taking Temple's character, Barbara, from her father's mansion to an exclusive rural boarding school. Barbara is unaware of the accident because it occurs outside the train station while she is still inside. Oblivious to what has happened, she wanders away from the train station to follow an Italian immigrant home to his basement apartment, where she is absorbed into the immigrant family. Thus, the car crash leads to Temple's fall and her movement across the city. One of the clearest allegories of the stock market crash plays out in *Bright Eyes*. The orphan status of Temple's character, Shirley Blake, occurs because, first, her father "cracks up" (i.e., crashes) in a plane, and then a bus crashes into her mother—her death signified by the broken plane on the birthday cake she was carrying—and then Shirley, with her soon-to-be adopted dad, falls from the sky when the plane he pilots has to crash-land.

Temple's fall from wealth to poverty in these films makes her mobile. Her mobility in the city leads her to have contact with strangers. Instead of risk, however, this contact ignites what Sharon Marcus has characterized as "the urban novel's emphasis on chance encounters, the interplay between isolation and community, and the sudden transformation of strangers into kin" (11). This renders a view of the urban as beneficent, open to encounter and contingency. It marks a difference between Temple's films and traditional orphan girl narratives in which "an orphan girl enters a home far from modern urban life, a home that is reluctant to accept her" (J. S. Sanders 6) and in which the orphan girl has to overcome hostility and win the hearts of those with whom she lives. Here, to meet Temple is to love her and want her.

The mode of encounter here differs markedly from that in the Dead End Kids films. There, the boys' encounter with adults could only be a one-way influence, for good or bad, from the adult to the child. The child's encounter with the adult was not transformative for the adult; indeed, transformation of any kind—away from delinquency, away from the block, away from poverty—was unlikely. Encounters only occurred within the boy's familiar realm. The boy only encountered those who entered his world. He did not have the mobility or freedom afforded Temple.

Unlike the Dead End Kids, Temple meets strangers, and they quickly become friends or, often, family. This development depends, clearly, on

FIGURE 8. Temple's affiliation with men in *Bright Eyes*. The men at the airport hold a special Christmas party just for Shirley.

Temple herself and the cuteness analyzed by Lori Merish. According to Merish, appreciating Temple's cuteness becomes a normative aesthetic response that not only leads people to want to admire her but draws out their maternal instincts. She writes, "Cute always in some sense designates a commodity in search of its mother, and is constructed to generate maternal desire" (186). In this sense Temple's cuteness transforms the urban into a space of encounter and kinship.

But whereas Merish emphasizes maternal desire, Temple's films are much more about paternal desire. Temple's primary relationships are with men. Either she has a single father, as in *Just around the Corner, Now and Forever, The Little Princess,* and *Poor Little Rich Girl,* or a grandfather, as in *Dimples;* or, orphaned, she meets a man whom she charms and who becomes her father, as in *Little Miss Marker, Little Miss Broadway* (Irving Cummings 1938), *Bright Eyes,* and *Stowaway.* Once fallen and moved out of sites of female containment, such as the posh schools of *The Little Princess* or *Just around the Corner,* the Temple character moves largely in the world of adults or male children. Her encounters with girls are generally marked by class division and end badly (like Mae West, she is aligned mainly with lower-class girls).

Temple was not generally photographed with other children because her mother believed it might make her seem "less cute" (Vered 56). Thus, most of her publicity photos show her with adults, especially male costars, furthering her association with adult males. The movement away from children in Temple's films and publicity marks an acceleration of the maturation process whereby the child is supposed to grow up and away from homosocial worlds to find a heterosexual mate. This movement away from children and toward adult men contributes to the sense that she is mature and knowing—growing not *up* but sideways, in Kathryn Bond Stockton's terms.

Temple's films hover on the edge of impropriety in scenes that place her in the wished-for role of wife. In *Poor Little Rich Girl*, for example, suffering neglect from her overly busy and successful single father, Temple, sitting in his lap, sings "When I'm with You" (Mack Gordon and Harry Revel 1936):

Oh Daddy how I miss you.
You're busy all your life.
I long to hug and kiss you.
Marry me, and let me be your wife.

In this, the child's neglect—her father's absence from her life—is wished away in an Electra complex fantasy. To have a father, Temple's character, Barbara, offers to become a wife. In other films Temple replaces the absent mother. In *Just around the Corner*, for instance, her character, Penny, declares that "a man without a woman around the house is quite a problem"; the film then cuts to an image of Temple with a rag around her head cleaning the apartment and attempting to produce a meal.

Temple's affiliation with men, and the way in which her films engender child loving in men, goes against not only the maternal logic of cuteness but also state and economic logic that links dependent children to mothers, not fathers. When Aid to Dependent Children (ADC) was developed as part of the 1935 Social Security Act, it grew from what *had* been mothers' pensions and carried many of the same assumptions as those pensions that "clung to the belief that parenting was primarily the mother's responsibility" (Ashby 114). ADC stitched support for dependent children to support for mothers and assumed that dependent children lived with a single or widowed mother. In Temple's films, by contrast, fathers are the primary caretaker, and mothers enter the narrative late, as a deus ex machina to marry the would-be father (thus blocking the inappropriate coupling of the child and man).

These films denaturalize maternal care but, in doing so, make clear a crisis in mothering. Ellen Key's Progressive feminist best seller *The Renaissance of Motherhood* argues that early feminism produces a disinclination for motherhood—birthrates decrease, and women increasingly view day care and outside care as better for the child's upbringing: "Motherhood has . . . ceased to be the sweet secret dream of the maiden, the glad hope of the wife, the deep regret of the ageing woman who has not had this yearning satisfied" (110). In Key's account, as women have been liberated from some traditional roles, they have lost their ability and interest in mothering: "The social activities of the mothers of the well-to-do classes and the outside work of the wage-earning mothers make mother-care only a figure of speech, and the children are neglected" (127). Neglect, according to this argument, emerges out of feminism and female self-interest.

Thus, Temple's films not only register the crisis in masculinity that Hatch and Studlar identify, a crisis related to the emasculating economics of the Depression, but also address a crisis in femininity, produced by modernization, urbanization, and feminism. Both problems are resolved within Temple's films through marriage and adoption. The man has to be taught, as Hatch says, and that leads him to maturity, understood as marriage. He engages "The New Fatherhood," a companionate model for fathers and children (Studlar 62–63). Temple operates within her films as an Oedipal accelerant, whose cuteness attracts the bachelor and transforms him from a man-child or an unproductive member of society—gambler in *Little Miss Marker*, con man in *Now and Forever*, rich playboy in *Stowaway*, aviator without a home in *Bright Eyes*—into a man ready for marriage. The woman is drawn partially to Temple and partially to the new more mature man—a man she has previously found unmarriageable. The arrival of the woman blocks the inappropriate coupling of Temple and the bachelor, reversing her precocious potential Oedipal trajectory so that she restores rather than replaces the mother. At the same time, the woman's marriage to the man and adoption of Temple rehabilitates her. As Claudia Nelson argues in relation to Victorian literature, adoption becomes "key to the moral reclamation of the new mother," offering a "solution" to the woman question and "taming women's desire for achievement within and beyond the home" (*Little Strangers* 124).

Marriage is not merely romantic in Temple's films. Instead, the status of the couple and of adoption has to be adjudicated by the law. *Stowaway*, *Bright Eyes*, and *Little Miss Broadway* each culminate in courtroom scenes in which Temple's character charms the judge, who not only places her in a family but plays matchmaker between the couple. As Priscilla Yamin argues, the early twentieth-century nuptial reform movement aimed to reestablish the "sense of security, morality, and community" that "pervasive poverty, rising dependence on charity, the growing visibility of women in the labor market, and the increasing influx of immigrants" threatened (41). Marriage was a tool to address social anxieties about social dislocation and urbanization.

Not coincidentally, the newly formed family in Temple's films is white and either aspiring to or firmly located within the middle class (Lury 71). Notably, in *Poor Little Rich Girl*, when the Italian immigrant Tony (Henry Armetta) falls for Temple/Barbara's charms, he wants to adopt her: "Can't we keep her, mama?" But his desire to adopt Barbara is treated as an absurdity in the film. This is partly because he already has a houseful of children, but also, I would argue, because he has a wife already and because he is a lower-class immigrant, not a figure of assimilation and class rise.

In *Dimples*, Temple's move away from other children into a largely adult world also entails a modification of her affiliation with blackness.[5] Her character is first seen in a multiracial environment. On the streets in the Bowery she sings and plays with a group of boys, including two African American children. She is initially not distinguished from these boys: all are identified as "street arabs." However, as the narrative progresses, Temple's cuteness enables her to be absorbed into a wealthy white family. Initially taken in by the rich dowager, she charms the nephew, too, who is inspired to become a theatrical producer. By film's end Temple not only performs in *Uncle Tom's Cabin* as Little Eva, thus underscoring both her white privilege and her transformative powers, but also appears in a blackface minstrelsy number. Her two friends from earlier in the film reappear here as "The Two Back Dots" (Jesse Scott and Thurman Black), reduced to a specialty act in her larger narrative.

In this sense Temple's films perform a version of whiteness closely aligned with ideologies of childhood innocence. Performing in Chinese costume in *Stowaway*, surreptitiously chatting with the Indian Ram Dass in

FIGURE 9. In *Dimples* Shirley performs with an all-male group of "street arabs," including two African American boys.

The Little Princess, dancing with Bill "Bojangles" Robinson in *Just around the Corner*, or performing with the Two Black Dots in *Dimples*, Temple does not exist in a wholly white world or without encountering racial others. However, she achieves the "unmarked status of whiteness" under what Robin Bernstein vividly characterizes as "claims of holy obliviousness" (8). Rather than an absence of knowledge, Bernstein views racial innocence and sexual innocence alike as "a state of deflection: a constantly replenishing obliviousness that causes sexual [and racial] matters to slide by without sticking" (41). Just as I have argued that Temple can be read as parodying the fallen woman, deflecting sexuality by teasing it, we can see her films construct racial innocence using childhood to mask interracial interaction even as the films covertly represent it.

Little Orphan Annie as New Girl

It is tempting to read Temple's parodic imitation of a fallen woman as a unique feature of her star image. Certainly, the particular mixture of cuteness and knowingness relates to Temple's performance style and her look. But the narrative structure and themes of the young star's urban films—the emphasis on a fall, female mobility, and girls' agency in transforming men, as well as maternal absence or failure—appear in numerous other contemporary texts and images.

The ur-text for representations of girls in the Depression is, of course, Harold Gray's *Little Orphan Annie* comic strip. The strip debuted on 5 August 1924, in the *New York Daily News* and moved within three months into syndication with the Chicago Tribune Newspapers Syndicate (later Tribune Media Services). The comic reached the height of its popularity in the 1930s. In 1930 a fifteen-minute radio show of *Little Orphan Annie* debuted on WGN Chicago and went national on NBC in 1931, initially with two separate casts, one for the East Coast broadcast and one for the West. The show ran six days a week at 5:45 p.m. and was on the air until 1942. Two film adaptations of the comic strip were made in the 1930s, both titled *Little Orphan Annie* (John S. Robertson 1932; Ben Holmes 1938), and "Little Orphan Annie" merchandise circulated widely. The strip continued with Gray's guidance until the 1960s but remains linked to the 1930s in the cultural imaginary, especially as the musical and film *Annie* (John Huston 1982) are set during the Great Depression.[6]

Little Orphan Annie is indebted to Victorian melodrama, especially Dickens. In 1938 Harold Gray made the link to Dickens explicit: "You can take *Great Expectations* or any Dickens book and put in running water and a telephone and you have Annie in a modern setting with a sound story" (Gray 2:11). As Jeet Heer explains, "Dickens' fiction is rife with orphans, lost children who roam the city streets, sudden reversals of fortune with characters finding and losing money rapidly, coincidental meetings, corruptly administered institutions like orphanages, hypocritical old people who pretend to be charitable but are only interested in their own personal self-aggrandizement, benevolent rich men who provide last minute rescue to those in jeopardy, and many other motifs that would be recycled in *Little Orphan Annie*" (Heer, "Dream Big" 24). As Heer suggests, Gray did not just borrow a few figures or plotlines from Dickens; he shared his sentimentality, his populist worldview, and what Sergei Eisenstein famously referred to as Dickens's propensity to portray the world in terms of irreconcilable divisions between rich and poor, good and evil (Eisenstein 234).

Rather than merely harking back to the past, however, Gray updates and Americanizes Dickens. When the Great Depression hits, especially, Annie's poverty and insecurity come to seem "closer to a newspaper headline than an outgrowth of Victorian fiction" (Heer, "Economy" 12). Similarly, although Gray borrows Dickens's view of the child as vulnerable and in need of protection, he revises the trope. Where orphans like Oliver Twist are passive characters, acted on for good or bad by forces they cannot control, Annie is "cast from a different mold. Her goodness is not passive but active. She doesn't let herself be pushed around, but is the mistress of her destiny. Alone in a city, she always finds work for herself" (Heer, "Dickens of a World" 17). In this sense Annie combines Dickensian melodrama with the generic demands of "new girl" literature.

Annie appeals as a "new girl," unmoored from conventional family life and able to have adventures. One version of the story Gray tells about Annie's origins emphasizes mobility and freedom as key to her character. Early versions of Annie's origins ascribe her gender to the newspaper publisher's input. In this early version Gray develops a character named "Little Orphan Otto," but *Tribune* publisher Captain Joseph Medill Patterson rejects him as a "pansy," suggesting that Gray change the feminine-looking character to a girl (Heer, "Dream Big" 24).[7] In 1951, however, Gray revised this story and claimed that Annie was based on a real-life model, a "street urchin he met while roaming the streets of Chicago": "I talked to this little kid and liked her right away," Gray said. "She had common sense, knew how to take care of herself. She had to. Her name was Annie. At the time some 40 strips were using boys as the main characters; only three were using girls. I chose Annie for mine, and made her an orphan, so she'd have no family, no tangling alliances, but freedom to go where she pleased" (Heer, "Dream Big" 24). This perhaps revisionist history matters less for its veracity—as Heer suggests, both stories are probably apocryphal—than for the analysis it provides of Annie's appeal: in this version Gray underscores her common sense, ability to fend for herself, and freedom from "tangling alliances." His description of Annie is echoed in Mitchell's description of popular "city arab" tales for girls. In these tales—a late nineteenth-century/early twentieth-century cycle of "new girl" fiction about "poor outcast waifs" (Mitchell 157)—the main character "lives on her own; she is cool, self-possessed, forward, independent; and she is also the highly visible bruised victim of abuse" (Mitchell 153).[8] Annie, then, both carries with her values of the Victorian age and updates the "new girl" paradigm—she is the new girl in a more modern setting.

Crucially, Annie is an urban girl. Although she frequently travels to rural areas as well as urban sites, she views the city as her home. In the 1936 episode "Those Who Are About to Die," for example, as Annie and her dog, Sandy, make their way back to the city from a rural workhouse, Annie proclaims, "I know some folks don't like th' city—plenty claim it's unhealthy—maybe th' air is bad—but what makes some folks dopey puts pep in others. . . . Sniff, sniff—Oh, Boy! Smell that Sandy? Smoke—Asphalt—Garlic—Gasoline—Old fruit—and look at th' people—Thousands of 'em, Sandy—Every breed on Earth—and noise— Boy it makes yer teeth chatter—Yep, it sure is like getting home again—eh, Sandy?" (Gray 2:22–23). Against those who view the city as intrinsically bad, Annie values the city for its diversity and liveliness, "havin' to think quicker and move faster than th' next guy" (Gray 7:22). She affiliates herself with the city and claims the city at large—rather than any single place—as home.

Like Shirley Temple, Annie evinces something of a category crisis with regard to her age. As Stella Ress argues, "Annie intrigues adults with her dual nature, a combination of youthful and mature qualities" (787–788). Annie appears childlike but acts like an adult: she frequently works for wages, sometimes lives on her own, even renting an apartment, often mouths "philosophies of a person of 60 years" (Ress 788), and is more caretaker than dependent. In one 1931 episode Annie even temporarily "adopts" an abandoned child she finds in the hallway of her boardinghouse. Rejecting the idea of an orphanage, Annie declares, "She'll be no factory product—this kid'll be hand raised and by me, or I'll know the reason why" (Gray 3:268). Rather than question Annie's ability to raise a child, the adults in her life praise her. "Good for you," says Maw Green; and her boss Jake declares, "Such a girl—Now she takes in a little waif to raise—she is young in years—yes—but she will raise that kid fine" (Gray 3:268).

Annie's combination of adult manners and childlike appearance and her status as "street arab," or what Joanne Hall calls a "female hobo," work together to parodically invoke the figure of the fallen woman. As in the Shirley Temple films, Little Orphan Annie can be seen as repeatedly enacting a fall. In the comic strip these falls are partially explained through market demands. In the early days of the strip, according to Heer, Gray and

Patterson argued over Annie's fate. Gray wanted her to stay with Daddy Warbucks, but Patterson thought the strip would have more appeal if Annie stayed poor. So they "split the difference" (Heer, "Dream Big" 26). Daddy would vanish repeatedly, "re-orphaning" Annie over and over again, leaving her to wander the streets or find a new home in poverty until Daddy would reappear, often rescuing Annie or being rescued by her, to start the cycle again.

Not only does Annie walk the streets, like Temple, but in many episodes she, like Temple, is assigned an exchange value that monetizes her appeal. For example, in the 1925 episode "Welcome Stranger," when Annie is separated from Daddy Warbucks and is living with the Silos, Warbucks posts a notice offering a $5,000 reward for her return. Annie is kidnapped by men who have seen the notice and aim to collect even more money: "This bird Warbucks would pay $50,000 for that brat if he'd pay a dime and I'm going to collect it" (Gray 1:120). In 1935, when Annie is discovered by the Hollywood talent agent Mr. Uptown, he declares, "This kid is the key to unlock millions in profits for Kolossal" (Gray 6:119). In 1933 Annie works as a street performer, singing alongside a blind fiddle player, and earns eleven dollars, but she soon meets an agent, Mr. Chizzler, who knows that Annie is "worth a fortune" (Gray 5:43). In "Easy Money" (Gray 7:155–217) swindlers attempt to murder Annie and collect $200,000 insurance money.

In many ways Annie's extended story plays maternal failure against paternal redemption. When Annie is first adopted, for example, she is taken in by Mrs. Warbucks on a trial basis (Gray 1:38). Mrs. Warbucks's interest in Annie, however, is only a masquerade of charitable behavior, intended to impress her friends: "Oh, I felt I should do something for charity, no matter what the sacrifice" (Gray 1:45). By contrast, as soon as Mr. Warbucks meets Annie, he insists she call him "Daddy."[9] He tells his wife, "Annie doesn't need charity. Just give her an even break and she'll do the rest" (Gray 1:51). Having made his fortune during the war in munitions, Daddy tells Annie, "Maybe I did wrong, Annie, but I did the best I knew." Confessing that he chased fortune to get his wife's love, and recognizing that his wife does not love him, he states, "I've made nothing but mistakes all my life. . . . If there were more girls like you in the world, there'd be a lot less old birds like me" (Gray 1:53). In a pattern that continues across the life of the strip, "those who help Annie, rich and poor alike, are rewarded by the fact that she helps them become young again and change their bad habits" (Heer, "Dickens of a World" 16). Soon, Daddy is playing cowboys with

Annie, taking Annie to a vaudeville show, rescuing Annie's friend Miss Fair from an unscrupulous loan shark, and giving his coat and a job to a homeless man (Gray 1:53–58).

Although Daddy and Annie state their mutual love, and Daddy admits his past mistakes, their union is impermanent. Daddy goes to Siberia on business, and as soon as he is gone, Mrs. Warbucks returns Annie to the orphanage (Gray 1:60), initiating the cycle of Annie's repeated abandonment. In short order Annie runs away and makes her way to the country. There she lives with Mr. and Mrs. Silo, kind country folk. But then Daddy returns and brings her home, until he and Mrs. Warbucks separate and he goes to Africa on business. Then Annie, thinking he is dead, joins a circus and is nearly crippled doing a trapeze act. Daddy returns and installs Annie at a country estate but ends up broke and on the road . . . and so on.

These cycles of abandonment and rescue in *Little Orphan Annie* each initiate new encounters and adventures. Many of these encounters put Annie at risk. For example, in "The Haunted House" Annie uncovers a gang of bank robbers, recovers the stolen money, and then is kidnapped by the bandits (Gray 1:367–374). In the remarkably similar story "Sherlock Jr." Annie catches a band of criminals and recovers the stolen money but then is kidnapped by the criminals shortly after (Gray 2:84–144). In another episode Annie is being escorted on her way to a private school by Daddy Warbucks's friend Wun Wey. But Wun Wey is killed by "competitors," who then take Annie hostage (Gray 6:111–115).

As often, though, Annie encounters strangers who quickly become friends and provide her temporary homes, becoming like family. In "The Girl Next Door" (Gray 2:248–272), for instance, she takes a walk, leaving the hotel where she and Daddy have been finally reunited, without paying attention to its name or address and promptly gets lost. She is found sleeping in a doorway by cab driver Monk Dooley, who takes her to his home. At home with his wife the next morning, Monk wonders if "maybe I should have taken her to the police station—they'd know what to do with her—I guess it was a mistake me bringing her here" (Gray 2:249). His wife, however, responds, "What else could you do? The place for that child is in a good home like ours" (Gray 2:249). Annie accepts them as they accept her: "Course th' Dooleys haven't all th' money in th' world, or th' swellest flat in town—but they have big hearts and I guess that's what really counts more'n anything else" (Gray 2:250).

FIGURE 10. In "On the Lam" Annie and Jack Boot opt to be "uncle" and "niece." © Tribune Content Agency, LLC. All Rights Reserved. Reprinted with permission.

Another episode, "On the Lam," shows Annie on the run from Chinese hit men (Gray 6:184–199). Hungry, tired, and with worn-out shoes, Annie wanders into a shoe repair shop and meets Jack Boot. After Boot feeds Annie and provides her with new shoes, she falls asleep in his shop. He takes her home to his bachelor house. There Annie cooks, cleans, and keeps a light on for him. Shyly, Annie and Boot each admit a desire to stay together. To keep neighbors from snooping, they decide to be "uncle" and "niece" to one another. For both, the feeling of kinship, if not the legality, is real. Annie says, "As far as that goes, you might *be* my *real* uncle, for all I know—Anyway, I'm going to really *believe* you *are*—Gee—a real *uncle*—folks o' my *own*" (Gray, 6:202; emphasis in original).

In "Justice at Play," from 1939, Annie finally travels with Daddy Warbucks to London: this, he assures her, will keep her safe from trouble. But criminals throw Annie off the ship, her feet and hands bound and her mouth gagged. Annie, however, executes a trick she learned from servant Punjab and frees herself before she hits the water. Then, floating down the English Channel, she is rescued by a young couple, John and Jill. Believing Warbucks to be dead, the young couple bring Annie home to their mansion, under pretense that she is their niece (Gray 8:217–294).

As Annie moves time and again from home to hotel to boardinghouse, from the country to the city and back again, she inhabits numerous spaces and encounters diverse people ranging widely in class and ethnicity. For an extended period in 1931, she lives in a boardinghouse run by the Irish-named Maw Green, while working at a store run by Jake, who speaks with a Yiddish inflection and has mainly customers with Jewish names. In 1936 she lives with Ginger, a former showgirl and countess, with neighbors Honest Al, a Jewish pawnbroker, and Barney, the landlord, who speaks with a cockney accent (Gray 7:27ff). Characters in *Little Orphan Annie* speak with accents that mark their ethnicity and neighborhood. This "melting pot ethos of Annie's world" (Heer, "Economy" 16) signals not only the populism of the strip, and provides a realist glimpse of multiethnic urban life, but also models an acceptance of diversity and tolerance—within whiteness.[10]

Just as Annie can be absorbed into good families, she also transforms bad ones. In an extended sequence, the Bleeks pose as her biological parents in a gold-digging scheme (Gray 5:91–219). Mrs. Bleek falls for Annie's goodness and charm, however, and tells her the truth: "I'm not your mother . . . but Annie . . . I wanted you to love me. . . . Annie, my darling—I'll be a mother to you, no matter what, I swear" (Gray 5:191). Annie eventually discovers the scheme and traps Mr. Bleek and his gang of thieves. Mrs. Bleek aids her: "This is my chance to go right, and I'm taking it. You're not alone against those heartless butchers any longer Annie" (Gray 5:215).

Little Orphan Annie underscores the contingency of not only urban living but also family. As a mobile and free child without "tangling alliances," Annie can forge temporary alliances with multiple adults, including bachelors, spinsters, and couples without children of their own, like the Silos and Dooleys. As Joanne Hall observes, "Annie often adopts and is adopted by couples who lack children just as she lacks parents; essentially, she is the last piece of the jigsaw to be willingly assimilated into the parent-child family structure" (38). Annie has no stable home life but drifts in and out of multiple homes, often with loving adults who take care of her. These adults come from different backgrounds, ethnicities, and classes. These alternative families render family as potentially queer—contingent and spontaneous, not organic or destined.

The comic strip takes the instability of families in the Depression and renders it not merely as a problem but as a virtue. If families are not stable and permanent, they can at least be malleable and accommodating. While highlighting the risks of urban living in Annie's frequent run-ins with criminals, kidnappers, and thugs, *Little Orphan Annie* simultaneously figures the urban as a site of possibility. In showing the perils of neglect and the possible susceptibility of girls to external influences and forces, *Little Orphan Annie* ultimately emphasizes the urban girl's freedom and capabilities.

The Jane Withers Variant

Like Little Orphan Annie and Shirley Temple, child star Jane Withers can be seen as a "new girl" who navigates uncertainties about immigration and poverty, while at the same time producing a version of the urban as a space of contact and encounter. Now remembered mostly, if at all, as "Josephine the Plumber" in commercials for Comet Cleanser throughout the 1960s and 1970s, Withers was an extremely successful child star, appearing in more than forty films between 1932 and her initial retirement in 1947. According to Quigley's annual Top Ten Money Makers Poll, Withers was among the top-ten box-office stars of 1937 and 1938 (Zierold 102), despite the fact that forty-six of her forty-seven films were B movies (unlike Temple, whose films were all considered A pictures).

In certain ways Withers appears to be the antidote to Temple's cuteness, "the yin to Shirley's yang" ("All Dolled Up!"). Her first big film role in *Bright Eyes* explicitly sets her in opposition to Temple: she plays a rich spoiled brat who torments Temple's sweet orphaned character. Withers has been described as "a tomboy rascal" ("All Dolled Up!") and "America's favorite problem child" (Zierold 97): "wild-eyed, mischievous, uncontrollable . . . the noisy, brawling youngster actually making a mess of the living room before departing, strictly against orders, for some neighborhood gangland mayhem" (Zierold 98–99). Zierold describes her as more ferocious and tomboyish than Temple, her characters often in trouble, or "fixes," and prone to brawls (Zierold 100–101). Physically, Withers differs from Temple: where Temple is pudgy but delicate, Withers is stocky and sturdy; where Temple has backlit ringlets of blonde hair, Withers has straight black hair, often worn in a bob or tight braids, with severe bangs. Withers is never eroticized in the same way that Temple is, and she does not face the degree of risk Little Orphan Annie faces. Her knowingness relates more to her toughness and her class—after *Bright Eyes* she is usually a lower-class character—than her sexuality.

Despite these differences, Withers's films bear remarkable similarity to Temple's. Although Withers is less conventionally pretty than Temple, her films nonetheless all assert her cuteness and show characters responding to her cuteness. And as Zierold notes, there is "great similarity in plot structure between Withers and Temple films" (100). Like Temple, Withers "could reform wayward characters . . . bring together troubled lovers . . . was often lost or orphaned, but for those who were kind to her, she could

FIGURE 11. In *Little Miss Nobody* Jane Withers plays niece and homemaker to her "Uncle" John.

accomplish near miracles" (Zierold 100). While Zierold attributes these similarities to the probably false claim that Withers was given Temple's sloppy seconds, after Temple turned scripts down, we can see both girls' roles as providing an effective response to the experience and uncertainties of the Depression.

Like Temple, Withers often plays an orphan, and she is generally cared for by men rather than women. Unlike Temple, however, Withers is primarily aligned with uncles rather than fathers. In *Pepper* (James Tinling 1936) she lives with Uncle Ben (Slim Summerville), a street sweeper. In *Little Miss Nobody* (John G. Blystone 1936) she is an orphan named Judy at the Sunshine Home for Children. When Judy runs away from the orphanage, because she is being sent to reform school, she pretends to be visiting her uncle so that a detective will not find out her true identity. She runs into a pet store and greets the owner as "Uncle John." Showing sympathy for the girl, the man, John Russell (Harry Carey) (himself on the run from the law), takes her in, and they live together as uncle and niece. In *Ginger*

(Lewis Seiler 1935), Withers lives with Uncle Rex (O. P. Heggie), a former actor whom she believes to be her uncle but who was a friend of her actor parents and took her in when they died.

This affiliation with uncles removes Withers from the Oedipal trajectory of Temple films and potentially queers the Withers character. As Eve Kosofsky Sedgwick avows, uncles and aunts are stereotypically associated with queer childhoods: "Because aunts and uncles (in either narrow or extended meanings) are adults whose intimate access to children needn't depend on their own pairing or procreation, it's very common, of course, for some of them to have the office of representing nonconforming or nonreproductive sexualities to children. We are many, the queer women and men whose first sense of the alternative life trajectories came to us from our uncles and aunts" (Sedgwick 63). In situating Withers with uncles, as opposed to fathers, her films skew the traditional family structure and offer a vision of alternatives. These alternative families are similar in many ways to the temporary formations in *Little Orphan Annie*. They render family not only as potentially queer but also as contingent and spontaneous, not organic or destined.

Like those of Temple and Annie, Withers's relationships with men are often accidental but transformative. Sometimes Withers bonds with men who carry some stigma of criminality or danger. In *Little Miss Nobody*, for example, "Uncle John" is being blackmailed by a criminal, "Dutch," who threatens to reveal Russell's past identity as a bond thief. When Dutch tries to rob the home of Judy's newly adopted friend, Uncle John shoots him. Then, to protect Judy, he turns himself in and admits his past crimes. In *This Is the Life* (Marshall Neilan 1935) Withers plays Geraldine "Jerry" Revier, a popular but unhappy vaudeville performer. She has been "rescued" from an orphanage by an unscrupulous couple who pose as her aunt and uncle and who abuse her talents for their own gain. An accused thief, Michael (John McGuire), breaks into Jerry's hotel dressing room when her cruel guardians are out. She first hides him from police, then runs away to join him as he seeks to clear his name. Disguising herself as a boy, Jerry joins Michael to hop a freight, then hike across country until they meet a traveling salesman and his male assistant who both help them travel.[11] Eventually Michael clears his name and makes Jerry's foster parents admit that they do not have legal rights to her, and then Michael takes Jerry home.

In some films Withers effects a transformation by teaching a wealthy man how to have fun. This remasculinizes the man who has been living an overly pampered existence. These films promulgate a populist vision in which being rich does not lead to happiness, and lower-class people are seen as more authentic and lively than the rich (and, in some ways, "better off"). In *Pepper*, for example, Withers runs with a gang of kids. When one kid's mother is given an eviction notice, the kids try to get $11 to cover her costs. While out begging in city streets, they see a flighty young heiress crash into an Italian immigrant's fruit stand. Later, the kids come across the mansion where she lives and decide to get money from her dad, a wealthy recluse. Rejected in their plea to see the old man, they throw tomatoes at his car. Later, Withers's Pepper returns to the mansion, first pushing her way into the front door, then, after being kicked out, returning to sneak in through a window. She meets the girl's father, John Wilkes (Irvin S. Cobb). He has been cooped up and coddled, forced to eat a strict bland diet and live quietly to prevent heart failure. Won over by Pepper's sincerity, Wilkes not only gives Pepper the remaining $5 she needs, but he loosens up, lets her play with his possessions, and complains that he never has any fun. She dismisses his health concerns: "Oh pooh, you look as strong as a horse." And she urges him to go with her to Coney Island to have fun. There they go on numerous rides and eat fourteen hot dogs. When they discover that Wilkes's wallet has been stolen, they wash dishes to pay for their meal. Then, needing money to get home, Pepper does a hustle—she blacks his glasses and has him pretend to be blind while she sings a song to earn money. Wilkes rides the subway with her (a change from his chauffeured car) and spends the night at her apartment, sharing a bed with Uncle Ben. In the morning they eat pancakes and sing old songs together. Revitalized by his association with Pepper, Wilkes works with Pepper and Ben to stop his daughter from marrying a phony aristocratic baron, thus enabling her romance with a working-class policeman.

In *Ginger*, similarly, Withers is an authenticating presence. She plays "Ginger," a nickname for Jeanette, an eight-year-old girl from the slums. When her "Uncle" Rex is put in jail and Ginger gets caught stealing, trying to earn enough money to bail him out, she is taken in by a wealthy woman who is writing a book on children titled *Are Children Human?* The woman, Mrs. Parker (Katharine Alexander), adheres to a behaviorist view, espoused by the judge in the case: "Most kids aren't delinquents really. It's merely a matter of environment. You might say parental neglect." She believes that if Ginger is put in the proper environment, she will learn to behave. Instead, Ginger changes the behavior of those around her. Initially, the woman's son, Hamilton (Jackie Searl), rejects Ginger's rough ways. He is effete, snobby, and removed from the everyday manners of working-class children. Soon, however, under Ginger's influence, he is sliding down bannisters, using slang, and roughhousing with boys. His father (Walter Wolf King) is also transformed. Not only does he praise his son for acting "like a hoodlum," but he also stands up to his controlling wife, critiques her ideas about child care, and tells her that "from now on" she has to "act human." Cured of her "crazy ideas" about kids, Mrs. Parker and family join Ginger and her "Uncle" for a celebratory bowl of mulligan stew in their Ninth Avenue tenement flat.

As with Temple and Annie, Withers's status as an orphan, her mobility, and the contingency of home in her films engages with life patterns in the context of immigration. Numerous Withers films explicitly combine the orphan theme with a narrative of immigration. In *45 Fathers* (James Tinling 1937), for example, her father dies in Africa, and she is sent to New York to be the ward of his former hunting club. In *Paddy O'Day* (Lewis Seiler 1936) Withers plays an Irish immigrant, a "plucky little girl traveling all alone to meet her mother," who discovers, upon arrival at Ellis Island that her mother is dead. In *Pack Up Your Troubles* (H. Bruce Humberstone 1939) her character, Colette, lives in France. Born in America, she came to France with her American mother and French father when her mother needed surgery. Her mother dies, and her father goes to the front, where, she believes, he also dies (we discover that he is alive and working as a spy for the Allies).

These immigrant plots exist partly to enable Withers to showcase her skills with accents and to perform novelty numbers about other countries. In *Paddy O'Day*, for example, she performs a Russian number in Russian costume and accent, "I Like a Balalaika" (Troy Sanders and Edward Eliscu), and sings "Keep a Twinkle in Your Eye" (Troy Sanders and Edward Eliscu) in an Irish accent. *This Is the Life* has Jerry perform "Sunday and Me" (Sam H. Stept and Sidney Clare) with a Scottish burr. But Withers's narratives of immigration also, and more importantly, promote a melting-pot politics. In *Paddy O'Day* her Irish character befriends a Russian family on board the ocean liner that brings her to New York. They plan to eat Irish stew and borscht together when they arrive. When Withers goes to the house where her mother worked as a servant, she meets an eccentric rich man, nephew to two prudish aunts. As in *Pepper* and *Ginger*, Withers frees the effete wealthy man from his pampered emasculating existence. Before meeting

Paddy, the nephew, Roy Ford (Pinky Tomlin), spends all his time alone studying his taxidermy birds. After Paddy arrives—hiding in his study from the aunts—she introduces him to her Russian friends. Taken with Tamara Petrovich (played by Rita Hayworth, billed as Rita Cansino), Roy begins frequenting her uncle's nightclub, Café Padushka. As with Wilkes in *Pepper* and the Parkers in *Ginger*, his introduction to lower-class life is authenticating and rejuvenating. By the time his aunts return home from a trip, Roy is drinking vodka and smoking, has replaced his dead birds with live ones, has become an investor in the club, and is writing songs for a revue. Ultimately Roy and Tamara marry, with the promise that they will adopt Paddy, thus forming a blended WASP American-Russian-Irish family.

Although *Paddy O'Day* has a central marriage plot, Withers's films do not usually include narratives of marriage or coupling. To be sure, in some films a couple will be formed, but this is much less central than in Temple's films and not a result of Withers's agency. In *This Is the Life*, for example, when Jerry and Michael try to steal food from a farm, they meet Helen Davis (Sally Blane), who first attempts to have them arrested but then decides to help them. At film's end it is implied that she and Michael have become a couple, but their romance is not central to the plot, and it is unclear if they will marry and raise Jerry together. In *Pepper* Wilkes's daughter eventually falls in love with the policeman who arrests her after she runs over the fruit cart. In some films, rather than help create a couple, Withers dismantles one. In *45 Fathers* she blocks the marriage of her guardian's wealthy employer, Roger Farragut (Thomas Beck), when she learns that his fiancée is only using him for money. In *Pepper*, similarly, she helps unmask the pretend baron who plans to marry Helen Wilkes (Muriel Robert).

As in Temple's films and *Little Orphan Annie*, Jane Withers's films denaturalize marriage and family. Where Temple's films emphasize legal definitions of marriage and family over bonds of love, Orphan Annie and Withers both emphasize the contingency of family. In these texts family depends on encounter and opportunity, and family can be temporary. Just as Annie emphasizes ethnic intermingling, Withers shows the possibilities of global mixing to create a sense of assimilation, accommodation, and conversion into something new. They work against feelings of alienation and loneliness engendered by poverty and, at the same time, work through anxieties related to immigration and the disintegration of conventional families.

Dorothy Gale as Yellow Brick Road Walker

Finally, these urban girl texts of the 1930s provide a different context and vantage for understanding Judy Garland's Dorothy in *The Wizard of Oz*. *The Wizard of Oz* is not generally considered an urban film, despite the centrality of the fantastic Emerald City to its imaginary.[12] We can, however, view the film as being about the urban. In queer readings Dorothy has been seen as the queer teen that travels to the city to find a "world in which her inner desires can be expressed freely and fully" (Creekmur and Doty 3). Here, Dorothy moves from a world of aunts and uncles to one with a "sissy lion, an artificial man who cannot stop crying, and a butch femme couple of witches" (Creekmur and Doty 3). She leaves the bland black-and-white world of Kansas poverty to discover a world of color, abundance, and diversity. In this sense Dorothy fits the pattern of myriad other queer children who escape the structures of rural or suburban communities to find new identities and alternative communities in the city.

Without denying this queer reading, I would emphasize the way in which Dorothy's move from rural to urban entails a fall that not only makes her mobile and frees her from the structures of home but also turns her into an immigrant and that her narrative relies on chance encounters with male figures whom she "picks up," and the transformation of those figures through her influence.[13] Salman Rushdie's reading of *The Wizard of Oz* is especially smart about the film as a tale of urban emigration. Rushdie places the film squarely in the tradition of neglect narratives. He describes the film as one "whose driving force is the inadequacy of adults, and how the weakness of grown-ups forces children to take control of their own destinies and, ironically, grow up themselves" (10). This reading emphasizes the ways in which Auntie Em (Clara Blandick) and Uncle Henry (Charley Grapewin) fail Dorothy—ignoring her at the start of the film when she tries to tell them about Miss Gulch's (Margaret Hamilton) threats to Toto and closing the door to the tornado shelter before she returns home. Their neglect leads to Dorothy's first running away then being carried away by the tornado, the event Rushdie refers to as her "*unhousing*" or "homelessness" (33). As he suggests, from the tornado to her arrival at the Emerald City, Dorothy "never has a roof over her head" but becomes one who walks, or rather skips and dances, the streets.

Once Dorothy lands in Munchkinland—falling from the sky in a house—and is given the mandate to "follow the yellow brick road" to find the Wizard, who can send her back to Kansas, her story becomes one of encounter. She faces risk in some encounters, such as the magic trees that throw apples, the Wicked Witch of the West (Margaret Hamilton), and the flying monkeys. But she also encounters strangers who become "kin"— the Tin Man (Jack Haley), the Scarecrow (Ray Bolger), and the Cowardly Lion (Bert Lahr). A stranger herself, Dorothy is a figure of immigration for whom everyone and everything is unfamiliar. Her status as outsider also makes her powerful. She kills the Wicked Witch of the East and liberates the Munchkins, then kills the witch's evil sister, the Wicked Witch of the West, and unmasks the Wizard. Along the way she also transforms the Tin Man, Scarecrow, and Lion, uncovering the powers they have inside but have not previously been able to access: a heart, a brain, and courage.

For Rushdie, *The Wizard of Oz* is an "anthem of all the world's migrants . . . a celebration of Escape, a grand paean to the Uprooted Self, a hymn, *the* hymn to Elsewhere" (23). Arguing against what he sees as the film's unsatisfying tribute to home, Rushdie underscores the way in which the film destabilizes notions of home and opens up alternatives: "The truth is that once we have left our childhood places and started to make up our lives, we understand that the real secret of the ruby slippers is not that 'there's no place like home,' but rather that there is no longer any such place *as* home: except, of course, for the home we make, or the homes that are made for us, in Oz: which is anywhere, and everywhere, except the place from which we began" (57). While Rushdie rightly emphasizes the power of the contingent alternative family structure Dorothy forges in the Emerald City, we can also see that Dorothy's return home does not mark a return to conventional understandings of family or home. Rather, it places her back with an aunt and uncle—stereotypical figures in queer narratives and orphan narratives alike—and with three unrelated men who have their identical counterparts in Oz: Hickory/the Tin Man, Hunk/the Scarecrow, and Zeke/the Lion. Dorothy's temporary displacement from one model of family has transformed—in our eyes—her family at home, making us see these seemingly marginal figures anew.

Real Fantasies

Dorothy's return home and her insistence on the reality of Oz—"It was a real place!"—reminds us that the vision of the urban as benign and girls as powerful exists primarily in the imaginary, as a myth of childhood. But it also reminds us how powerful that imagining is. *The Wizard of Oz*, along with *Little Orphan Annie* and films starring Shirley Temple and Jane Withers, produces a potent and prevailing fantasy of the urban girl as mobile, free, and powerful, an adventurer rather than a victim. These texts challenge conventional views of the limitations placed on girl protagonists. For example, Ina Rae Hark claims that being "on the road" is an adventure generally reserved for boys: "In American home-leaving narratives, both literary and cinematic, woman as protagonist is rare; woman as protagonist who escapes either redomestication or ruin is rarer still" (29). These urban girls, however, are all "unhoused" or home-leaving figures who are neither ruined nor, in any simple way, domesticated. These texts each, to differing degrees, parodically invoke the figure of the streetwalker by showing girls who roam city streets and have frequent "pickup" encounters with men. These texts stitch together the contradictory narratives of the fallen woman and the "new girl." They show girls being unmoored from home—as orphaned, lost, displaced—and then finding themselves on streets where they encounter men. Their encounters, however, enable the girl to have significant agency to transform and improve not only her situation but also that of the men and to create new alternative families.

Here, I have grouped these "new girls" together, to show the prevalence of mobile urban girls in Depression era popular culture. In viewing the films of Shirley Temple and Jane Withers alongside such paradigmatic texts as *Little Orphan Annie* and *The Wizard of Oz*, we see consistent patterns in the representations of urban girls in the 1930s. These patterns show that girls in this period function to alleviate the sense of crisis around masculinity engendered by the Depression, as Hatch and Studlar argue, but also point to anxieties about maternity, marriage, the status of family, and immigration. Rather than ignore these problems, these films—like their counterparts in boy-centered narratives of the period—articulate, mediate, and make emotionally vivid the anxieties of the Depression and of modernity. But where the boy-focused narratives tended to engage issues of modernity within a limited sphere—showing the boys as trapped within their block, only able to encounter a limited range of people—these narratives, surprisingly, show the girls as more mobile than the boys and even global in their movements through various urban spaces. Where the Dead End Kids films tend to produce a fatalist view of the effects of poverty on children's life chances, these girl-centered narratives offer a more optimistic view. They provide a utopian solution to the traumatic effects of modernity in the figure of the "new girl," a girl whose movements mimic those of the fallen woman but whose own unmooring from traditional familial structures shows alternatives and possibilities in the upheaval and instability of modern life.

At the same time, these narratives also show the girls being forced, as Rushdie says, to grow up and away from innocence. In entering a world of mainly men, these girls leave the world of other children. Unlike the gangs of boy-centered narratives, the "new girl" is a singular figure. As a state that depends on being unhoused and unmoored, the girls' freedom exists in the space between being a child at home and the assumption of wholly adult responsibilities. Existing in a provisional space between the child's home and the married woman's home, the "new girl" finds her freedom in a liminal and transitive space, one that is also defined temporally, as a moment (similar, in ways, to the moment of stardom afforded child actors, before they grow up out of cuteness and into sexual maturity). The new girl's freedom exists within a world of white privilege and "obliviousness" to race; she is afforded a mobility that is not available to nonwhite girls; and she can queer the family but cannot erase color lines. In returning to the moment of her invention and dominance in popular culture, through reading these texts, I hope to preserve that moment, to reimagine the urban girl's freedom and mobility, and to imaginatively revive this important myth of childhood without whitewashing its limitations and boundaries.

3

Neglect at Home

Rejecting Mothers and Middle-Class Kids

In the 1930s, as discussed in previous chapters, neglect was portrayed largely in terms of social and economic factors: the neglected child lived in poverty and was homeless, orphaned, or otherwise displaced or removed from traditional structures of family and home. Such 1930s Hollywood texts as *Little Orphan Annie*, *The Wizard of Oz*, and films starring the Dead End Kids, Jane Withers, and Shirley Temple link neglect to ongoing concerns about urbanization, overpopulation, immigration, tenements, and slums that date back to the nineteenth century, and they stitch those concerns to issues specific to the Depression, such as unemployment, child abandonment, child homelessness, and the disintegration of the family (Ashby 2). By midcentury, however, in America, the discourses both on the child and on neglect move away from issues related to social and economic factors toward an emphasis on individual personality and psychological well-being.[1] Where the 1930s texts could be described in terms of vernacular modernism, by midcentury texts are less concerned with global traumatic effects of modernity and more with individual psychology and psychological trauma.

This shift in perceptions of neglect was noted at the 1950 White House Conference on Childhood and Youth. This conference was the fifth such meeting. The first White House Conference on the Care of Dependent Children, convened in 1909, had as its main topic concerns over the institutionalization of dependent and neglected children. The 1919 White House Conference on Standards of Child Welfare addressed children's health and welfare. The 1929 conference continued its examination of child welfare, with particular emphasis on action items such as providing better training to pregnant and nursing mothers. In 1939 the White House Conference on Children in a Democracy "highlighted the democratic values, services, and environment necessary for the welfare of children" (Child Welfare League of America, "The History" 2). In 1950 the Fact Finding Committee of the White House Conference on Childhood and Youth noted: "The first two conferences were concerned chiefly with the problems of particular groups of socially disadvantaged children in the United States; the next two gave major attention to certain social and economic aspects of the well-being of all American children" (Witmer and Kotinsky xv). "In the meantime," the report continued, "a new conception of children's needs developed, and we now know that even if the recommendations of the previous conferences were fully carried out it would not be enough. The new ideas, which are still in the making, have to do with the qualitative aspects of human relations" and "children's feelings" (Witmer and Kotinsky xv; see also *A Healthy Personality*). The 1950 conference, then, focused not on social and economic causes of neglect but on developing "the happy personality." To the degree that class, poverty, or other social and economic factors were taken into account, the emphasis was on how those factors handicap a child's personality and psychological well-being: they were not addressed as problems in their own right. The next two conferences furthered the emphasis on individual personality over social cause: in 1960 the White House Conference on Children focused on developing the child's creativity and, in 1970, on enhancing and cherishing the child's individuality and identity (Michael and Goldstein).

In swinging the emphasis from child welfare to the child's personality, the 1950 White House Conference on Childhood and Youth marked a shift in concern from primarily impoverished, orphaned children in the 1910s, 1920s, and 1930s to a concern with primarily white middle-class children in the postwar period. Rather than address the problems of children who might lack access to school, health care, or stable homes—the emphasis of the first four White House conferences—this conference focused on how schools, health services, family, churches, and synagogues could hinder or foster the middle-class child's healthy personality.

The idea of a happy personality was defined at the 1950 White House conference largely through Erik Erikson's ideas of stages of personality development. Erikson claims that personality is formed through a series of conflicts that, if resolved successfully, move the child from one stage of development to the next (Witmer and Kotinsky 6). Thus, the child progresses from a sense of trust as an infant to a sense of autonomy, to a sense of initiative, then senses of duty and accomplishment, then, in adolescence, a sense of identity, and, finally, "the parental sense," which means, literally, being ready to reproduce but also, figuratively, being productive and creative members of society.

In this Eriksonian model of development parents are crucial: "It is in and through the family that the main components of a child's personality develop" (Witmer and Kotinsky 174). The report cites many factors that influence the family's success or failure in fostering a healthy and happy personality, particularly rifts between husband and wife. These include the high divorce rate, the frequency of sexual incompatibility, worry and discontent over money, and concerns or disagreements over child rearing. But, the report concludes, "wives and mothers are commonly regarded as most at fault" (Witmer and Kotinsky 195). In particular, the absence of the mother is perceived as damaging (Witmer and Kotinsky 94).

In blaming mothers for hindering the child's development, the 1952 report on the White House Conference on Childhood and Youth avows a midcentury crisis in femininity. In a prescient anticipation of what Betty Friedan will call "a strange yearning" in *The Feminine Mystique* in 1963, the report identifies and describes women's dissatisfaction with their roles as mothers:

Many middle-class American women are dissatisfied with marriage and family life. Many of these women say they have little fondness for the job they are called on to do—though few of them try to avoid it by avoiding marriage. What these women complain of is the "boredom" and uselessness of household tasks, the perplexities of child rearing, the lack of appreciation on the part of husbands, the sexual dissatisfaction, the ingratitude of children. . . . A possible explanation of this unsatisfactory situation is found in the vagueness of the current American definition of the feminine role and, particularly, the lack of prestige attached to the job of wife and mother. (Witmer and Kotinsky 195)

This passage seems to open up a feminist discourse about the limitations and frustrations of being a housewife. Deflecting that critique, however, in the report findings, the solution to the mother's dissatisfaction is to promote individuality in child rearing, to better accommodate the child's unique personality, and to get more involvement in parenting from the father, "with the result that the wife finds her domestic tasks more satisfying, since she can feel that her accomplishment 'rates' in the American way of life" (Witmer and Kotinsky 202).

Unexpectedly, this sympathetic reading of women's dissatisfaction quickly shifts, in the report, to a castigation of women under the rubric of "momism." *Momism* is a term invented by Philip Wylie and popularized through his best-selling 1942 book, *Generation of Vipers*—and adopted by Erikson—that figures mothers as harmful to their children, especially their sons. According to the White House Report, American women, bored by motherhood, reject their roles as loving mother and instead become nagging and controlling. The mother aims to dominate and repress the child. Her attempt to control the child restricts the child's freedom.

Momism is associated with overmothering, which prevents the child from attaining growth and independence, but the White House Report interestingly allies momism with its seeming opposite in the concept of "rejecting motherhood." As psychologists state in 1970, maternal over-protection reveals the "suppressed hostility of the mother," and her over-protection of the child can be "a defense against guilty feelings aroused by rejection" (Anthony and Benedek 374). In tandem with this, mothers who give the child too much freedom, under so-called permissive-parenting models—notably Dr. Spock's child-led care—are also viewed with suspicion: "Both theory and observation indicate that 'permissiveness' can be carried too far. . . . Children not only need but even want to be kept under reasonable and kindly control" (Witmer and Kotinsky 93). Thus, too much mothering and too little are one and the same.

This tendency to blame mothers was noted at the time. In a 1950 *Parents Magazine* editorial, entitled "In Defense of Mothers," Herschel Alt claims: "There is an overemphasis at present on making parents, and especially mothers, the scapegoats for anything that goes wrong with children, from nail biting to juvenile delinquency. . . . There is too much talk of rejection these days; everyone is busy either rejecting or being rejected." Rather than dismantle the concept of the rejecting mother, however, Alt suggests that we consider the "whole" mother, her role as daughter and wife, as well as mother, and look to the influences on her that might "affect her ability to love her own child in a variety of ways."

While "momism" dominated much popular discourse on motherhood in the 1950s, the figure of the rejecting mother came to the fore increasingly in the context of second-wave feminism. As feminists extended their critique from first-wave concerns with voting rights and legal equality issues, such as property rights, to broad areas of de facto inequalities related to work, family, reproductive rights, and more, the women's liberation movement, as it came to be called, appeared in popular discourse to promote a rejection of the role of wife and mother (along with bras). Popular discourse would tend to knit together feminism and maternal rejection.

Popular discourse on feminism often maps feminism onto the figure of the discontented housewife. As I have noted, Betty Friedan's *The Feminine Mystique* located an undercurrent of dissatisfaction in married suburban women's lives, a sense of boredom and frustration, particularly for those who had gone to college and worked but had given up work and careers to be stay-at-home moms. As Victoria Hesford explains, Friedan's book appealed, in part, because it tapped into the very same discourses of psychology and the happy personality that underpinned much postwar thinking about the child: "The story Friedan offers as the necessary counter to that of the discontented wife—the story that would clear the mists of the feminine mystique and allow women to see their possibilities anew—was that of individual 'self-actualization.' The rhetoric and terms Friedan used to articulate this story of liberatory autonomy were rooted in the existential-inflected work of midcentury American psychology, particularly the work of human potential psychologists like A. H. Maslow and Erik Erikson" (108).

Women had been pushed by a conformist society to adapt to ideals of domesticated femininity, Friedan argued, and thus had not reached their full potential as creative human beings: "The goal of self-actualization," in contemporary psychology and in Friedan, was based on "the idea that life was an adventure and that people lived through a cycle of development. The potential to change and to achieve an 'authentic' self not only propelled people through their life adventure but was 'actualized' through the creative work they undertook" (Hesford 108). Although Erikson identified the "parental sense" as key to human development, this sense involved not only having children but also being productive and creative members of society. While motherhood and housewifery fulfilled one side of this important stage of development, Friedan pushed for women to be able to achieve the other.

Although this view of women's "self-actualization" relied on the same model of human development as that applied to the child in the 1950 White House Conference on Childhood and Youth, the mother's development was, in much popular discourse, set against that of the child. The mother's self-actualization and need to be, in the words of the heroine of *Stella Dallas* (King Vidor 1937), "something else besides a mother" was often pitted against her maternal obligation to shepherd the child through his or her self-actualization. Friedan does not recommend that women leave their husband and children, per se, but she does suggest that they leave home to go to work or school and craft an identity separate from that of mother and wife.

Friedan's ideas percolate from the mid-1960s forward, but the discourse of women's liberation, as such, does not explode until the 1967 protest against the Miss America pageant and, especially, what Hesford calls the "watershed" year, 1970, when women's liberation became "a nationally mediated event" (3, 5). In the 1970s, especially, the "women's libber" is linked to the trope of the rejecting mother in popular discourse (a linkage that seems still to underpin much conservative discourse today).

A *Life* magazine article from 1972 makes the connection explicit. Titled "Dropout Wife: A Seattle Woman Who Walked Out on Her Family Is Part of a New Class," the article makes one woman's story of leaving her family stand in for a "new class" of woman. The article begins: "One evening nine months ago, 35-year old Wanda Lee Adams, college graduate, wife of a middle-level Seattle executive and mother of three, walked out on her family to begin a new life of her own." Noting that there was "no great animosity" between husband and wife, that husband Don "was considerate, attentive, and devoted," and that money was "not a factor," the article says that Wanda had begun to find life "increasingly frustrating and suffocating." Starting to work again and going back to school, à la Friedan, Wanda "encountered the women's liberation movement" and realized "I was experiencing what a lot of women experience."

Life presents Wanda's story as exemplary of the women's liberation movement and, partly, as a cautionary tale. The story portrays Wanda as an educated woman whose plans were "totally traditional: to have a family and to be a good wife and mother" (36). But she has no life of her own. When she begins to take classes, she feels alienated from Don, who feels threatened by her newfound freedom and "radical new views." Not content to merely connect Wanda's experience of frustration to broader trends, the article claims that her leaving home also signals wider patterns: "The breakup of a home for such cool reasons is no longer rare. *No accurate statistics exist*, but around the country, interviews with marriage counselors, psychiatrists, detective agencies—as well as women's liberation groups—confirm the growth of what is called the phenomenon of the dropout wife. Most dropouts are middle-class, educated, highly motivated women who have been married a number of years. Some, but by no means all, are also women's liberation converts like Wanda Adams" (34B; italics mine).

Wanda is not just a symptom of a trend but a causal agent of change: she is an active member of Seattle's Radical Feminists, runs "rap sessions" with teenage girls, and "counsels wives caught in her own predicament" (37). In a largely sympathetic article that notes how often Wanda and Don bring the whole family together, the pull-quotes nonetheless underscore the damage she has done to her children: "The boys miss having me around" (38). At the same time, Wanda's story of maternal abandonment redeems husband Don as father: "He began to discover some unexpected joys in his new relationship with his children. . . . He found that caring for them gave him a sense of closeness that he had never felt before" (40). This narrative of maternal abandonment, on the one hand, and paternal redemption, on the other, becomes a paradigmatic narrative of neglect in the context of feminism.

Feminizing Neglect

I begin with the twin poles of the model of the "happy personality" and the trope of the rejecting mother to delineate a shift in ideas about parenting and neglect that mirrors trends in representations of the white urban child in American films and literature from World War II forward. (Representations of African American and minority children differ markedly as the following chapter will show.) This chapter spans a longer period than the last chapters, on the Depression. M. Keith Booker uses the term "the long fifties" to cover the years 1946 to 1964, arguing that in terms of periodization it makes sense to link these peak Cold War years. Of course, these are also the peak years of the baby boom that begins during World War II and lasts until 1964. My analysis extends into the late 1970s, to suggest ways in which tropes of maternal separation established in the "long fifties" shift and intensify over time. Fundamental shifts in the way childhood was being conceptualized had been under way since the early 1950s; they begin to take shape in films made in the early 1960s and then culminate in the 1970s, when the feminist mother becomes synonymous with the negligent mother.

While neglect narratives of the 1930s addressed a crisis in masculinity brought on by the Depression and cast fathers and father figures as either failures or in need of rehabilitation—unable to succeed financially, unable or unwilling to take on the role of husband and father—mid- to late-century narratives tend to chastise mothers and blame the mother for neglecting the child's emotional needs. Children in these texts are, by and large, not suffering the effects of poverty or, if they are, poverty is not determining. Rather, children in these texts suffer from a lack of maternal care and some form of rejecting motherhood, often directly linked to feminism. Momism, or overmothering, tends not to be represented in relation to children but figures prominently in narratives of adult masculinity gone wrong, such as in *White Heat* (Raoul Walsh 1949), *Psycho* (Alfred Hitchcock 1960), and *The Manchurian Candidate* (John Frankenheimer 1962). In child-focused films, by contrast, mothers are presented as detached, distracted, or absent; they are less often redeemed or rehabilitated than replaced with other caregivers. And against the recommendation of the White House report, fathers are not partners with mothers but are either absent themselves or rivals with the mother.

Mid-to-late twentieth-century ideas about neglect and parenting are not limited to urban scenarios and in many ways speak more to suburban notions of family and home. But the notion of neglect described in the White House Conference pervades representations of urban children. At the same time that the discourse on neglect changes to become more individuated and family-based, notions of the urban also become problematized as running counter to the needs of family. As I have discussed in *The Apartment Plot: Urban Living in American Film and Popular Culture, 1945 to 1975*, popular mid-to-late twentieth-century discourse tended to foster the idea that suburban living was better for families and children. Much popular culture fed on an ideal of the stereotypical 1950s cocktail of a white, heterosexual middle class, rising marriage rates, the baby boom, and suburban living. As Elaine Tyler May argues, there was some sense in which "in the postwar years, Americans found that viable alternatives to the prevailing family norm were virtually unavailable" (15). In her analysis the emphasis on home and family reflected and refracted Cold War policies of "containment," U.S. ambassador George Kennan's 1947 term for U.S. foreign policy apropos the Soviet bloc. No matter that many people were left out of the suburban imaginary, including single and divorced people, African Americans, working-class whites, ethnic minorities, and gay people; or that urban living was, as well, the preferred option for many married, middle-class families with urban or bohemian tastes. Urban living in popular mid-to-late twentieth-century discourse is often represented as inherently bad for the child or is suburbanized to match contemporary ideals of home. As we will see, discourses of containment and isolation underpin many child-centered films.

This home-bound emphasis in mid-twentieth-century American film differs from postwar European film, which tends to focus on what Michael Lawrence characterizes as the "pitiable child"—disposed, displaced, or orphaned during World War II. Films such as Vittorio De Sica's *Shoeshine* (1946), René Clément's *Forbidden Games* (1952), and Andrei Tarkovsky's *Ivan's Childhood* (1962) portray the traumatic effects of war on children and their communities. While the damage to the child may be emotional as well as physical, the causes are understood to be social and global, not individual- or family-based. American films such as *The Pied Piper* (Irving Pichel 1942) and *Little Boy Lost* (George Seaton 1953) take up similar themes but are still placed in a European setting. The former, made during the war, depicts an Englishman on vacation in France who becomes caretaker for a group of children lost during the war; the latter represents an American father's search for his son in France after the war. Despite these examples, the majority of postwar and mid-to-late-century American child-centered films set in America investigate the effects of parenting in lieu of war or any other large-scale social cause.

This chapter considers the difference between 1930s American texts and mid-to-late-century ones by comparing two texts that rework texts from the 1930s: *The Champ*, in its original 1931 version, directed by King Vidor, and its 1979 remake, directed by Franco Zeffirelli; and P. L. Travers's 1934 book *Mary Poppins* and its Disney film adaptation from 1964. In examining Travers's book, I am shifting briefly from an American focus to a British text. I do so because the transition from a British context to an American one underscores the particularity of the American film as revision. These texts will serve to inaugurate my discussion of the rejecting mother across four texts: the films *Kramer vs. Kramer* (Robert Benton 1979) and *Little Fugitive* (Morris Engel and Ray Ashley 1953) and two examples of children's literature, *Eloise* (Kay Thompson 1955) and *Harriet the Spy* (Louise Fitzhugh 1964). Each text shows a variation of the rejecting mother; but where some texts show parental neglect as disabling and restricting, others emphasize the enabling effects of neglect.

A Tale of Two Champs

In both versions of *The Champ* we find an eight-year-old boy being raised by his father, his mother having left when the son was a baby. The father, whom the boy calls Champ, is a former boxing champion who is now down on his heels, a drunk and a gambler. In both films the father wins a horse for his son by gambling and then loses it in another game. In both versions the mother is rich and remarried. She accidentally encounters the son at a race track when he races his horse, and she attempts to become his mother again. The child resists and opts to return to his father. The father goes back in the ring to win enough money to properly care for the boy and get back his horse but dies after winning the championship bout. The child is reunited with his mother.

While the basic plot of the two films is the same, and both are tear-jerkers, details shift in such a way as to alter the film's overall meaning. As Leger Grindon observes, "Both films address social problems arising from shifting gender roles typical of their respective eras" (130). In particular, he notes that "the 1931 film sympathetically portrays a failure of masculinity," whereas the 1979 film "offers a hostile treatment of the career woman." This shift in emphasis not only marks changing views of gender and an antifeminist backlash but also reorients the viewer's understanding of the child, the nature of his neglect, and the interpretation of his relation to his urban setting.

As Raymond Durgnat and Scott Simmon argue, the 1931 version of *The Champ* is "progressive and reformist" (131), concerned with "the class powerlessness of down-and-out men, reinforced by the social powerlessness of children" (124). Comparing it to another King Vidor film, *Stella Dallas*, Durgnat and Simmon describe *The Champ* as primarily about class: "A parent coming to grips with his/her own inadequacy, must force class status and wealth on the unwilling child" (124). In 1931 *The Champ* could be read as a common story of masculine failure under economic pressure. As Grindon suggests, the Champ's troubles represent a "catalogue of fears haunting working class men during the Depression" (133). Out of work, abandoned by a wife who left to marry a more prosperous man, the Champ's drinking and gambling register as a response to "the masculine anxiety engendered by joblessness and the economic threat of the Depression" (Grindon 134).

By contrast, the 1979 version of *The Champ* makes the Champ's problems psychological. Class differences are in the mix, certainly, but rather than being representative of a class of men all suffering the effects of similar social and economic forces, Jon Voight's Champ (Billy) is psychologically destroyed by individual circumstances. When Wallace Beery's Champ (Andy) encounters his ex-wife in the original film, he shows little emotion, except perhaps annoyance. In the 1979 version, by contrast, Voight's Champ clearly still loves his ex-wife and, weeping, tells her, "You can always come back." His grief over the loss of her seemingly breaks him.

This difference relates to a key difference between the two films regarding why the mother leaves the child in the first place. In the 1931 version the relationship (similar to that in *Stella Dallas*) is marked by class. In the film we are told that the wife, Linda (Irene Rich), was initially "fascinated" by the Champ because he was in vogue as a champion. Durgnat and Simmon describe their union as "a hasty romantic affair between cultural incompatibles" (125). They describe Linda as a "wealthy WASP who has now outgrown her bold-flapper's pseudo romanticism" and the Champ as "rejected by the socialite world because of his failures in the ring, now returning to the asphalt jungle from which he came" (Durgnat and Simmon 125). This reading appropriately suggests that the Champ's problems lead his wife to leave him. Having been attracted to him in a moment when he was financially and culturally ascendant, she leaves when he falls from a position of power to one of inadequacy. Unable to win fights, thus unable to function as a breadwinner, the Champ reverts to working-class pleasures and dangers. No longer starry-eyed, Linda leaves and secures a more stable home with upper-class Tony (Hale Hamilton). Why she gives Andy custody of their son, Dink (Jackie Cooper), is unclear. With Tony she has a daughter, thus indicating her favorable disposition to motherhood.

In Franco Zeffirelli's rendering of *The Champ* the division between the couple relates to gender and feminism rather than class. The wife, Annie (Faye Dunaway), leaves because she is dissatisfied with the role of wife and mother and has ambition. Annie is now not only married to a wealthy man but is herself a successful fashion designer. Unlike Linda, she does not have any children with her new husband and thus appears to have rejected not just Billy and son, T. J. (Ricky Schroeder), but motherhood. In her taxonomy of rejecting mothers, Anna Freud identifies one variant in which the mother rejects the child because of her own "masculinity," defined as "longing for a career" and "competition with the husband" (379). In the logic of the film Annie fits this profile. Calling Annie a "big shot now," Billy acknowledges that he wanted a woman who would be home waiting for him and that "today, I feel exactly the same way." In case there is any question about where the film's sympathies lie, Zeffirelli labels Annie "the hard-bitten self-centered bitch whose return sparks all the trouble" (qtd. in Grindon 136). When Billy asks Annie why she left, he cries, "What do I tell him? That you wanted a career? And that's why you left your son and husband!" In 1931, when Linda is asked to explain why she left the Champ, she says that they had a disagreement, thus faulting both parties. Annie, by contrast, says, "I made a mistake," taking all the blame. Where Andy, in the original, fails as a boxer and thus loses his wife, Billy's fall is caused by his wife's leaving: the timing of her departure and his last bout are identical, seven years.

In the two films the stepfather's role differs markedly. In Vidor's film Linda's husband, Tony, is much more prominent in the narrative than Linda. Tony runs into Andy at the track before Linda sees him. Tony offers Andy money, which he accepts, to allow Linda to see Dink. After Linda hosts Dink at her posh apartment, she tells Tony, "We've got to get that baby away from him." Tony then finds Andy at a bar, gambling. He asks Andy to let them have Dink for six months. Andy initially refuses, then later accepts money from Linda and agrees to ask Dink if he wants to live with her for "a good home, decent environment, friends." When Andy is arrested and put in the drunk-tank, Tony bails him out. Andy pretends that he does not want Dink anymore and forces Dink to go live with Linda and Tony. From the time Dink runs away, returning to the Champ, until the Champ's death, we do not see Linda. Tony appears in Andy's dressing room before the fight and tells him that he and Linda will not try to take Dink again. When the Champ dies, we see first Tony, then Linda, enter his dressing room. In the last seconds of the film, nonetheless, Linda sweeps Dink into her arms and he cries, "Mother, mother."

In contrast to stepfather Tony's active role in the narrative, Annie's husband, Mike (Arthur Hill), stays much more in the background. As in the earlier film, Mike sees Billy at the track, but in this version he does not speak to him. Then, when Annie spots Billy and realizes that T. J. is her son, Mike looks chagrined, as if he had not planned to tell her the truth. Annie, without Mike, goes to see T. J. and confronts Billy, who reminds her that *she* gave *him* custody. When T. J. visits her, this time on a fabulous yacht (her wealth much grander than Linda's), T. J. talks to Mike and learns that he is a gerontologist, fascinated by age, but clearly not by children. After this, we barely see Mike and T. J. together, but we see lengthy romantic shots of T. J. swimming with his mother, who lovingly cradles him in the water. The contrast between Tony and Mike suggests a similar contrast between the two women. Where Linda is in the background, letting her husband function as her negotiator and mediator, Annie's role is foregrounded. Tony runs his family—as Andy failed to do?—whereas Mike is diminished or castrated by Annie.

Mike does visit Billy at the gambling hall, but Billy does not know or recognize him. When Tony finds Andy gambling, Dink is in the gambling hall, asleep on a pool table. Tony does not chastise Andy for bringing Dink out to a gambling joint at night but merely turns off a light above the sleeping child and states that Dink may benefit from a "different environment." By contrast, when Mike reminds Billy that T. J. has a mother, Billy reminds Mike that Annie abandoned her son and did not perform her role as mother: "Never did she change his pants or wipe his nose or teach him his prayers or give him a bath. Some goddamn mother." Thus, where the Vidor film used the scene between father and stepfather to emphasize the need for "a different environment," the Zeffirelli film uses the same scene to emphasize the woman's neglect and failure to nurture the child.

Along with the difference accorded the stepfather role, the mother's role differs significantly in the two films. While Linda is absent from the narrative after Dink returns to the Champ and the Champ trains for his fight, Annie features prominently in the latter part of the film. After T. J. refuses to stay with Annie (crying, "I want Champ! Champ! Champ!"), she goes to see Billy and asks him to tell T. J. "how it was, and how it is," meaning that she is T. J.'s mother. This scene allows Billy to confront Annie and ask why she left. It also allows him to voice his pain: "What about me, Billy Flynn? What about me? I'm real, too." While Billy trains for his return to the ring, T. J. tentatively corresponds with Annie and invites her to the fight. She comes, without Mike, who is upset and seemingly jealous. Whereas the first film did not show Linda or Tony until after the fight, the 1979 film shows Annie at the bout. T. J. sees her, waves, and tells the Champ "She's here!" Frequent reaction shots show both Annie's concern for the Champ and her admiration of him. At film's end, when Annie enters the Champ's dressing room, we hear T. J. crying, "I want Champ! Champ! Champ! Champ!" just like he did when he rejected Annie. Now, however, he approaches Annie slowly, then hugs her. But instead of ending with the image of mother and child, as in the Vidor film, this version shifts to a high-angle shot of Billy dead and in the spotlight, an image of Christological sacrifice. As Grindon avows, "The delinquent woman learns the value of parenting, the emotions of motherhood, from the man's self-sacrifice" (139).

Tellingly, the boy's understanding of what constitutes a mother changes between the two films. In both films the Champ has told the boy that his mother died. When the boy is first told that the woman is his mother, alive, he refutes that fact. To Linda Dink says, "You're not married to the Champ anymore. Then I guess you're not my mother." To Annie T. J. first says, "You don't live with us. You're not married to the Champ." But then he shifts from this legal or practical view of marriage and motherhood to ask, "Do you love the Champ? Do you? No? You're not my mother." In both films the boy, Dink or T. J., measures the woman by her relationship to the Champ. But where Dink applies a simple rule of "the woman who is my mother must be married to my father," T. J. raises the bar and asks for not just marriage or cohabitation but love. Loving the Champ seems a requirement to be T. J.'s mother, and coming to love the Champ again is what redeems Annie. She goes to the fight because, she tells Mike, "I don't think Billy would go back in the ring if I hadn't come back in their lives." She understands that the fight is as much for her as it is for T. J. Her appearance at the fight is taken as her support of Billy and makes her available to be a mother to T. J.

Along with changes in the representation of the parents in the two versions of *The Champ*, there are significant differences in the way the child's world is represented. In particular, they represent his relation to urban space, and, thus, the way we understand his neglect, differently. In the 1931 film Dink is a figure of neglect that shows simultaneously the way in which he is impoverished and also the way in which his neglect gives him freedom. By contrast, T. J., in the later film, seems much more isolated and unhappy.

To be sure, Dink shows signs of poverty. He wears rags and is dirty. He lives in a one-room apartment with his dad, with whom he shares a bed.

And he is rendered knowing by experience. In many ways Dink is the adult in the family. When Andy goes missing before an important meeting that may restart his career, Dink tracks him down in a bar, sobers him up with coffee, and escorts him home. There, Dink witnesses Andy blow the meeting, his drunkenness still evident. Then, Dink undresses Andy and puts him to bed before undressing himself. The next day, we see Dink cleaning the one-room apartment.

In the class logic of the film Dink will be "better off" with his mother. Certainly, he lacks the amenities she can provide. He has not yet gone to school or traveled beyond his immediate neighborhood. But the film makes clear that Dink is happy in his current life and that, in certain ways, his life is better with his father than it would be with his mother. For one thing, Dink and his father have a physically affectionate relationship. When Dink puts Andy to bed, he crawls into bed with his father. Andy rolls over and steals the covers, but Dink spoons him. Furthering the physicality of their relationship, whenever Andy makes a bet, he has Dink spit on his hand. In contrast, when Linda wants to undress Dink for bed, he refuses and asks for privacy. In addition, life at his mother's is presented as rather dull and rigid by comparison to his life with Andy. Durgnat and Simmon note that Tony hints that Dink may be sent to military school if he lives with them (128). Andy, trying to dissuade Dink from going, compares the school to "a prison. Everybody wears uniforms." Whether that is true or not, it is clear that Dink will have less freedom. When Dink sees his mother's apartment, he recognizes the class difference: "The Champ and me aren't fixed up as well as this." But he also suggests that her home is lacking: "Our joint is more lively. It's right above the Greek saloon. . . . I like to listen to the piano when I wait for the Champ to come home at night." What might represent a miserable existence—the young child living above a saloon, waiting for his drunken dad to return—is here presented in positive anti-elitist terms; it is lively.

Durgnat and Simmon claim that the original film's location in Tijuana functions to displace the action away from Prohibition laws, still in force in the United States, so that Andy's drinking is immoral but not illegal (124). In addition, Tijuana establishes the seediness of Andy's life, away from America and the neighborhood where he grew up. It is a border town, which implies a certain lack of stability and tradition. For Dink, however, Tijuana provides a strong sense of community. Dink has a group of six male friends with whom he roams the streets and plays. This group of kids provides support to

FIGURE 12. Dink and his friends roam the streets looking for Andy in *The Champ* (1931).

Dink throughout the narrative. We see them together, arm in arm, walking the streets looking for Andy. They are with Dink when Andy gives him the horse. They are with Dink when he witnesses Andy being arrested. Together with Dink they watch the Champ train and check out the competition. Dink has an especially strong friendship with an African American boy, Jonah (Jesse Scott). Jonah helps Dink sober up the Champ, rides in the truck at the start of the film when we see the Champ and Dink jogging, and waits in the car when Dink goes to visit his mom. At the end of the film Jonah enters Andy's dressing room with Dink after the fight. When the Champ dies, Dink hugs Jonah, crying, before Tony and Linda arrive. Because Dink has friends, his situation seems potentially shared by the other boys. He is no more unmoored than Jonah, whose family we never see. His community of friends, along with Andy's male friends, provides another instance of a queer family, what Durgnat and Simmon call an "improvised or asymmetrical family" that "complements the disruptions in melting pot films" (128).

In the 1979 film T. J. also has a warm and loving relationship with his father. But, presumably owing to changed mores in relation to childhood sexuality and pedophilia, they are not as physically affectionate as Andy and Dink. Like Dink, T. J. finds his father drunk in a bar, drumming. He brings him home from Miami to the backstretch at Hileah, where they live. But when he starts to undress his father, Billy stops him and says, "The day a man can't take off his own pants is the day he's not a man anymore." T. J. and Billy have separate beds.

More important, T. J. is isolated from other kids. The people who live in the backstretch are all adults who work with the horses. Nobody besides Billy seems to have children. Thus, T. J. circulates in an adult world. This adult world never quite adheres to become a melting pot alternative family. Rather than streets, T. J. lives in an artificial world attached to the race-track, isolated from city streets. Unlike Dink, who has Jonah, T. J. has no close friend besides his father, which emphasizes his dependence on him. When his father runs off in Miami, panicked at the prospect of fighting again, T. J. runs through the unfamiliar streets alone. This reads as a scene of endangerment. T. J.'s isolation makes his situation seem unique and uniquely bad. It is caused by parental failure (on both parents' parts), not by social or economic conditions. His isolation also blocks the possibility of producing an alternative family and makes the film seem more insistent about the need for a traditional family. Where neglect makes Dink at least partially free and open to encounter, T. J.'s neglect makes him lonely and impedes his development.

Poppins in Context

While the original Frances Marion screenplay for *The Champ* is largely Dickensian and melodramatic in its imagination of a child suffering neglect and poverty at the hands of a drunken father, P. L. Travers's *Mary Poppins* harks back more to J. M. Barrie in its emphasis on imagination, make-believe, and play. Against the wretchedness and tears of *The Champ*, *Mary Poppins* offers light entertainment in a middle-class milieu. But, similar to the adaptation of *The Champ*, the film adaptation of *Mary Poppins* shifts the text's meaning to emphasize the children's emotional neglect and parental failure.

Echoes of Barrie can be heard in the description of the father in Travers's *Mary Poppins*. Like the father in *Peter Pan*, he is "absent-minded" at home (Travers 15), focused on making money, and concerned about costs.

Like the father in *Peter Pan*, who purchases a dog to serve as a nurse to save costs, Mr. Banks in *Mary Poppins* tells his wife that she can *either* have "a nice, clean, comfortable house *or* four children" (Travers 13; emphasis mine). Thus, the Bankses' home is not only the smallest but also the most dilapidated house on Cherry-Tree Lane. Despite, however, Mr. Banks's claim of financial privation, the Banks family has a cook, a housekeeper, a gardener, and, "of course," a nanny for the children.

In the original book the nanny is described as necessary both for the children and for their mother. Despite his cost-cutting measures, Mr. Banks does not question the need for the nanny or any other servants. At the start of the story the nanny, Katie Nanna, has quit. Readers are given no reason for her actions.[2] Almost as soon as Mrs. Banks begins writing advertisements for a new nanny, Mary Poppins appears, carried in on the East Wind. She stays with the Banks family until the wind changes.

Mary Poppins introduces the four Banks children to numerous adventures, or encourages them to imagine that they happened, depending on whether one reads the story as pure fantasy or as magic realism. As Mary Poppins asserts at one point, "Everybody's got a Fairyland of their own" (Travers 36). Like *Peter Pan*'s Neverland, Fairyland is an imaginative construct that children carry with them, but, as with Neverland, it requires a free and mobile Other to enable the children to find it. In these adventures the children are magically transported to places they would not otherwise go and have encounters with strange characters: they visit Mary's uncle, who floats to his ceiling when he laughs via laughing gas that makes the children float as well; they meet a tiny gingerbread woman and her two giant daughters, who break off fingers as treats for the children; they speak to animals; and they visit the zoo at night, when humans are in cages and animals are their masters.

At the end of the book, when Mary Poppins departs, the children, distraught at her leaving, are cheered when they realize that she has said "au revoir" and not good-bye. Thus, they hold out the promise that she will return (and she does in three sequels). For Mrs. Banks, however, Mary Poppins's leaving merely repeats the cycle that Katie Nanna's leaving begins, "leaving me high and dry with nobody to help me and not a word of notice" (Travers 188). Left without a nanny, Mrs. Banks nonetheless goes out to dinner, kissing the children "absent-mindedly" (Travers 188), and sending the cook up to take care of the children.

If, in the original story, Mr. and Mrs. Banks are, much like the Darlings in *Peter Pan*, a bit distracted, they are not much criticized as parents. Mary Poppins is taken to be a much more fun and interesting nanny than Katie Nanna, certainly, but Mary Poppins herself has flaws. She is vain, easily offended, sometimes sharp with the children, and often cross. Although she shows some tenderness in giving Michael a compass and Jane a self-portrait, she leaves the children abruptly, without saying good-bye. Mrs. Banks has the same relationship to Mary Poppins as to other nannies and is unchanged by her coming or going.

The Disney film adaptation of *Mary Poppins*, famously disliked by Travers, alters the story in some significant ways. Travers objected to the use of animation in one scene, the use of songs, and the overall softening of Mary Poppins. Along with those changes are ones that shift the logic of the narrative to strongly emphasize the children's emotional neglect and parental failure and to render Mary Poppins a psychological necessity and not just a diversion.[3]

The most symptomatic changes in the film adaptation have to do with the rendering of Mrs. Banks (Glynis Johns). Whereas before, in the novel, Mrs. Banks's need for a nanny was seen as a natural part of running a household, the film makes Mrs. Banks seem to be rejecting motherhood. In Anna Freud's influential analysis of the rejecting mother, mothers who entrust the care of their children to nurses are often described as rejecting (because the mother can turn off her attachment to the child) (379), and the film seemingly supports this view. Instead of four children, two of whom are infants in the book, the film's Banks family has only two kids. While the book suggests that Mrs. Banks specifically desired her children—choosing them over a nicer house—the film eliminates the sense of choice and cuts out any indication of Mr. Banks's pecuniary concerns. Most important, the film links Mrs. Banks to first-wave feminism, particularly the suffrage movement. In leaving her children to fight for a women's cause, Mrs. Banks seems to be adopting "masculine" values, like Annie in the remake of *The Champ*, and turning against hearth and home. Whereas the book *Mary Poppins* was set in the present, the film places the action in 1910—neither the time of the book's publication nor the film's present but at a peak moment for women's activism for suffrage in England. When Katie Nanna (Elsa Lanchester) quits, Mrs. Banks is away from home at a suffrage meeting. As she returns home wearing a sash with "Votes for Women" imprinted on it, she is so caught up in "the cause" that the servants cannot interrupt to tell her the news. Singing "Sister Suffragette" (all songs Richard M. Sherman and Robert B. Sherman 1964), Mrs. Banks claims an affinity with the cook and housekeeper, draping them in "Votes for Women" sashes and gleefully proclaiming that "While we adore men individually / We agree that as a group they're rather stupid" and "No more the meek and mild subservients we, / We're fighting for our rights militantly." Despite her fantasy of herself as a militant, however, it becomes clear that Mrs. Banks has no control whatsoever in her home; and despite her claim of solidarity with the women who work in her home, she does not share their load or point of view.

In making Mrs. Banks a would-be suffragette, the film makes the role of nanny function as a mother substitute. Katie Nanna is the sixth nanny in four months. She leaves because the children have run away from her, their fourth disappearance in a week. In *Peter Pan*, being lost is blamed on distracted nannies who do not pay sufficient attention and thus allow children to fall out of their carriages. Here, in contrast, being lost is taken to be an act of defiance on the part of the children: Katie Nanna considers them to have run away from her. Again, the film seems to rely on popular psychological explanations of the rejecting mother. In her analysis of the rejecting mother, for instance, Anna Freud links running away and being lost to the rejecting mother. She identifies one type of rejecting mother as rejecting the child by separation: "Separations between mother and infant are *rejections*, whether they are brought about for good or bad reasons, whether they are long or short" (381). In this light, when Mrs. Banks leaves her children to attend suffrage meetings, she rejects them. Freud suggests that the child feels tied to the mother when he feels her love, but when he feels rejected, the child feels lost: "When the infant is old enough to be capable of independent movement, he may even get lost physically, i.e., he may venture away from the mother into what is normally for him 'out of bounds' and not find his way back to her" (A. Freud 382). Bluntly, Freud asserts that when the mother rejects the child by separating from him, the mother "may lose her emotional hold on [her] young children; this, in turn, may induce the child to stray, to lose himself, to run away" (A. Freud 382). The child "cannot live without a mother substitute" (A. Freud 382) and will search for a replacement shortly after being rejected by the mother. In *Mary Poppins* the children are given a series of unsatisfactory mother substitutes in nannies and run away repeatedly, frustrating the nannies, who then quit, thus furthering the cycle of rejection.

Mary Poppins is not antifeminist per se, in large part because it treats suffrage as a superficial diversion rather than a serious issue. Rather than castigate Mrs. Banks, the film suggests that her involvement with suffrage, and her status as a rejecting mother, is a response to her husband's domination. Mr. Banks (David Tomlinson) adheres to traditional ideas of masculinity: he defines himself primarily as a breadwinner and (like Billy in the remake of *The Champ*) supports the separation of spheres. When he returns from work, he, like his wife, is too distracted to notice Katie Nanna's leaving. He even helps her into a cab. In "The Life I Lead" he sings a paean to masculinity:

I feel a surge of deep satisfaction

.   .   .   .

When I return . . . to hearth and wife

.   .   .   .

King Edward's on the throne
It's the age of men.

Mr. Banks adheres to a strict model of parenting that emphasizes discipline over emotion and firmness over affection or play. When the police bring the children home, he stops Mrs. Banks from running to them: "Don't be emotional." Here, and throughout the film, we see that Mrs. Banks has loving instincts toward her children but that Mr. Banks does not allow her to exercise those impulses because he views them as weak. In this he echoes early twentieth-century views of parenting, such as those of John Watson and Arnold Gesell, who promote independence and self-reliance in children, against parental coddling and affection. The film, however, speaks from a 1960s perspective influenced by Dr. Spock that promotes less restrictive parenting and portrays Mr. Banks's attitude as out of date and in need of adjustment. More than Mrs. Banks, the children blame Mr. Banks for their running away. They say that their kite blew away, that it was not a good kite because they made it themselves: "Perhaps if *you* helped us," they suggest, establishing a need for his involvement.

Although Mary Poppins arrives at Cherry-Tree Lane in both the book and novel because the East Wind carries her there, the film shows her arrival as specifically responsive to the children's needs and especially their need for a more loving and playful mother figure. When Mr. Banks dictates an advertisement for a nanny to Mrs. Banks—taking over the job because he claims that she failed in her previous efforts to hire a nanny—he asks for a "firm, respectable, no-nonsense" nanny who "can give commands." The children, however, proffer their own advertisement. In "The Perfect Nanny" they ask for "a cheery disposition," someone who is kind, witty, sweet, "Never . . . cross or cruel," and crucially, someone who will play with them: "Play games, all sorts." In direct opposition to the father's desire for a nanny who commands, Jane (Karen Dotrice) and Michael (Matthew Garber) state that they want to be loved, not disciplined: "If you won't scold and dominate us, / We will never give you cause to hate us."

In a sense Mary Poppins blends the father's desires and those of the children: she dominates and controls everyone she meets, but she does so through imagination and play rather than tough discipline. Although Mr. Banks tears up the children's ad and throws it in the fireplace, when Mary Poppins (Julie Andrews) arrives, she has a copy, the fragments reassembled. Reading to him from the ad, she reads the list as suiting her qualifications, then heads directly upstairs, magically riding the banister up, while the father remains flummoxed below. Soon, she gets the kids to clean their room by making it a game in "A Spoonful of Sugar":

In ev'ry job that must be done
There is an element of fun.
You find the fun, and snap!
The job's a game.

She forces the children to take their medicine, but each kid's spoonful has a unique taste suited to them (and Mary Poppins gets rum punch flavor). As in the book, Mary Poppins can appear to be stern, but in the film her sternness seems a pose—as Julie Andrews shows a flicker of amusement or small smile behind her stern mask—and her sweetness and love are foregrounded.

In her use of creativity and play rather than an emphasis on discipline and punishment, Mary Poppins embodies the ethos of the creative child, a key component of developing a healthy personality. Amy Ogata notes that midcentury discourse on childhood emphasized the importance of creativity: "Inverting the norm of training children to assume the conventions of adulthood, the discourse on creativity valued the child's unique insight, which the parent labored to reveal, sustain and then emulate" (xi). The ideal of creativity encouraged parents to foster the child's healthy personality through play and to downplay restrictions. In part, this emphasis on creativity was pitched as a counter to totalitarianism, thus fitting Cold War ideology by making the American child seem less rigid and controlled than the Russian. In addition, Ogata argues, creativity was placed in opposition to postwar conformity as analyzed by David Riesman in *The Lonely Crowd* (1950) and William Whyte in *The Organization Man* (1957).

In this film, as in many 1930s texts, the father has to be reformed and rehabilitated. But, as opposed to those films in which the father has to be redeemed by accepting his role as father and breadwinner, here the father has to become more childlike and playful. In a key scene Mr. Banks fails his children by allying himself with his employer and his corporate values over his children. When the children visit their father at the bank, they want to stop and give money to the Bird Woman, whom Mary Poppins has described to them (in a change from the book in which they tell Poppins about her, thus asserting their own prior knowledge of the city). Their father views this as wasteful and going against the seriousness he wants to instill. When Michael refuses to give up his tuppence for a deposit, he accidentally causes a run on the bank. The children run away, terrified of their father as much as of the other bankers.

Just as the film establishes Mary Poppins as a mother substitute for the absent rejecting mother, it provides a father substitute. The film amplifies the role of Bert, the Match Man (Dick Van Dyke). He opens the film doing a one-man show in the park and then guides the viewer, in a direct address, to Cherry-Tree Lane. He and Mary, together, take the children on a "Jolly Holiday" into one of his chalk drawings—of a picnic in the park with a merry-go-round and a horse race—a trip reserved for Mary and Bert alone in the book. Bert shows only affection, no sternness. When the kids get lost, having run away from their father's bank, Bert finds them, scared in a dark alley, and promises "Bert'll take care of you like I was your own father." He takes them home and is pressed into babysitting as Mrs. Banks heads to a suffrage meeting. Working as a chimney sweep, he shows them the chimney, "doorway to a land of enchantment" and leads them out onto the rooftops of London along with Mary Poppins and a host of chimney sweeps. Later, alone with Mr. Banks, who has been summoned to the bank for his own scolding, Bert subtly urges him to attend to his children, by undercutting his corporate values, in "A Man Has Dreams":

You've got to grind, grind, grind
At that grindstone,
Though child'ood slips like sand through a sieve.
And all too soon they've up and grown,
And then they've flown,
And it's too late for you to give
Just that spoonful of sugar
To 'elp the medicine go down.

Mr. Banks's transformation occurs in stages. First, he is stripped of his status as breadwinner. He loses his job at the bank. Then he is stripped of the symbols of his success and conformity to traditions of masculinity and work: his boutonniere, his umbrella, and his bowler hat are all broken. But, finding Michael's tuppence in his pocket—a sign of Michael's childlike desire to give money to the birds rather than the bank—Mr. Banks finally recognizes the value of childishness. He bursts into song, singing the nonsensical "Supercalifragilisticexpialidocious," which he had previously dismissed. When he returns home, he kisses Mrs. Banks on the mouth and swings her around playfully, then leads the whole house in a dance around the room. Emerging from the basement with the now-repaired kite, he leads Jane and Michael outside to "Let's Go Fly a Kite" but not before Mrs. Banks rushes to get a proper tail for the kite: her "Votes for Women" sash. The family is thus restored. The father has discovered the value of affection and play. He becomes a guide for his children: rather than commanding by scolding, he holds their hands (the film emphasizes this as he releases and regrips Jane's hand as they go around a streetlamp). The rejecting mother gives up her interest in suffrage because she can now love her children. At the park they meet the bankers, who have themselves been inspired by Banks's outburst to go fly a kite. Mr. Banks gets his job back.

In the original Travers book, the wind determines Mary Poppins's actions. In the film the wind functions as a metaphor. At the start of the film, neighbor Admiral Boom (Reginald Owen) warns Bert that there is "heavy weather brewing" at the Banks's. By film's end the storm has passed. As Mary prepares to leave, it is she, not the children, who has been left behind. The parrot head on her umbrella voices the sentiment she cannot express, complaining that the children seem to prefer their father to her. Mary agrees but knows that this is "as it should be."

The remake of *The Champ* and the film adaptation of *Mary Poppins* both show a transition from dominant tropes of neglect in the 1930s related to poverty to an understanding of neglect as emotional and related to bad parenting in the postwar period. These two revisionist texts largely ignore social or economic causes of neglect and focus instead on neglect as an individual issue requiring individual solutions. Both the remake of *The Champ* and the film *Mary Poppins* align the trope of the rejecting mother with feminism. In *The Champ* Annie's feminism is implicit in her dissatisfaction with the role of housewife and her desire to have a career. In *Mary Poppins* Mrs. Banks's work for suffrage casts her as a first-wave feminist—focused primarily on the vote and issues of gender equality such as property rights—but her militant discourse on women's rights and her frequent exits from home would echo in an early 1960s context of second-wave feminism. In each film a mother's rejection produces an emotional gap that must be filled. Fathers are partly to blame for the mother's feelings of unhappiness and her rejection of the child(ren), but, more important, fathers are valued for their love, attention, and ability to engage the child(ren). Compared to their source texts, and compared to films from the 1930s discussed in previous chapters, these films place much less emphasis on the child's mobility or ability to colonize space, and much more emphasis on traditional family structures. Despite, then, contemporary ideals of creativity and play, the child in these texts is relatively restricted in movement, isolated from a community of children, and tethered to parents or parental substitutes. This model of neglect extends to numerous other films of the period, especially films produced in the context of American second-wave feminism.

Women's Lib and the Rejecting Mother

As Lucy Fischer has suggested, motherhood in cinema has often been "a site of 'crisis'" (30), but the nature of that crisis changes across genres and in different historical periods. The "crisis" of the rejecting mother, particularly, comes to the fore in the context of second-wave feminism. *Kramer vs. Kramer* presents a paradigmatic rejecting mother plot that directly echoes much of the "Dropout Wife" scenario. In the first few minutes of the film Joanna Kramer (Meryl Streep) leaves her husband, Ted (Dustin Hoffman), and son, Billy (Justin Henry), telling her husband that she no longer loves him and does not think she is a good mother to her son. Thereafter, the narrative mainly focuses on Ted's acceptance of his role as primary care-taker. At the start of the film Ted embodies stereotypical masculine values: he is ambitious, more attached to his career than family, and views his primary role in the family to be that of breadwinner. When Joanna first leaves, he does not know where the frying pans are, how to crack an egg, or how to make coffee; his son must instruct him at the grocery store about which brands to buy. Initially, he fails at his parental duties, showing up twenty minutes late to pick Billy up from a birthday party, long after "all the other mothers." He is tense and impatient with Billy. Ted's newfound role as primary caregiver causes problems for him at work and challenges his adherence to the stereotypical breadwinning role. In a series of scenes we see that family obligations pull Ted's attention away from work, to the dismay of his boss, who fires him.[4] Eventually, however, he acclimates to the role of single parent and shapes his life around Billy. Deciding that Billy matters more than his career, Ted takes a lesser job and a significant pay cut at another advertising firm.

Kramer vs. Kramer links Joanna's rejection of Billy to feminist concerns. Initially, Ted angrily denounces a friend, Margaret (Jane Alexander), whom he believes influenced Joanna with her "women's lib." When Joanna writes to Billy to explain her actions, she says, "I have gone away because I must find something interesting to do for myself in the world." Later, when she returns to New York, Joanna explains that she was always defined in relation to others—daughter, wife, mother—and that she needed to find herself. At the custody trial, she says that she had worked after graduating from Smith—at *Mademoiselle*, of course!—but that Ted never wanted her to work. Now, she works as a sportswear designer and makes more than Ted.

For women, Joanna's various statements might ring familiar, as her complaints about feeling constricted in the role of wife and mother and wishing to engage more in the world of work, intellect, and creativity would underpin much popular feminist discourse. The film, however, is somewhat ambivalent about Joanna's feminism. Early on, when her friend Margaret tells Ted that it took a lot of courage for Joanna to leave, he asks, "How much courage does it take to walk out on your kid?" Because Joanna leaves Billy and not just Ted, her actions seem selfish, not empowered. The character of Margaret, initially identified as a feminist who left her husband, is modified over the course of the film. She tells Ted she hoped her husband—who cheated on her—would stop her from divorcing him, and by film's end she has called him to reconcile. Over the course of the film

Ted and Margaret become close friends, and she serves as his witness at the custody trial, praising Ted as a father. Also, after Ted's initial transition into being primary caregiver, the film does not make parenting seem very hard for him: we never see how Billy gets home from school on a day-to-day basis or who takes care of him when his father goes on a date. The labor of babysitters or other help is obscured so that Ted seems able to do it all—attend Halloween pageants, buy groceries, cook, read stories, teach Billy to ride his bike, and hang out at the playground. Even when Billy has an accident at the park, it is Margaret, not Ted, who fails to catch his fall from the jungle gym, whereas the scene emphasizes Ted's commitment as he runs all the way to the hospital carrying Billy and insists on staying with him while he gets stitches.

The film's feminism leans more toward altering definitions of masculinity than sympathizing with women. At the custody trial Ted acknowledges his mistakes as a husband and makes an impassioned speech in which he applies feminist principles to male concerns:

> My wife used to always say to me, "Why can't a woman have the same ambitions as a man?" I think you're right [looking at Joanna]. And maybe I've learned that much. But, by the same token, I'd like to know what law is it that says a woman is a better parent simply by virtue of her sex? I've had a lot of time to think about what it is that makes a good parent. It has to do with constancy. It has to do with patience. Listening . . . It has to do with love. . . . I don't know where it's written that says a woman has a corner on that market, that a man has any less of those emotions than a woman does. Billy has a home with me. . . . I'm not a perfect parent. . . . But I'm there.

Here Ted appropriates feminist principles to argue for his own ability to be a parent. He acknowledges his own newfound understanding of Joanna's views. He also asserts his superiority to Joanna in terms of presence, "constancy," not leaving. In the end, in line with legal conventions of the time, the court grants Joanna custody. On the day when she is supposed to pick up her son, however, she decides to leave Billy with his father because she realizes that that is his "home." She thus rejects him, again, and seems to acknowledge Ted's superiority as a parent.

Kramer vs. Kramer is, certainly, an urban film. Ted exists in a high-powered Madison Avenue world that fuels his ambitions. The Kramers live in a nice co-op on the Upper East Side. Scenes are shot on location in

Central Park, the Chrysler Building, Federal Hall, and Tweed Courthouse, as well as on various streets in Manhattan. When Joanna returns, she is able to hide in plain sight in the city, spying on Billy from a coffee shop near his school. We see Billy in city playgrounds, riding his bike, and meeting with his mother in Central Park. But Billy's relation to urban spaces is entirely circumscribed by his parents. Billy is tethered to his parents, and we never see him walk down a street, play in the playground, or ride his bike without his father nearby watching. Billy has no scenes in which he interacts with other kids or encounters strangers. When his father picks him up at the birthday party, he sits alone, waiting. When his father attends his Halloween pageant, a teacher lurks nearby, feeding him lines. Mainly, we see Billy in the apartment, and always with a parent.

In this film, rather than be unhomed, as in many Depression era films, the child experiences emotional neglect. He is unmoored psychologically, not literally displaced. The experience of the mother's leaving—motivation for the fort/da game in Sigmund Freud's analysis—here does not facilitate the boy's mastery or allow the boy to delight in her absence. Rather, the boy is given an immediate substitute in the father, who promises never to leave.

Kramer vs. Kramer, like the remake of *The Champ* and *Mary Poppins*, castigates the mother and shows her neglect as psychologically damaging to the child. These films also show the child's mobility in the city to be significantly restricted and posit mobility as risk—as when T. J. runs through the streets of Miami in *The Champ*, Jane and Michael get lost in the city in *Mary Poppins*, and Billy falls from the jungle gym in *Kramer vs. Kramer*. Other postwar texts, however, show maternal neglect as more enabling than disabling and show the child's mobility to be key to his development of a healthy personality.

Untethered

Little Fugitive, by documentarians Morris Engel, Ruth Orkin, and Ray Ashley, is perhaps the quintessential example of the mythical urban landscape of childhood combined with a fantasy of neglect. The plot is simple and exists only to set up the child's solo wanderings. A boy and his older brother are left alone in their Brooklyn apartment while their single mother goes away for two days to visit a sick relative. At first, the boys and their friends are shown colonizing urban spaces—playing ball in the street,

FIGURE 13. Lennie and friends read comics in the alley in *Little Fugitive*.

FIGURE 14. Joey, Lennie, and friends play ball in the street in *Little Fugitive*.

reading comic books in the alley, and playing with a toy gun in a vacant lot. Then, miffed that his sudden babysitting duties preclude his birthday trip to Coney Island, the older brother, Lennie (Richard Brewster), and his friends play a trick on the younger brother, Joey (Richie Andrusco), and lead him to believe that he has shot and killed his older brother. Scared, the younger boy, Joey, runs away, takes a subway to Coney Island, and stays there for two full days before his older brother finds and retrieves him. They return home minutes before their mother does, and she remains unaware of the adventures that have befallen her children.

On the surface *Little Fugitive* would appear to be a story of a rejecting mother and a child's risk. The mother's leaving (according to contemporary psychoanalysts) counts as rejection, no matter her motivation. Brother Lennie is a poor mother substitute. But the film does not treat the mother's leaving as in any way bad, and Joey's trip to Coney Island seems more adventurous than risky. In Bosley Crowther's original review of *Little Fugitive* Crowther described it as "a wondrous illustration of the eccentricities of a small boy, adrift on his own resources in a tiny and tawdry mob playground," and claimed that "the heart and body of the picture are views of this little boy as he rambles around Coney Island, cut loose from his family and quite alone." The film renders his urban odyssey with location shooting that shows the boy competently navigating his way amid the crowds of Coney Island, buying hot dogs, picking up bottles to redeem for nickels, riding the ponies, hiding underneath the boardwalk, and sleeping on the beach. Joey does not ask for help or seek escape from Coney Island. Rather, the man renting the ponies (Jay Williams) questions him and contacts Lennie, who then tracks Joey by writing clues for his brother to follow on various surfaces in Coney Island.

In many ways the mother's absence and the brother's trick enable Joey to grow and develop his personality. *Little Fugitive* shows the boy achieving mastery over his circumstances away from and without his mother's knowledge. In Erikson's terms Joey develops a sense of autonomy in taking the train by himself to Coney Island. He develops a sense of initiative as he watches another boy sell bottles and then begins redeeming them himself. In taking the bottle money to buy food and pony rides, he shows a sense of accomplishment. And in following his brother's clues to get home, he shows trust in the brother. In contrast to the films I discussed above, Joey is not only untethered but also, crucially, open to contact— with the pony-ride man, with other boys on the beach, and with the larger community of the beach. He navigates his contacts carefully but without fear.

Little Fugitive predates the other films discussed here and thus does not situate its narrative of maternal leaving in the context of second-wave feminism. In addition, it locates its action in working-class white ethnic areas: Brooklyn and Coney Island. It differs both from the seediness of the setting in *The Champ* and the urban middle-class settings of *Mary Poppins* and *Kramer vs. Kramer*. An oddity in some ways, *Little Fugitive* can nonetheless be taken as an emblematic film of mid-twentieth-century urban childhood. With its bare-bones emphasis on neglect, mobility, and social space, it creates an urban pastoral—an emphasis underscored, literally, by the film's ironic repetition of the song "Home on the Range" within the Lester Troob harmonica score, as well as by Joey's chalk drawings of horses on the sidewalk and frequent pony rides.

Neglect of Affluence

Postwar children's literature is especially rife with narratives of benign neglect that enables the child to be mobile and free. In many of these tales the mother's rejection is less explicitly linked to feminism than affluence: she neglects her child by outsourcing the child's care. *Eloise*, for example, features a paradigmatic urban character whose quirky creativity and domination of the space of the Plaza Hotel depends on her mother's absence. Eloise is a figure of privilege who experiences the neglect of affluence. Her mother exists only tangentially in the narrative as a wealthy single mother, described by Eloise as having a charge account at Bergdorf's; owning stock in AT&T; knowing Coco Chanel, an ad man, and the owner of the Plaza; traveling with her lawyer to Virginia and to Europe on her own; and occasionally sending for Eloise "if there's some sun." There is no mention of a father. Eloise has a nanny, "my mostly companion" (Thompson 19), with whom she orders room service and watches TV, who bathes her and dresses her, and whom she calls when she can't sleep. She has many friends in the hotel, all adults, whom she visits daily.

Described as a "precocious grown up," six-year-old Eloise announces herself as a "city child" (Thompson 8). Her "neighborhood" consists of the interior spaces of the Plaza Hotel, a space that blurs public and private. In her wanderings through the hotel Eloise visits the lobby, including the various desks and services there, and rides the elevator, where she encounters crowds and strangers. She dines in the Palm Court, where she is served by Thomas the waiter, visits Bill the busboy in the Persian Room, watches debutantes in the Terrace Room and businessmen in the Baroque Room, attends weddings in the White and Gold Room, checks on packages in the Package Room, visits the Men's Room for a pretend shoeshine and the barber for a trim, and so on. She describes her route through the hotel and provides a personalized pullout map of it in the book—elevator to fifth floor, stairs to eighth, elevator to fifteenth floor, stairs to twelfth, elevator to lobby then all the way back up to the top floor, where in a mirror, she looks at herself.

In some sense a lonely child, abandoned by her mother, *Eloise* emphasizes the child's freedom and creativity over any sense of unhappiness. Over and over, Eloise declares, "Oooooooooooooooooooooo I absolutely love the Plaza." Within the world of the Plaza she plays with dolls, skates, sings, laughs, plays dress up, and generally messes about in the hotel. Fabulously rich, she masquerades as "an orphan" (Thompson 36), wandering into open hotel rooms: "I limp and sort of bend to the side and look sort of sad in between the arms" to get "a piece of melon or something." For Eloise the hotel is a playground where she is never bored but exercises her intelligence and creativity. Her mother's absence facilitates rather than constricts.

Harriet the Spy, similarly, portrays a girl of imagination and intellect in an upper-class milieu. Like Eloise, Harriet relies on her nanny, Ole Golly, much more than her mother or father. Her family also has a cook and a maid. Harriet's parents are more distractedly absent than actively rejecting. As opposed to Ole Golly, Harriet's parents are described frequently as absent-mindedly talking to her: "She never got the feeling with Ole Golly that she did with her parents that they never heard anything" (Fitzhugh 82). When Ole Golly leaves—initially fired over a misunderstanding and then quitting to get married—Harriet's parents discover their distance from her: "It makes me feel I don't even know my own child," her father says. And her mother answers, "We must try to get to know her better now that Miss Golly is gone" (Fitzhugh 162). Instead of a narrative of parental rehabilitation, however, *Harriet the Spy* focuses more on Harriet's personal growth, as Harriet loses then regains her friends both by learning to be more empathetic and by learning to lie, to make others feel better.

Parents get rather short shrift in *Harriet the Spy*, but they are not seen as causal factors in a child's development. Early in the book, Ole Golly takes

Harriet and Sport to visit her mother in Rockaway. Rather than demonstrate an emotional investment in her mother, Ole Golly shows Harriet her mother as an anthropological curiosity: "I want you to see how this person lives, Harriet. . . . I brought you here because you have never seen the inside of a house like this. Have you ever seen a house that has one bed, one table, four chairs, and a bathtub in the kitchen?" (Fitzhugh 11, 15). Less an exposure to a person of a different class, Ole Golly views her mother as offering Harriet a view of an entirely different personality and approach to life. While Ole Golly is well-read, attuned to the importance of intelligence and study, her mother is an idiot: "Behold, Harriet," Ole Golly said, "a woman who never had any interest in anyone else, nor in any book, nor in any school, nor in any way of life, but has lived her whole life in this room, eating and sleeping and waiting to die" (Fitzhugh 17–18). Neither Ole Golly nor the narrative make any sense of how Mrs. Golly would have parented her.

Elsewhere in the book Harriet describes a statue, purchased by a couple, the Robinsons, who are described as obsessed with consumerism, living just to show people their acquisitions: "They never worked, and what was worse, they never even read anything. They bought things and brought them home and then had people in to look at them" (Fitzhugh 63). The statue they buy resembles the sculptor Marisol's *Baby Girl*, which was exhibited in New York at the Museum of Modern Art in 1963: "The strangest thing Harriet had ever seen. It was an enormous—but enormous— perhaps six feet high—wooden sculpture of a fat, petulant, rather unattractive baby. . . . The baby sat on its diapered bottom, feet straight out ahead, and fat arms curving into fatter hands, which held, surprisingly, a tiny mother" (Fitzhugh 150). As J. D. Stahl points out, Marisol's statue, which shows an oversized baby holding a tiny Marisol marionette, emphasizes the power of children to manipulate adults ("Louise Fitzhugh" 159). In addition to critiquing modern art and vain consumerism, this episode serves to mock child-led parenting that lets the child rule over the parents and reduces them to puppets or children themselves. In the case of the Robinsons the object itself rules: they do not have any children but purchase this absurd substitute.

As a substitute parent, Ole Golly is neither distracted from nor dominated by Harriet. She provides guidance to Harriet, mainly by quoting aphorisms to her such as, "Solitude, the safeguard of mediocrity, is to genius the stern friend" (Fitzhugh 101), without explaining them or drawing out a moral. When she gives advice, it generally prods Harriet to observe, write, and be engaged with the world around her, to foster Harriet's intellect and imagination. Ole Golly leads Harriet by example and word, but gives Harriet freedom and respect. At the same time, Ole Golly lives her own life, much to Harriet's surprise, and finds love and a home of her own.

Harriet is very much a city child. In the opening pages of the book she plays "Town," a game that consists of imagining the sort of small suburban town that would be the cultural norm for many kids in the 1960s but that, for her, is an unfamiliar space. In her imagination, the town has a mountain, a filling station, a lawyer, and a doctor. She adds someone who works in television, like her father, and someone who is a writer, like her friend Sport's father. Everyone in the Town goes to bed at 9:30, enforcing its mundane ordinariness and opposing it to her life in New York, where Sport says his father "goes to bed at nine in the morning" (Fitzhugh 6). But then Harriet infuses the sleepy town with a soap opera sense of melodrama and coincidence—just as a baby is being delivered in the town hospital, robbers hold up the gas station and leave the owner bound and gagged, then proceed to beat and rob an old farmer, while the police chief gets a bad feeling—indicating her inability to imagine ordinary small-town life.

Where Eloise's adventures are circumscribed by the walls of the hotel, Harriet is much more mobile and free to roam city streets. Eric Tribunella characterizes her as a child flâneuse (77). He notes the importance of her freedom of movement in the city and the contrast Harriet establishes between her school-year city life and her summer in the country. In her notebook she associates city life with being a pedestrian, the density of people, and the proximity of buildings to each other, whereas she links her summer country life with not only a lower-class, less concentrated population and greater separation between buildings, but also a lack of freedom, as her movements require adult supervision and car travel (Tribunella 77). As Sonya Sawyer Fritz notes, *Harriet the Spy* characterizes the city "as a space that enriches rather than endangers" and that offers readers "captivating models of childhood competence and autonomy" (86).

A would-be writer and spy, Harriet is the opposite of Mrs. Golly: her life is all about observation and seeing different things: "Ole Golly told me if I was going to be a writer, I better write down everything, so I'm a spy that writes down everything" (Fitzhugh 34). She carries a notebook at all times and writes down her observations about strangers and friends. She observes people everywhere she goes and tries to imagine their lives:

MAN WITH ROLLED WHITE SOCKS, FAT LEGS. WOMAN WITH
ONE CROSS-EYE AND A LONG NOSE. HORRIBLE LOOKING
LITTLE BOY AND A FAT BLONDE MOTHER WHO KEEPS WIP-
ING HIS NOSE OFF. FUNNY LADY LOOKS LIKE A TEACHER AND
IS READING. I DON'T THINK I'D LIKE TO LIVE WHERE ANY OF
THESE PEOPLE LIVE OR DO THE THINGS THEY DO. I BET THAT
LITTLE BOY IS SAD AND CRIES A LOT. I BET THAT WOMAN
WITH THE CROSS-EYE LOOKS IN THE MIRROR AND JUST
FEELS TERRIBLE. (Fitzhugh 11; all caps in original)

Each day after school, Harriet changes into her spy clothes—hoodie, jeans,
flashlight, tool belt, and sneakers (which Kathleen Horning reads as rather
butch "cross-dressing" [49])—and goes on her "route," a regular rotation of
people she watches each day, recording events and dialogue as she observes.

Like Eloise's route through the hotel, Harriet's route is a child-oriented
map of her neighborhood, a play space, a space hidden from adults, and
meaningful only within Harriet's imagination. As in *Eloise*, Harriet's route
is conveyed in the book with a great deal of specificity, creating a strong
sense of place. Her route exposes her to different ways of living, different classes, and different family structures. She travels from her school
on East End across from Carl Schurz Park to her home on East Eighty-
Seventh Street, where she ritualistically has cake and milk before going on
her route. Then, once dressed, she walks to the deli and living space of the
Italian immigrant Dei Santi family and their employee Little Joe Curry on
York Avenue, to the aforementioned Robinsons' duplex on Eighty-eighth
Street, to the home of bachelor Harrison Withers, who lives in a two-room
apartment filled with twenty-six cats in one room and handmade birdcages
in the other, to the mansion of wealthy dowager Mrs. Plumber. To spy on
these characters, Harriet traverses city streets, scrambles onto a window-
sill in the alley by the Dei Santis' store, climbs up onto Harrison Withers's roof to peer in his skylight, sneaks into the Robinsons' garden to see
in their ground-floor window, and, riskily, slips into the kitchen dumb-
waiter at Mrs. Plumber's, then hoists herself up in it to spy on the bedrid-
den woman. Along the way, one day she stops to see her friend Sport, who
lives with his divorced dad in an apartment in a four-story building that
Harriet describes as smelling like old laundry. "IT'S NOISY AND KIND
OF POOR LOOKING," she notes (Fitzhugh 49).[5] Another day she visits her friend Janie in "a renovated brownstone off East End Avenue on

Eighty-fourth Street" (Fitzhugh 69), where Janie keeps a science lab in her bedroom.

At just the same time that Ole Golly leaves, Harriet experiences a crisis: her notebook falls into the hands of her classmates. Horrified at her often unkind observations, her friends, including Sport and Janie, turn against her. Learning for the first time about Harriet's notebook, and the trouble it has caused, her mother takes away Harriet's replacement notebook. Ostracized at school and unmoored at home, Harriet begins to act out at home and school, mistreating those she encounters. Her parents respond by sending her to a psychiatrist, directly importing the discourse of psychology and personality in the narrative. Instead of castigating her, the doctor determines that Harriet is intelligent and curious and could be a writer. He suggests channeling her energies into writing for the school paper. There, she initially uses the paper to gossip meanly about classmates and people on her route. Her parents also turn to Ole Golly, however, who writes to Harriet that she should apologize and lie: "Remember that writing is to put love into the world, not to use against your friends. But to yourself you must always tell the truth" (Fitzhugh 263). Harriet then uses the paper to issue an apology and deny the veracity of her notes. More important, she begins to be a proper fiction writer and drafts a story about Harrison Withers for the *New Yorker*. The "moral" of the story Harriet writes is "THAT SOME PEOPLE ARE ONE WAY AND SOME PEOPLE ARE ANOTHER AND THAT'S THAT" (Fitzhugh 265). This observation, along with her ability to "be an onion"—using Method acting style identification to feel like an onion—for the school play, conveys Harriet's new-found sense of respect and empathy for others. Not only does she regain the friendship of Sport and Janie, but she also feels "calm, happy, and immensely pleased with her mind" (Fitzhugh 281).

Whose Fantasy?

Many postwar texts imagine maternal neglect as crippling and assume that a well-cared-for child will be tethered to her parents. In films such as the remake of *The Champ* and *Mary Poppins*, or *Kramer vs. Kramer*, it is assumed that the child should be at home or closely watched by a parent at all times. Children in these films are largely isolated from other children and are constricted in their movements. When they are detached from family and on the streets, they are seen to be in danger. The child's proper development depends on proper parenting.

But *Little Fugitive, Eloise*, and *Harriet the Spy* offer a model in which parental neglect enables the child to be creative and autonomous and facilitates the child's growth and mastery. In these texts spatial mobility goes hand in hand with psychological well-being. Urban spaces open these children to encounters with a range of people. Joey meets people on the beach and at the amusement park and navigates hordes of strangers on the subway and at Coney Island. Eloise comes across—and often literally bumps into—not only adults who work in the hotel but also strangers who visit the hotel. Harriet observes a wide range of people and learns to have greater sympathy for them. These encounters do not alienate them from home but empower them and foster their emotional and psychological growth. Against the tendency in other texts to chastise parents for leaving their children, and viewing them as "rejecting," these texts suggest that the child can leave home and be untethered from his or her parents without being completely unmoored.

In part, we might consider these texts as being aimed at different audiences. *The Champ* and *Kramer vs. Kramer* are both rated PG (Parental Guidance Suggested) by the Motion Picture Association of America (MPAA), while *Mary Poppins* and *Little Fugitive* are both rated family films (G for General Audience). *The Champ, Mary Poppins*, and *Kramer vs. Kramer* are big-budget Hollywood films, whereas *Little Fugitive* is a small art-house film. *Eloise* and *Harriet the Spy* are both children's books. Thus, rather than audience per se, we might consider the various texts' point of address. As I discussed in my introduction, children's texts are generally double-voiced, speaking both a child's perspective and an adult's at the same time. In *Eloise* we hear Eloise's point of view as she narrates the book and understand it from an adult vantage. Similarly, in *Harriet the Spy* we encounter satiric humor that presents a "caustic attack on adults" that is "radically grounded in the assumption of [a] child's interests" (Stahl, "Satire" 121), but we also see Harriet's flaws and missteps. *Little Fugitive* is focalized around Joey's experience and, to a lesser degree, that of his brother, but it also enables adults to peer into the child's world. *The Champ, Mary Poppins*, and *Kramer vs. Kramer* are similarly double-voiced, but the emphasis shifts somewhat, so that the children in these texts are less agents in the narrative than objects or victims. We have sympathy *for* them more than we identify *with* them. The narrative is as much, if not more, about the adults as about the children.

Ultimately, we need to ask what function the fantasies of neglect in these texts perform and for whom. *Little Fugitive*, *Eloise*, and *Harriet the Spy* each provide both the child and the adult spectator or reader with a fantasy of childhood mobility and play. They are not about maternal failure but about children being left alone to explore the world. Their explorations are not problem-free, but they enable the children to achieve mastery. In *The Champ*, *Mary Poppins*, and *Kramer vs. Kramer*, by contrast, the fantasy is not, primarily, it seems, for the child. To be sure, *Mary Poppins* provides the child a fantasy of a perfect mother substitute. But *Mary Poppins*, along with the other texts, proffers a range of adult fantasies related to feminism—a male fantasy about the deleterious effects of feminist yearnings, female fantasies of punishment for wanting more, and fantasies about damage to the child's psyche if left alone. These fantasies become self-fulfilling prophecies as the child is imagined as increasingly inadequate to navigate the world and thus requires increasing attention from and harnessing to parents. They are fantasies about not only a child's neglect but also a woman's proper place.

4

"The Odds Are against Him"

Archives of Unhappiness
among Black Urban Boys

The goal of the "happy personality" discussed in the last chapter was, as I suggested, largely limited to white middle-class children. As Sara Ahmed brilliantly elucidates, understandings of what constitute happiness not only vary historically and culturally but also depend on systems of exclusion, dividing happy from unhappy, good objects and good lifestyles from bad, and, I would add, persons deserving to be happy from persons unworthy or unable to access happiness. In the texts I discussed in the previous chapter—*The Champ*, *Mary Poppins*, and *Kramer vs. Kramer*—the child's right to happiness conflicts with the mother's, whose attempt to secure happiness is viewed negatively as selfish and misdirected.

Ahmed suggests that happiness is prescriptive more than descriptive: "Happiness is looked for where it is expected to be found, even when happiness is reported to be missing" (7). In particular, happiness is often aligned with "stable families and communities" (Ahmed 7). As Ahmed notes, the discourse on happiness participates in an ideologically conservative project: "If certain ways of living promote happiness then to promote happiness would be to promote those ways of living. Thus happiness promotion becomes very quickly the promotion of certain types of families" (11). At the same time that happiness has been historically linked to certain ideologies of family—heterosexual marriage and reproduction—it also relates to being fortunate. As Ahmed delineates, "the word *happy* originally meant having good 'hap' or fortune" (22), to be lucky or fortunate. Thus, it comes as no surprise that when the 1950 White House Conference on Children shifted its attention to "the happy personality," it elided social and economic causes of neglect or the needs of socially disadvantaged or unfortunate children who did not have the prerequisites, or fortune, to be happy.

Poor and minority children are seemingly left out of the midcentury discourse on the "happy personality." In part, minority children, and especially African American children, are perceived at midcentury as existing outside conventional family structures. The infamous Moynihan Report from 1965 (*The Negro Family: The Case for National Action*), for instance, linked black poverty to the relative absence of nuclear families, the predominance of single-mother households, and the weakening of black men's roles as husbands and fathers. Despite being critiqued in myriad ways—as poor sociology, as blaming the victim, as antiwoman, as racist, as stereotyping—the Moynihan Report both mirrored and shaped much discourse on black children for decades, and it placed African American children on the wrong side of ways of living associated with happiness.

In part, African American children are excluded from the discourse on happiness because, in mid-to-late twentieth-century discourse, the black child and the white child are seen as radically different in kind. For example, in their 1972 book *Children of the Storm: Black Children and American Child Welfare*, Andrew Billingsley and Jeanne M. Giovannoni argue that "the racism that characterizes American society has had tragic effects upon Black children. It has given the Black child a history, a situation, and a set of problems that are qualitatively different from those of the white child" (vii). Similarly, justifying the need for a book specifically about black child care, as opposed to a race-neutral child-care book, James P. Comer and Alvin F. Poussaint argue that black children and white children need to be viewed differently. Until recently, they claim, "blacks and whites alike, for different reasons, pretended that all children—in fact, all people—were the same. Rearing a black child was just like rearing a white child. Some people still make that claim. We believe there *is* a difference. Growing up black in America, where policy-making and attitudes are largely influenced and controlled by whites who are often antagonistic or indifferent to the needs of blacks, poses many special problems for black parents and their children" (1).

Defined and constrained by racism, poverty, and confinement to the ghetto, as well as broken families, black children, Comer and Poussaint argue, grow up integrally and systemically neglected. Providing a history of black childhood, the authors argue that black children under slavery "were abused and denied a happy childhood and the opportunity to develop to their fullest potential" (7) and that "even after slavery was legally abolished, black children were one of the most mistreated and neglected groups in American society" (8). Not only were many black parents forced to neglect their own children to care for white children, both during and after slavery, but black children also suffer "economic and social deprivation" (Comer and Poussaint 9). In articulating a difference between black children and white children, dependent upon the black child's different experience and history—spoken from within African American culture and from an activist standpoint—these claims dovetail with Robin Bernstein's argument that the figure of the conventional ideal child in popular discourse is white and that innocence is ascribed to white children, whereas black children are excluded from discourses of innocence and viewed as, in effect, not children.

In claiming that black children were denied a "happy childhood," and could not "develop to their fullest potential," Comer and Poussaint employ Eriksonian language of the happy personality. But they underscore that the black child does not have access to this developmental model of a happy and healthy personality because black parents themselves are blocked from happiness. For parents to "help their children develop," Comer and Poussaint argue, parents themselves must have a "sense of belonging in the larger society. This sense of belonging can only be felt when parents are protected and obstacles to earning a living and respect are not placed in their way" (Comer and Poussaint 2). Racism denies "blacks a oneness with society and the security that comes with this feeling" (Comer and Poussaint 2). As stated in a special issue of *Ebony* titled "The Black Child," "the major problems concerning the quality of life relate to the inequality of life imposed on many children in the United States" (Ellis 38).

In suggesting that the different contexts in which black children and white children grow limit the opportunities for black children, these various texts imply that black children do not have access to the building blocks of happiness that are generally available to white children. In a parallel case Ahmed argues that black feminists raise the question of "who is entitled to happiness" and that they "teach us that some women—black and working-class women—are not even entitled to be proximate to the fantasy, though they may be instrumental in enabling others to approximate its form" (51) (for example, freeing white middle-class women to go back to work by performing household labor in white women's homes). Narratives about black children, similarly, raise the question of who is entitled to happiness.

Happiness, in Ahmed's reading, is not a static state but a promise: "The promise of the object is always in this specific sense ahead of us; to follow happiness is often narrated as following a path (it is no accident that we speak of 'the path of happiness'), such that if we follow the path we imagine we will reach its point" (32). Happiness, then, depends on futurity and hope, an open-ended tomorrow. Rather than this sense of promise, however, narratives of black childhood emphasize blockage, imprisonment, entrapment, and a sense of fate, all leading to unhappiness. In *No Future: Queer Theory and the Death Drive* Leo Bersani argues that narratives of reproductive futurity are heteronormative and that the queer child is viewed as not only existing outside narratives of futurity but as a future-negating force. In this sense we can think of the African American child as queered. Whereas the imagined happy child grows up and forward into the future, the unhappy African American child is denied that upward movement.

In contrast to the futurity of happiness, the association of black children with the urban ghetto, and particularly Harlem, situates them within discourses of entrapment, containment, and failure. The black child's segregation in public space corresponds to what Bernstein describes as the child's segregation from discourses of childhood innocence. Along with Moynihan's *The Negro Family*, texts including St. Clair Drake and Horace R. Cayton's important *Black Metropolis*, Kenneth Clark's *Dark Ghetto*, James Baldwin's "Fifth Avenue, Uptown," Oscar Lewis's "The Culture of Poverty," Lee Rainwater's *Behind Ghetto Walls: Black Families in a Federal Slum*, and Richard Wright's *12 Million Black Voices* each, in different ways, offers an assessment of the ghetto as "pathological" in both its objective and subjective dimensions (Massood, *Black City Cinema* 84). These texts focus on the feelings of entrapment engendered by the ghetto, as well as problems of drugs, poverty, and the disintegration of the black family; they argue that segregation produces a uniquely limiting urban experience. They bring to light what Oscar Lewis describes as a subculture of poverty, a "way of life" that is an "adaptation and a reaction" to structural inequalities that marginalize and separate ghetto inhabitants from the dominant white society (19, 21). Echoing in many ways laments about the white ethnic ghettos of the Depression, descriptions of the black ghetto ultimately differ from those in their sense of lives shaped by racist policies and actions and in their marked difference from *all* white life, poor or rich.

In the majority of mid-to-late twentieth-century discourse on black childhood, a strong sense of predetermined fate, rather than futurity, dominates. Kenneth Clark analyzes the "institutionalized pathology" of the ghetto as "chronic, self-perpetuating" (81). In his analysis the ghetto produces symptoms that are neither reversible nor controllable: "One kind of pathology breeds another. The child born in the ghetto is more likely to come into a world of broken homes and illegitimacy; and this family and social instability is conducive to delinquency, drug addiction and criminal violence" (Clark 81). Although Clark prescribes various fixes to the ghetto's problems, his language emphasizes inevitable cycles of repetition and failure.

Similarly, Richard Wright expresses a sense of hopelessness in his discussion of ghetto life. Contrasting the progress of white immigrants who move from tenements in the ghetto to rooming houses in slightly better neighborhoods to nicer apartments and even suburban homes, he characterizes life for African Americans as being trapped in the ghetto, kept in place by racism and "the Bosses of the Buildings" (Wright, *12 Million* 102–104). Describing the typical Harlem apartment as "the kitchenette"—a seven-room apartment cut up into seven separate tiny apartments with five or six people living in that one room (*12 Million* 104–105)—Wright ascribes to it a terrible agency to encourage crime, blight hope, and engender resentment. The kitchenette, controlled by the Bosses of the Buildings, "is our poison, our death sentence without a trial" (Wright, *12 Million* 106), "the funnel through which our pulverized lives flow to ruin and death on the city's pavements" (Wright, *12 Million* 111). Regarding children, in particular, Wright claims that the kitchenette "fills our black boys with longing and restlessness, urging them to run off from home, to join together with other restless black boys in gangs, that brutal form of city courage" (*12 Million* 111): "We watch strange moods fill our children, and our hearts swell with pain. The streets, with their noise and flaring lights, the taverns, the automobiles, and the poolrooms claim them and no voice of ours can call them back" (*12 Million* 136). Like the kitchenette, the streets seemingly have agency: they attract the child and lead him away from home and into trouble.

The effects of ghetto life are seen to particularly impact African American boys. For instance, as Paula Massood has indicated, a 1940 *Look* magazine photo essay titled "244,000 Native Sons" suggests that Harlem youth are predestined to become delinquents (Massood, *Making a Promised Land* 94–97). A page titled "Harlem Delinquents in the Making" distinguishes Harlem boys from other (presumably white middle-class) kids, using the familiar discourse of the happy personality: "Every child, no matter how fortunate, finds it hard to adjust himself to his environment. The Harlem child finds it doubly hard. His problem is complicated by poverty and race discrimination" (Carter 10). Placing the African American child in opposition to those who have "hap" or fortune, the author, Michael Carter, argues that while poverty creates "a desire for betterment," racism "kills opportunities to fulfill that desire" (10). Blocked from the path to fulfill desire, or to pursue happiness, the African American child finds "the odds are against him" (Carter 10). A photo credited to the Photo League shows five young black boys labeled "Five Social Problems." Claiming these boys as "typical Harlem boys," the caption details the obstacles they face and have overcome, including high infant mortality rates, poor schools, poor health care, and lack of playground space. Ominously, the caption concludes: "They don't know that they will probably be living within Harlem's boundaries for the rest of their lives" (Carter 10).

Massood notes that in mid-to-late twentieth-century film and photography black male youth come to embody the problems of Harlem as both symptom and cause of the area's problems (*Making a Promised Land* 97).[1] Likewise, in fiction and film of the period, African American boys are the focus and are seen both as symptoms of a crisis and as social problems. Narratives such as the quasi-documentary *The Quiet One* (Sidney Meyers 1948), Ann Petry's 1946 novel *The Street*, Warren Miller's 1959 novel *The Cool World* (later a play, then a 1964 movie directed by Shirley Clarke), and Virginia Hamilton's 1971 children's book *The Planet of Junior Brown* each tell a story of urban black boys and together make up what Ahmed refers to as "unhappy archives" (17). These archives of unhappiness each map the child's failed home life, his lack of opportunity, his alienation from school and family, his entrance into delinquency, and his sense of entrapment in the ghetto. These narratives deploy common assumptions about the black family in linking the child to either a single mother or no parents at all. These texts render the mother as inadequate to help her child or as downright cruel. Each child is drawn, in one way or another, to delinquency and criminality. And, crucially, each narrative stages some kind of rescue for the child from his family and, in some cases, from the city itself. *Bush Mama* (Haile Gerima, made in 1975, released in 1979) presents a twist on these archetypal narratives by looking at neglect in relation to a black girl.

These texts thus disseminate not only the assumption that black male children will become delinquents but also what Billingsley and Giovannoni refer to as a series of wrongheaded stereotypes about black families. First, in rendering the child as having no father or no parents at all, these texts advance the claims of the Moynihan Report that the black family had deteriorated, an assumption challenged by the 1970 U.S. census, which showed the majority of African American children were living with two parents (Billingsley and Giovannoni 16). Second, they duplicate a "major misconception in child welfare" that "a major problem within the Black community is parental inadequacy whatever the number of parents" (Billingsley and Giovannoni 17). Third, they mimic the impulses of child welfare services that seek to rescue black children from inadequate parents, viewing adequate homes as hard to find in the black urban community owing to "pervasive internal pathology" (Billingsley and Giovannoni 17). These various myths and misconceptions produce a fantasy of neglect that locates the problems of the black community within the black community itself, as a self-perpetuating cycle of misery caused by weak family structures and bad parenting.

Nonetheless, rather than entirely defeatist narratives, these texts each, in different ways, work to produce a conscious recognition of unhappiness. They expose the limitations of life for the African American child and the ways in which the black child is blocked from happiness. They show that white fantasies of neglect in the black community serve to obscure the large-scale social and institutional mechanisms of neglect that underpin a racist and segregated society. In this way, they mark white happiness as injustice.

Home Is No Refuge

The Quiet One is a curious amalgamation. Made collaboratively by street photographer Helen Levitt, her brother William Levitt, writer James Agee, film editor Sidney Meyers, painter Janice Loeb, and cinematographer Richard Bagley, the film mixes professional and amateur actors and blends fictional and documentary modes to produce a docudrama that is at once a social problem picture about child neglect and promotional material for the Wiltwyck School for Boys, a residential school for delinquent youth in upstate New York. Directed by Meyers and written by Agee,[2] the film explicitly aligns itself with midcentury psychological discourse in having a white male school psychiatrist (actor Gary Merrill) serve as the film's voice-over narrator. Although the film shows both white and black boys at Wiltwyck,[3] the narrative focuses on an African American boy, Donald Peters—played by nonactor Donald Thompson[4]—and places much of its action in Harlem, thus racializing the story.

The film's opening establishes the interrelatedness of neglect, psychology, and environment: the opening title describes Wiltwyck as a school for boys "who have reacted with grave disturbance of personality to neglect in their homes and in their community." The film identifies the boys as nonnormative and noninnocent from the start. As we see a mixed-race group of boys playing hide-and-seek in a natural wooded environment, a voice-over by the school's unnamed male psychiatrist states, "When I watch them playing, they seem like ordinary children. By all rights they are ordinary children, but circumstances have deformed them." Explaining that some of the kids have criminal records and "nearly all of them are sick enough" to require the psychiatrist's help, the narrator claims that the "root of most of their problems is that nobody has ever wanted them."

As the film shifts its focus to Donald Peters, the "quiet one" of the title, we learn his story in a series of flashbacks. Born of a father who has vanished, "whose face he can't even recall" (because Donald only has a poorly cropped and thus faceless photo of him), and a mother "who has no room for him in her life," Donald lives with his grandmother in Harlem, "a woman he hates so much that even at night he seldom comes back." We see Donald's grandmother search city streets for him as he sleeps in a coal bin, then witness the scolding and violent beating he receives when he returns home and "the sick quiet that follows violence and duty without love."

FIGURE 15. Donald, bottom of frame, wanders the streets of Harlem alone in *The Quiet One*.

Quasi-documentary footage shows Donald skipping school and wandering the streets of Harlem alone.

Levitt was known for her still images of exuberant life in the ghetto and especially of children playing, images that challenged the pathological view of the ghetto and ascribed to it an expressive power (Massood, *Making a Promised Land* 106). But the footage here contrasts Donald to the everyday activities of the ghetto and shows him as isolated.[5] We see shots of racially and ethnically diverse adults talking, smoking, hanging out on stoops, working, playing ball, or at the barbershop, as well as a few shots of kids, smiling or walking with an adult. These documentary shots are intercut with shots of Donald. Some shots show him walking alone through busy scenes or looking through shop windows, whereas others show him alone in shots that are not clearly filmed at the same time or place as the other ghetto images but that rely on the Kuleshov effect to create a spatiotemporal connection and imply his reaction to or separation from the activities around him. While these scenes could, in a different context, be read as showing the child's mobility and freedom in the city, the voice-over narration makes clear that Donald's is a negative freedom: "Of course, the streets can be a wonderful school. Freedom is wonderful, too. But if you're as lonely as Donald is, all you learn is loneliness. Donald's kind of freedom is solitary confinement." Aligned with confinement and entrapment, even as he wanders freely, Donald's move into delinquency seems inevitable. Alienated from those on the street who have "some place to go, some definite thing to do," Donald goes home, but, the narrator tells us, "home is no refuge." At home Donald steals money from his grandmother; then, on the streets, he is robbed by bullies. He goes to visit his mother, but she ignores him as she tends to her boyfriend and new baby. Enraged, Donald first smears makeup all over a mirror in his mother's flat, blocking his own image from view, then returns to the streets and smashes a car with a rock.

As in the narratives discussed in the last chapter, Donald's unhappiness is ascribed to a rejecting mother and, in this case, a rejecting grandmother as well. Once Donald is at Wiltwyck, his mother abandons him entirely, disappearing from the city and leaving no forwarding address or contact information for the school. After angrily acting out at school, Donald initially "transplants his affections" from his mother and seeks a father substitute at the school, latching on to one of the school counselors, Clarence (Clarence Cooper). Through his friendship with Clarence, Donald begins to imagine a future. Putting on Clarence's jacket, Donald looks in the mirror. The voice-over states that the mirror here is "no longer a focus for misery and self hatred," as it was at Donald's mother's apartment, but now functions "more like a window on a happy present and a hopeful future, an image of a happy child and the man he hopes to be like."

But before Donald can be fully cured, he must sever even his mental ties to his family and home. Jealous of Clarence's attention to another boy, Donald steals Clarence's lighter and runs away from school. As it gets dark and cold, and Donald is nearly hit by a passing train, we see a montage of images, treated as Donald's thoughts—images of his mother smiling warmly at him, countered by images of his grandmother beating him and his mother's now deserted apartment. Now, according to the voice-over, Donald sees the "home he broke his heart over for what it really was." As Donald accepts "his motherlessness, his homelessness, this temporary home," he is made new: "The baby in Donald began to die. A child was born." Donald can now return to Wiltwyck. There, he gives back the lighter and "his extravagant emotional claims on Clarence."

A redemptive narrative in some ways, *The Quiet One* stops short of promising happiness. "There is no happy ending to Donald's story," we are told. Donald, and the other boys will be "equipped against the future," which is "the most that we can hope to do." The school can help "clear away the harm of the past" and make the boys "a little better able" to go forward and "to care for their children better than their parents" had. But rather than a promise of reproductive futurity, these boys' futures seem dim, as the film ends with the evocative descriptive image of "generations of those maimed in childhood each making the next in its own image . . . an infinite corridor of despair."

The City of No Future

Like *The Quiet One*, *The Cool World* is something of a hybrid text. Initially a novel by the white novelist Warren Miller, the book offers a first-person narration by Duke, a fourteen-year-old African American boy, written in a vernacular style that captures his lack of grammar, inability to spell, and accent. The novel was adapted into a play by Miller and Robert Rossen, then made into a film by Shirley Clarke. The film blends Clarke's affiliation with documentary and New American cinema to present a realist art film that adopts a largely observational style, though it maintains occasional use of first-person narration in voice-over. All three versions of the text revolve around Duke Custis (Rony Clanton in the film), a black teen and member of a gang whose main goal is to buy a gun from a local gangster named Priest (Carl Lee) and who kills a member of a rival gang. Both film and novel portray Duke's home life as inadequate and his environment as debilitating.[6]

As in *The Quiet One*, Duke has an absent father and a rejecting mother. Both Duke and his mother live with Duke's grandmother in Harlem. Grandma Custis (Georgia Burke) is not abusive, but when she catches Duke stealing from her purse, she spouts fire-and-brimstone warnings of the terrible judgments that will come down upon him. Duke has no memory of his father and can't even sort the many "husbands" his mother has had. Recalling a dream he had in which "one of my mother's husbands carried me on his shoulders" at the zoo, Duke asks his mother, "Whut was the name of that husband who took me to the zoo when I was a little kid?" (Miller 53, misspellings in original). But Duke's mom (Gloria Foster) can't

FIGURE 16. In *The Cool World* Duke and friends make a home away from home in an abandoned apartment.

recall such a trip, even after rattling off the names of numerous men. Duke's mother apologizes for abandoning him early, when she came north and left him in Alabama with his grandmother, and for her inability to care for him properly now: "I ain't got the strength to take care of you and look after you like I should." She complains about having to work for so little money and having so much of her money taken for taxes, taxes that never go to anything that improves her life. After Duke asks about her various "husbands," Mrs. Custis goes to the mirror, in the film, and mumbles a critical soliloquy about men. "I never wanted but the one husband," she says, "but things got too much for him. Things always get too much for men. Thinking all day of what they comin' home to. And one time they just don't come home." This scene simultaneously reinforces the stereotype of the vanishing black father and gives space to the black mother's anger, articulating the failed promise of men and marriage.

It is not just the instability of Duke's individual family that blocks his happiness: his problems are endemic and inescapable. In the novel Duke considers how mothers try to protect their kids from danger: "Usely they move . . . to a new place in Brooklyn or Queens or some where like they think changing the neiborhood gonna make some difference. Neiborhoods all the same" (Miller 144–145). The neighborhoods available to African Americans are limited and "all the same"; changing from one to another does not change one's situation or offer a way out of one's problems. The sense of sameness applies to buildings as well. "Apartments make me sad," Duke's narration states. He describes how bleak, depressing, and poorly built all the apartments he knows are, and, he claims, "Lots of guys feel that way. They just as soon stay out in the hall" (Miller 222). Rather than stay at home, Duke and his gang establish a home away from home, a clubhouse, a parody of domesticity in an abandoned apartment stocked with weapons, drugs, comic books, and a live-in prostitute.

The film, in particular, offers a critique of the pervasive racism and inequalities that structure Duke's life. The first shots of the film show an African American man in close-up speaking in direct address to the camera: "Do you want to know the truth about the white man? The white man is the devil!" The camera moves back to reveal this as a scene of sidewalk preaching, and we hear the man critique the "white devil" for his history of persecuting, jailing, and beating the black man and for creating a slavery of "not just the body" but "of the very soul" of black men. Largely ignored by bystanders in the film, the preacher nonetheless articulates for us, the film audience, a history of white injustice, a history that stands as a kind of expository prelude to the events about to unfold. In a film almost exclusively populated by black characters, this opening invites us to read the narrative in relation to white culture, understanding the segregated world we view as produced in and through racism.

Both novel and film emphasize the limited worldview of ghetto inhabitants. When Luane (Yolanda Rodriguez), a prostitute girlfriend of Duke's, says she wants to go to San Francisco to see the ocean, Duke tells her that there is an ocean in New York: she at first does not believe him, so he takes her to Coney Island to prove it. In the film the scenes at Coney Island serve as something of a respite from the cramped apartments and streets of Harlem, but the sequence ends with Duke alone and abandoned on the beach, as Luane apparently leaves for good. At the start of both the novel and the film Duke's class goes to visit Wall Street on a field trip. The book accentuates the gap between Duke's experience and the things his white teacher shows him: as the teacher talks about George Washington, the boys pay no attention; as they walk to the Stock Exchange, the boys focus on sneaking a smoke; as they watch a film about America that showed "factories & farms & mountains & a working man in a blue shirt buyin stocks," the boys slash and damage the chairs. The film emphasizes the boys' distance from white New York by having the teacher, Mr. Shapiro (Jerome Raphael), serve as tour guide to them as their bus leaves Harlem and approaches Wall Street. Near Central Park and Fifth Avenue, the teacher says they are passing some of the most expensive residential real estate in New York, then points out the Plaza Hotel, Bergdorf Goodman, Radio City, the Public Library, and Greenwich Village, assuming correctly that none of the boys know or have seen these places. A bus full of white school kids appears next to Duke's all-black bus, further marking the distinction between white and black worlds. A voice-over of Duke's interior thoughts, all about guns and gangs, also emphasizes the difference between Duke's life experience and the sights he sees.

The Cool World highlights not just the limited worldview of the ghetto inhabitants but their limited ability to imagine the future. Most tellingly, in the book, when the students on the field trip visit an exhibit called "The City of the Future," Duke is not "fooled" by the rockets flying over it, their wires showing. He sees it as "jes a big housing projeck" (Miller 15). Duke's view of the City of the Future as a housing project underscores not only his cynical worldview but also the text's lack of faith in his futurity. Later in the book, on his way to visit Priest to try to buy a gun, Duke stops to have his Tarot cards read by a gypsy. When she shows him the death card, he says "Friend of mine got killed yestaday. . . . That mus be him" (129). But the gypsy says she is not talking about the past but about his future: "It the Future when you gonna be near some body dead" (130). This curious statement reads as simultaneously "the death card shows a future in which you will be near someone who is dead," "a future in which you will be dead, near someone," and "the future is defined as being near someone dead," all of which suggest a future of death, not reproduction; fate, not hope.

The only future Duke can imagine involves his getting the gun from Priest. Like Chekhov's gun, planted in the first act and required to go off in the next, the gun Duke desires structures his future; but rather than fulfilling its role, the gun functions as another form of blockage and failure for Duke. In one stream-of-consciousness voice-over, Duke's thoughts wander, and he fantasizes about getting the gun. Although he does not have the $50 required to purchase the gun, he thinks, "Supposin I had the bread." He imagines himself with "the piece," congratulated by Priest, and able to kill Angel, a member of a rival gang. But his fantasy quickly shifts: "Suddenly I feel cold all over. I see death everywhere. I feel like nothing's gonna go right." In this moment, rather than imagining success, in which he kills with the gun, he imagines the death that will follow from his not getting the gun: "No bread, no piece." Both possible futures, though, end in death—Angel's death at Duke's hands or "death everywhere." In the end Duke does not have the cash necessary to purchase the gun.

The Cool World fulfills the gypsy's bleak prediction for Duke's future: "You gonna be near some body dead." Without the gun, Duke and his gang battle a rival gang, the Wolves, with knives and makeshift weapons. Duke drops his knife in a confrontation with Angel (Joe Oliver). Fellow gang member Rod (Bostic Felton) stabs and kills Angel, who says "thank you" when Duke removes the blade—whether it is thanks for killing him or taking the blade out is unclear.

In both the novel and film Duke is arrested for the murder, but the two texts diverge significantly at the end. The novel imagines Duke being placed in a rural reform school akin to Wiltwyck. Duke says that the judge in the case insisted that the school make room for him: "I aint sendin him back to the streets" (239). At first, Duke says, he missed the city, "but now I don't so much any more. I mean Man who need it" (241). The novel imagines Duke being rescued from the city and from his ghetto environment, relocated to the country and "a real house" (239), with a baseball diamond and flowerbeds for him to tend. Here, as in *The Quiet One*, the black child must be removed from family and community to have any sense of futurity. In this environment he begins to learn to read and write and gets his first job. Doc Levine from the school tells him that he can "do any thing. Be any thing," and Duke looks forward, at least as far as spring, when he can see if the bulbs he has planted will grow.

The film ends on a less redemptive note, with Duke in the back of a police car. Duke is taken away from his family and community but is seemingly stuck in the past, as we hear his interior thoughts as the police car speeds away, imagining others saying, "There goes Duke Custis. He's a cool killer." Whether relocated to a rural institution or jail, *The Cool World* suggests that the city is a dead end, offering no future.

The Agency of the Street

Both *The Quiet One* and *The Cool World* represent the single male child of a single mother. In *The Quiet One* we see the mother from Donald's perspective and have no real understanding of why she has him stay with his grandmother or why she ultimately abandons him, except for one scene that shows her with her new boyfriend (or husband) and an infant son. The boyfriend is clearly resentful of Donald's visit and takes the mother out, leaving Donald to babysit, even though he has just arrived for a visit. The critique of unhappiness in *The Quiet One* is framed by the white narrator and within psychosocial discourse. *The Cool World* briefly gives the mother a voice and provides some understanding of her situation but mainly focuses on Duke's perspective. Serving as one of an archive of unhappiness, the critique in *The Cool World* is implied through Duke's actions and delusions, but except for the anonymous preacher at the film's start, no character articulates racial resentment or a sense of injustice. In the novel *The Street*, by contrast, the narrative about a single mother and her son in Harlem conveys the mother's internal thoughts and feelings, and it articulates clearly her resentment and understanding of oppression and the myriad ways in which her life chances and those of her son are blocked and how the two of them are denied happiness and futurity.

Written by African American author Ann Petry, *The Street* offers an omniscient narration that is focalized through the experiences of various characters, primarily those of the mother, Lutie Johnson, but also her son, Bub; Jones, the super in her building; and his mistress, Min. The narrative begins with Lutie finding a new apartment on 116th Street in Harlem and then details her travails within the apartment building, including a near rape by the super, her son's move into delinquency under the tutelage of the super, her dealings with local gangsters, and finally her murder of one of the gangsters. Much of the narrative details Lutie's feelings about the ghetto, white injustice, and her fears for the impact of ghetto life on Bub.

Like Duke in *The Cool World*, Lutie expresses an understanding of the inadequacy and sameness of apartments in the ghetto. When she first goes to view the apartment, even before she enters, Lutie knows what it will be like. Reading an advertisement that says "three rooms, steam heat, parquet floors, respectable tenants," Lutie decodes the terms using her knowledge of similar apartments, echoing in many ways Wright's description of the kitchenette and the oppressive "Bosses of the Buildings." She thinks,

"Parquet floors here meant that the wood was so old and so discolored that no amount of varnish or shellac would conceal the scars and old scraped places, the years of dragging furniture across the floors, the hammer blows of time and children and drunks and dirty, slovenly women" (Petry 3). She understands that steam heat means "a rattling, clanging noise in radiators early in the morning and then a hissing that went on all day" (Petry 3). "Respectable tenants," she knows, must be modified to "in these houses where colored people were allowed to live" (Petry 3) and thus includes anyone who can pay the rent. Looking at the building from the street, she knows the rooms will be small and dark, with no sunlight, and that hallways will be dark and narrow.

More than individual apartments or apartment buildings, Lutie recognizes the sameness of all streets in the ghetto. Thinking that 116th Street is a "bad street," Lutie corrects herself: "It wasn't just this street that she was afraid of or that was bad. It was any street where people were packed together like sardines in a can" (Petry 206). She broadens her critique from the street to the city: "It wasn't just this city. It was any city where they set up a line and say black folks stay on this side and white folks on this side, so that the black folks were crammed on top of each other—jammed and packed and forced into the smallest possible spaces until they were completely cut off from light and air" (Petry 206). Here, Petry grants Lutie a sense of injustice, as well as resentment. Petry's discussion of "the line" echoes similar passages in Wright's *Native Son*: "We live here and they live there. We black and they white. They got things and we ain't. They do things and we can't. It's just like living in jail. Half the time I feel like I'm on the outside of the world peeping in through a knothole in the fence" (20). But Lutie's critique extends beyond race to encompass gender. She thinks, "It was any place where the women had to work to support the families because the men couldn't get jobs and the men got bored and pulled out and the kids were left without proper homes because there was nobody around to put a heart into it" (Petry 206). Here, Lutie relates her personal experience to broader trends. As we learn in the course of the novel, her husband, Jim, could not find work, then resented her work for a white family in a white suburb and, left home alone, cheated on her. But Lutie also acknowledges the ways in which the conditions of poverty induce single motherhood. In a world where people have to work all the time, she thinks, their only source of pleasure or relief is "their bodies," and "the crowding together made the young girls wise beyond their years" (Petry 206). But rather than blame black people, Lutie links the dynamics of gender and family in the black community to white oppression: "It all added up to the same thing, she decided—white people" (Petry 206).

Just as Wright attributed agency to the streets—saying that the streets "claim" boys "and no voice of ours can call them back" (*12 Million* 136)—Lutie endows the street with the power to ensnare her son. She views the street as inherently dangerous. "She didn't know which was worse," Petry writes, "his being alone in those dreary rooms or his playing in the street where the least of the dangers confronting him came from the stream of traffic which roared through 116th Street" (60). While the traffic is one danger, Lutie views "gangs of young boys" as a worse threat and one that Bub is "too young to recognize and avoid" (Petry 60). Against the notion that African American boys are knowing and not innocent, Lutie acknowledges that Bub would not see the street the same way she does. "It was impossible to know how this street looked to eight year old Bub," she thinks. "It may have appealed to him or it may have frightened him" (Petry 415). Lutie sees it from an adult perspective: "She tried to see the street with his eyes and couldn't because the crap game in progress in the middle of the block, the scraps of obscene talk she heard as she passed the poolroom, the tough young boys with their caps on backward who swaggered by, were things she saw with the eye of an adult and reacted to from an adult's point of view" (Petry 415). Lutie acknowledges that children may have a different experience of the city—a child's view that finds play spaces amid disorder or that will be blind to dangers—but she cannot access or celebrate his view because she sees all the ways in which the street will harm her son.

Lutie envisions the street as not just dangerous but as determining both her fate and Bub's. Lutie is tricked by a local gangster, Boots, to think she is being hired to sing in a nightclub. Instead, it turns out that both Boots and his boss, Junto, have designs on Lutie and want her to be Junto's mistress. As she ponders her choice, Lutie thinks of all the things she has done to better herself—leaving her husband, going to high school, working as a housemaid, getting a certificate to get a better job as a file clerk—yet she recognizes the inevitability of her downfall: "All those years she'd been heading straight as an arrow for that street or some other street just like it" (Petry 426). The street becomes a stand-in for the ghetto as a whole and, more than that, for the blocked opportunities and bad fate that are endemic to the ghetto. When Bub gets into trouble—lured into a scheme to steal mail by the super who is resentful of Lutie after he is caught and stopped from trying to rape her—Lutie views this, too, as the work of the street, thinking that "he would have gotten into trouble sooner or later, because the street looked after him when she wasn't around" (Petry 427).

Lutie eventually abandons Bub, fulfilling the mandate of all these texts to "rescue" the child by severing ties between mother and son. Lutie's abandonment emerges from her sense that she will no longer be able to care for Bub. When Lutie resists the plan to have her be Junto's mistress, Boots attempts to force her but decides, "I'll have mine first" (Petry 428) and attempts to rape her. Lutie becomes angry, and "this quick surface anger helped to swell and became a part of the deepening stream of rage that had fed on the hate, the frustration, the resentment she had toward the pattern her life had followed" (Petry 428). "A lifetime of pent-up resentment" (Petry 430) leads Lutie to grab a candlestick and bludgeon Boots to death, taking out all her anger in a brutal attack that finally strikes at "the white world which thrust black people into a walled enclosure from which there was no escape" (Petry 430). Recognizing that she will have to go to jail and will not be able to care for Bub, Lutie takes cash from Boots and flees to Chicago, leaving Bub, who is still in jail for the mail theft: "So he will go to reform school, she repeated. He'll be better off without you. That way he may have some kind of chance. He didn't have the ghost of a chance on that street" (Petry 435). If happiness requires hope and a sense of futurity, Bub can only access that through being cut off from his family. His only "chance," or "hap," is—like Donald's in *The Quiet One* and Duke's in *The Cool World*—institutional life outside the ghetto.

Becoming Militant

The Quiet One, *The Cool World*, and *The Street* all end with a solitary boy, removed from family and from community, thus redoubling the problem of the broken family that presumably creates the crisis. *Bush Mama* similarly ends with a child alone but, in this case, a girl, both of whose parents wind up in jail.

Made for his UCLA thesis by Haile Gerima, who credits himself not as "director" but as "answerable," the film combines documentary footage, location shooting, surrealist images, complex layered soundscapes, found footage, and found sound in a fiction film that approximates Godardian aesthetics and leftist politics. The film opens with footage of Gerima and his crew being harassed by the LAPD while sounds recorded from welfare offices play—a cacophony of callous institutional-ese. As the scene shifts, and Dorothy enters the frame, the throbbing nondiegetic score by Onaje Kareen Kenyatta overlaps with these voices and the sounds of both helicopters and police sirens. Elsewhere, Gerima adopts Soviet-style intellectual montage, jump cuts, and scenes of direct address as he explores white violence against blacks, the culture of blacks blaming blacks for their troubles, and the oppressive welfare system.

In contrast to many postwar narratives of black life, *Bush Mama* starts with a happy family: mother, Dorothy (Barbara O. Jones); father, T. C. (Johnny Weathers); and daughter, Luann (Susan Williams). In early scenes we see T. C. and Luann playing together and all three dancing in the living room. T. C. is a discharged Vietnam vet. Expecting a "hero's welcome" on his return, he faces instead unemployment. Heading out to a new job, he is arrested for a crime he did not commit and imprisoned. Left alone, a pregnant Dorothy is pressured by different views and voices: social workers who want her to abort the baby, friends who want her to give up on T. C., associates who view her as a drunk, T. C.'s emerging militant views, and her own growing awareness of state-sponsored abuse of African Americans. Ultimately, she shifts from a passive acceptance of her situation to a revolutionary militant view.

For much of the film Dorothy remains uninterested in politics. When a neighbor girl hangs a poster of a militarized and heavily armed African mother and child in her apartment, she allows it because she has nothing else on her walls. But when T. C. is arrested, and her social worker pressures her to get an abortion, threatening to take away her welfare, Dorothy begins to get angry. Ultimately, she shifts from passivity to action in order to protect her daughter. One day, when Dorothy is out looking for work, a policeman finds her daughter alone on a street corner waiting for her. Accusing Luanne of being a vagrant or prostitute, the white policeman forces her to take him to her home. There, he handcuffs her to the bed and rapes her while Luann screams "Mama mama" repeatedly. When Dorothy returns and finds the policeman attacking her daughter, he says he came to arrest her for "taking really rotten care of your little whore daughter." She bludgeons him to death. In prison she is beaten and miscarries. The film ends with a long take of Dorothy framed, without her wig, with the poster of the African mother and child behind her. In voice-over we hear a letter to T. C. in which she complains of his false imprisonment and her mistreatment in jail and says, "We got to make changes." Admitting that she previously thought she was "born to be poor, to be pushed around and stepped on," she says she now knows her problem is "the place I was born into," a place that is unjust. "I have to get to know myself," she says, and that "we all" have to learn to talk to each other. Recalling that she used to wear a wig all the time, she tells T. C., "The wig is off my head. I never saw what was under it. . . . The wig is off my head." As Dorothy begins to imagine a future via revolutionary politics, daughter Luann's future remains uncertain. Raped by the policeman, she is left alone, with both parents in jail.

Imagining Tomorrow

In functioning as archives of unhappiness, but with little or no promise of futurity, *The Quiet One*, *The Cool World*, *The Street*, and *Bush Mama* resemble the cycle of films Christopher Sieving describes as "racial impasse" films. Sieving uses the term to cover late 1960s and early 1970s black-themed films that do not fit into the category of either the Hollywood "problem picture," in which race is a problem to be solved by white liberalism, or later blaxploitation films, which adopt a black nationalist stance. In the racial impasse film black-white relations are seen to be "damaged perhaps beyond repair . . . bogged down in a stalemate" (Sieving 162). In the texts I have discussed, black life itself is "bogged down"—trapped and blocked from happiness. The texts dissect an impossible present and articulate anger but hold little hope for a more promising tomorrow.

The Planet of Junior Brown differs from these texts in offering an Afrofuturist vision to counter African American boys' alienation and unhappiness. Mark Derry first coined the term *Afrofuturism* in an essay addressing the question of why there was so little African American science fiction. For Derry, science fiction seemed a natural fit for African American writers "in light of the fact that African Americans, in a very real sense, are the descendants of alien abductees; they inhabit a sci-fi nightmare in which unseen but no less impassable force fields of intolerance frustrate their movements; official histories undo what has been done; and technology is too often brought to bear on black bodies" (180). For Derry, an Afrofuturist vision consists of "speculative fiction that treats African-American themes and addresses African-American concerns in the context of twentieth century technoculture" (180). Because there was not much explicit science fiction at the time Derry was writing, he found Afrofuturism in "unlikely places" (182) and expanded the notion to include music by Sun Ra's Arkestra, George Clinton, Herbie Hancock, and others, as well as paintings by Jean-Michel Basquiat, and films such as John Sayles's *Brother from Another Planet* (1984) and Lizzie Borden's *Born in Flames* (1983). Following Derry, others have extended the notion further to define *Afrofuturism* as both an "artistic aesthetic and a framework for critical theory" and have expanded its generic affiliation beyond science fiction to include hybrid mixes of "science fiction, historical fiction, speculative fiction, fantasy, Afrocentricity, and magic realism" (Womack 9). In one of the broadest statements, art curator Ingrid LaFleur defines *Afrofuturism* as "imagining possible futures through a black cultural lens" (quoted in Womack 9).

The Planet of Junior Brown is not generally considered among the pantheon of Afrofuturist texts. But author Virginia Hamilton is one of the few African American female authors who has written science fiction (Hampton and Brooks), and the book draws on various themes and ideas related to science fiction, as well as combining elements of fantasy in a text that is largely realist. Hamilton, as Gregory Jerome Hampton and Wanda M. Brooks argue, "allows alienation to be imagined outside of the traditional definitions of the term" (71) in science fiction, to consider aliens not as something existing outside our known world but as ones who are alienated from or marginalized within the known world. In *The Planet of Junior Brown*, Hamilton not only troubles the categories of alienation and Otherness, but also imagines an alternative world, a city beneath the city, and an alternative reality for homeless boys. This alternative reality evokes science fiction in its use of a terminology of planets to name the various underground spots the boys inhabit. Moreover, in contrasting this underground world to the known world, the novel creates what novelist Nalo Hopkinson describes as "a science fictional world" (A. Nelson 100): "I can directly manipulate the metaphorical structure of the story. . . . In other words, what I can do is to intervene in the readers' assumptions by creating a world in which standards are different. Or I can blatantly show what values the characters in the story are trying to live out by making them actual, by exaggerating them into the realm of the fantastical, so that the consequences conversely become so real that they are tangible" (A. Nelson 100–101). In Hopkinson's account a "science fictional world" need not take place in a world completely removed from the known world but will invert, exaggerate, or otherwise alter aspects of the known world to distance readers from their everyday assumptions and expectations. In *The Planet of Junior Brown*, Hamilton creates a sense of two worlds, through a narrative contrasting the lives of two boys; in that contrast she produces a world in which "standards are different" and stereotypical assumptions are turned on their head. As Roberta Seelinger Trites notes, Hamilton examines the "social effects of inclusion and exclusion on people" but shows marginalized people transforming their "outsideness" into "insideness" (147); thus, she destabilizes the categories of inside/outside, included/excluded, dominant/marginal, and even human/inhuman.

The Planet of Junior Brown tells the story of two eighth-grade boys: Junior, an obese musical prodigy; and Buddy, a street-smart homeless boy with a penchant for advanced math. At the story's start the two boys have been skipping school for some months, spending their school days with the school's janitor, a former math teacher, Mr. Pool, in a hidden room that Mr. Pool has made to look like a broom closet, and which nobody besides them knows how to enter. Junior lives with his mother in an apartment; his father works in Jersey and is supposed to visit on weekends, but it is clear that he rarely does and that he may have abandoned the family altogether. Buddy tells Junior and Mr. Pool that he lives with his aunt and that his mother in Texas will come soon, but in truth he is homeless.

In many ways the novel situates the two boys in conventional narratives of rejecting mothers. Buddy's mother has abandoned him: "Rarely did Buddy trouble himself about his mother, whom he hadn't seen since the age of nine. He knew she had abandoned him because his presence reminded her how completely unable she was to care for him. Out of desperation she had walked away from him" (Hamilton 64). Buddy's mother resembles the mothers in *The Quiet One*, *The Cool World*, and *The Street*, all women who feel inadequate to the task of motherhood and are beaten down and defeated in their own lives. Junior's mother is presented as overly controlling and protective, which, as we saw in the last chapter, is understood in psychological discourse of the time as evidence of the mother's hostility toward the child.

From Buddy's perspective, Junior's mother is like other women whose husbands have left: lonely and anxious, she "had all the time she needed to get her insides confused and to make the life of her favorite child over to suit herself" (Hamilton 25). Beyond being overprotective, Junior's mother is seen as manipulative and selfish. She pretends to be sick (or convinces herself she is sick) to control Junior. When Junior brings Buddy home to dinner and says he wants to go to a movie with him, she suddenly starts coughing and wheezing with a severe asthma attack (Hamilton 124). Junior instantly becomes his mother's caretaker, quickly slipping an oxygen mask onto his mother and injecting her with epinephrine. Beyond being needy and demanding, Junior's mother is also marked as selfish and castrating. Junior has a Baldwin piano in his apartment, but when he plays, it is silent. In order that she can have rest and quiet, Junior's mother has taken out all the wires meant to vibrate and produce sound so that when Junior hits the keys "the hammers struck against nothing . . . rose and fell senselessly" (Hamilton 115).

Music makes Junior happy, but his music lessons outside the home have also become compromised. Each week, Junior travels from his school near Ninety-Seventh Street and Broadway to an apartment at Seventy-eighth and Amsterdam Avenue to take a piano lesson. But for the last few weeks Junior has not had a lesson because his teacher, Miss Peebs, is having some sort of breakdown. Convinced that a diseased and contagious relative is living in her apartment, she has covered most of her furniture with tarps and has violently wrecked her piano, keeping music out of Junior's reach. By novel's end Junior has come to believe in the "relative," too, begins speaking to him, and asks Buddy to help take him out of the claustrophobic apartment.

Buddy has what would normally be considered a lesser life than Junior's. Although Junior's mother is controlling, she still cares for him, feeds him, and clothes him. Buddy is homeless, does not have adequate clothing, and must work and scrounge to get what little food he eats. In the logic of the book, however, Buddy's life is looked upon as more desirable than Junior's. When Buddy considers Junior's mother, he thinks, "I'd take the street any day" (Hamilton 34). Later, when he imagines telling Junior about his life—his efforts with homeless kids and his paid employment at a newsstand—he thinks, "You going to want to be as free as me" (Hamilton 114). While readers may be uncertain whether to value Buddy's life as he does, Junior certainly envies Buddy's freedom. Trapped at home after his mother's asthma attack, Junior wonders, "How come Buddy was so free all the time? How come he could go to a movie or just walk around? Buddy had it all free. . . . Buddy had taken what had been free in Junior's house when he went away. He had taken the noise and left Junior with the quiet room" (Hamilton 135). Unlike Buddy, who moves freely in the city, Junior's mother tries to control his movements in the city and "think[s] they gonna lynch you if you go downtown too far" (Hamilton 31). Though Junior loves the city, "loved Broadway" and "knew he belonged to it the way the fixtures of newsstands and traffic lights belonged to it" (Hamilton 36), "he accepted . . . the fact that freedom ended for him once he went home to his mother's house" (Hamilton 58). More than just freedom, Buddy opens worlds to Junior. Contemplating the solar system they have built with Mr. Pool, Junior admits to himself that "what he knew about the universe had come from his friendship with Buddy Clark" (Hamilton 15).

Buddy offers an inverse perspective on the city. Buddy and the other homeless children are invisible in the everyday city: "It was simply that no one had any idea they existed" (Hamilton 63). They inhabit secret spaces, and in this, as in their invisibility, they echo Ralph Ellison's *Invisible Man*, whose "invisible" narrator lives in a secret hidden space (Stewart). But whereas invisibility can function as a "metaphor of disillusionment and disempowerment" (Stewart 195), Buddy views the invisible community as invisible only because of the city's indifference: "For Buddy, the city of darkness was deeply familiar and as fine a treasure as any he could have dreamed. He had accepted its mindless indifference to life because he knew it was he, alone, and others, as alone as he was, who gave it what little humanity it had" (Hamilton 63). Far from feeling disempowered, Buddy attributes to himself and other homeless boys the ability to imbue the city with humanity.

The homeless boys in *The Planet of Junior Brown* show their humanity in the way they care for each other. When Buddy first finds himself among the homeless, he is scared, but they welcome him: "This is the planet of Tomorrow Billy," an older boy tells him. "If you want to live on it, you can" (Hamilton 72). Tomorrow Billy, we learn, is a name given to older boys who look after younger ones, teaching them how to live, feeding them, giving them clothing, and visiting them each night, as they ask, "Tomorrow, Billy? Will we see you again tomorrow night?" (Hamilton 73), until one day they forget to ask and Tomorrow Billy knows they are okay and can live on their own.

Mr. Pool recognizes this humanity in Buddy, and he positions it within a futurist vision. Recalling how he had grown indifferent as a teacher—"I lost heart" (Hamilton 13)—Mr. Pool finds that through the "example of Buddy Clark's devotion to Junior Brown," he "slowly began to believe in himself again" (Hamilton 13). Buddy's caretaking awakens something in

Mr. Pool and makes him view normal human life as somehow alien: "He could no longer remember when he arrived at the curious notion that two legged beings on earth were only disguised as men" (Hamilton 13). Mr. Pool considers Buddy to be an alien creature—"He sensed a whole new being lying in wait within the boy"—but one who will reveal true humanity: "Perhaps the human race is yet to come, thought Mr. Pool. We must make life ready" (Hamilton 13).

Junior expresses his desire for freedom in his art, particularly a large canvas on which he paints the Red Man, a giant red figure in whose outlined body he draws myriad tiny urban figures and spaces, including the school and the planet of Junior Brown and the "streets with Buddy Clark free and tough, knocking his way through them . . . everyone flowing free" (Hamilton 139). In the Red Man, Junior "had been in the painting, like a single brown ball bouncing on street corners, jiving in school yards. Junior had painted himself everywhere in the city where he had no business being" (Hamilton 165). His mother discovers the canvas and, disgusted with the images, incinerates it. At the same time, Mr. Pool is fired, his secret room discovered and the solar system and plant of Junior Brown disassembled. And shortly after, Junior encounters "the relative" and has a breakdown.

To help Junior, Buddy exposes the world of Tomorrow Billy to Mr. Pool and Junior. Mr. Pool fixes a hoist to lower Junior into the basement of a boarded-up building that serves as Buddy's planet. Mr. Pool joins them, bringing the solar system with him. Buddy tells the other homeless boys that Junior will live with them. Buddy's Tomorrow Billy had told him, "The highest law is to learn to live for yourself" (Hamilton 73). Buddy now revises this and teaches the inhabitants of his planet, "We are together . . . because we have to learn to live for each other. . . . The highest law for us is to live for one another. I can teach you how to do that" (Hamilton 210). The promise of tomorrow thus becomes a promise of a caring collective. Against the idea that African American boys are trapped and doomed, *The Planet of Junior Brown* posits an alternative universe in which boys find a more caring universe outside the strictures of family and institutional life and in which a descent into a hidden basement becomes an access point to "new light" and "faith in one another" (Hamilton 210).

Texts such as *The Quiet One*, *The Cool World*, *The Street*, *Bush Mama*, and *The Planet of Junior Brown* articulate anger at the way in which social and institutional mechanisms underpin racist practices and block the African American child's happiness. *The Planet of Junior Brown*, however, offers a counternarrative to the chronicles of familial neglect and delinquency that dominate mid-to-late twentieth-century representations of African American children. To do so, however, requires imagining an alternative universe or a subterranean city beneath the city. While we disengage the stereotype of delinquent black boys in need of rescue by white society, we also revert to fantasy for a solution to their unhappiness and anger. The problems that denied the black child access to hap or good fortune are not resolved but symbolically buried. To move forward, into a future that is not science fiction, we need to imagine black and other minority children as mobile and free figures in an urban landscape linked to play and encounter, not criminality or misery.

5

Helicopters and Catastrophes

The Failure to Neglect
and Neglect as Failure

As we have seen, this book takes as its subject the abiding imaginary of the mobile urban child in conjunction with fantasies of neglect. The city street is key to this imaginary and to my project. Thus, it is worthwhile to consider the quintessential urban street of American childhood: *Sesame Street*. Changes in how this show portrays childhood mobility and urbanism are indicative of the broad changes I have outlined here.

In its original conception *Sesame Street* (1969) presented a progressive counter to narratives of urban neglect. The makers of *Sesame Street* aimed their show explicitly at kids in poor urban environments who might not get enough early education. The show's creator, Joan Cooney, hired Evelyn Payne Davis, formerly director of fund development at the New York Urban League, as an outreach director to garner the attention and viewership of the target audience (which she did, handing out flyers at churches and day-care centers, organizing evening community meetings with free child care, getting corporations to supply day-care centers with free TVs, and more) (Davis 153–154, 179–181).

Producer and writer Jon Stone, a former associate producer on *Captain Kangaroo* (1955), decided that the best way to target inner-city kids was through "unflinching realism" (Davis 155). Ironically, Stone got the idea to set the show on a city street from a sardonic public service announcement (PSA) aimed at getting urban kids out of the city in the summer. According to Michael Davis, in his history of *Sesame Street*:

> The PSA opened with a printed message: "Send your kid to a ghetto this summer." It then cut to a street scene in Harlem, where a black actor named Lincoln Kilpatrick narrated a mock travelogue of an inner-city neighborhood, touting its supposed amenities. "We have all kinds of facilities here," he said, pointing out "pools" (fire hydrants gushing into gutters) and "ball fields" (a car-lined street where children played stickball), not to mention "field trips" (to fetid trash-strewn lots), and "cozy camp cabins" (where black children slept three or four to a bed).
>
> The actor pointedly asked, "You don't want your kids to play *here* this summer? Then don't expect *ours* to." (Davis 154)

For Stone, while this PSA aimed to underscore the lack of opportunity in the ghetto, it sparked a more auspicious view of urban streets. "For a preschool child in Harlem," Stone said, "the street is where the action is" (Davis 155). He viewed the street as "Utopia" with "kids hollering, jumping double Dutch, running through the open hydrants, playing stickball" (Davis 155). The set, he believed, had to be an inner-city street with a brownstone "so the cast and kids could 'stoop' in the age-old New York tradition" (Davis 155). Stone's remarkable inversion of the PSA message led him to create a set and environment aimed at presenting a positive spin on urban living instead of the artificial world of most children's TV to date: Stone insisted on "no Treasure House, no toymaker's workshop, no enchanted castle, no dude ranch, no circus" (Davis 154).

The show's realism and emphasis on inner-city children can be seen in the first episode, which aired on November 10, 1969. Claymation figures spell out the words *Sesame Street*; then, as the theme song begins— promising a "sunny day," where "Everything's A.O.K."—live-action footage shows kids playing in various urban settings—a playground with graffiti, the zoo, parks. Then, we cut to a studio lot built to look like an urban street. It shows different building materials and textures, faded signs, doors painted a variety of colors, fire escapes, and garbage cans in front of buildings. We meet Gordon (Matt Robinson), an African American man with mutton-chop sideburns and an Afro, wearing a suit and carrying a briefcase. Gordon, a teacher home from work for the day, escorts a young mixed-race girl, Sally (the kids on the show are uncredited nonactors who are not given a script but respond to whatever the grown-ups say to them). Sally is new to the neighborhood, so Gordon shows her around. "You've never seen a street like Sesame Street," he tells her. "Everything happens here." Indeed, after meeting a young white girl named Ariana and an African American boy named Ronald, who are playing on the sidewalk, Sally is introduced to adults Bob (Bob McGrath); Mr. Hooper (Will Lee); and Gordon's wife, Susan (Loretta Long), and then to the Muppets Big Bird (Caroll Spinney) and Ernie (Frank Oz) before we cut away to a Bert (Jim Henson) and Ernie segment set in their basement apartment. Following a segment on the number 3, Sally and Gordon go to Gordon's house, where Susan gives them cookies and milk. Over the course of the episode, Sally meets Oscar the Grouch (Caroll Spinney), and we see various segments on milk, the birth of chickens, the letter E, the number 2, and more.

In another segment, teaching kids about spatiality (over, under, through), we see live-action footage of a mixed-race and mixed-gender group of kids playing Follow the Leader. While a child's voice-over narrates their actions, they run through yards, going past a clothesline, then through an empty lot strewn with construction materials and garbage. They climb through a pipe, pile up cardboard and old broken crates, and run over saw-horses that have buckets of paint and water on them. One kid goes under, instead of over, the saw-horses and ends up with a bucket of dirty water dumped over his head.

Initially, the series continues to show children playing in city streets, encountering both grown-ups and Muppet others. In season 2, episode 131, which aired on 9 November 1970, for instance, we see kids riding bikes, jumping rope, and using a rope swing on the sidewalk with laundry hanging in the background; Big Bird leads a parade of kids and grown-ups through the street; two kids ride their bikes alone through city streets, to the beach and the zoo; and kids and Big Bird alike learn how to cross the street safely. Episode 276 from season 3, which aired on 8 November 1971, shows kids using a box spring on a city sidewalk as a trampoline and playing basketball with Gordon. In these early seasons the street becomes an alternative family. The children are never shown with their parents but are attached to various Muppets and adults, including Gordon, Susan, Bob, Mr. Hooper, and later the Spanish-speaking Rafael (Raul Julia) and Maria (Sonia Monzano).

These early episodes of *Sesame Street* are found on a DVD compilation called *Old School* that was released in 2006. At the start of the DVD, before we see the first episode, a cartoon character named Bob announces that the shows are "intended for grown-ups and may not suit the needs of today's preschool child." Since counting to three and knowing which of these things are not like the others seem to still suit a preschool curriculum, the show's "adults only" label seems to be motivated by the show's realism and its contrast to contemporary mores. As Lenore Skenazy points out in her book *Free-Range Kids*—describing the first episode with its images of kids playing in vacant lots, wiggling through a pipe, and scrambling to the top of a jungle gym, and with its narrative of a little girl being taken home by an adult male stranger—what seemed "nice and normal" in 1969 "today looks like a trailer for *Saw II: This Time It's Preschool*" (69). *Old School* represents as strange and distant a vantage on childhood as the Dead End Kids or Shirley Temple films.

Nowadays, *Sesame Street* places much less emphasis on its urbanism; it shows many fewer children; it shows those children in much more controlled environments; and it seems less targeted to inner-city children than an ideal generic conception of childhood. In episode 4520, for example, which aired in season 46 on 19 February 2015, the theme song begins with a live-action image of kids making chalk drawings on a city sidewalk but quickly morphs into an animated sequence in which drawn cityscapes lead them to a drawn image of a street. The episode celebrates the word of the day, *artist*, so this emphasis on drawn images is not entirely out of place. But in other recent episodes the opening theme shows Big Bird escorting children through city streets rather than showing them merely playing on their own. The street set, when it is shown, looks to be a cleaner, more gentrified space than the gritty realistic space Stone imagined. In the first segment of episode 4520, for example, Bert sits at a sidewalk café. Behind him, we see flowering trees, window boxes, and lots of planters with mainly red brick buildings in good repair. After this segment, we do not return to the street set. Instead, transitions such as a paint brush covering the screen or a wipe move viewers from one segment to the next. Most segments feature

Muppets in direct address talking or singing to the camera. Occasionally a live-action adult mixes with the Muppets but they are also filmed frontally and speaking directly to the camera. Instead of a neighborhood in which one can map exactly where Bert and Ernie live in relation to Gordon and Susan, or Oscar or Big Bird, *Sesame Street* thematically connects a series of discrete segments with Muppet characters like Elmo (formerly Kevin Clash, now Ryan Dillon), Ernie, and Grover (formerly Frank Oz, now Eric Jacobson). Kids appear, but not on the street. In episode 4520 we see kids and grown-ups in a segment about art: they stand in a space with white walls in the background and glass in the foreground, and they paint on the glass to cover the screen. In another segment kids are shown in an overhead shot drawing on pavement but their drawings turn into cartoons, and they are seen running through an impossible animated world of cartoon boats, roads, and trees. A segment focused on jogging shows kids running in what appears to be a school gym, then briefly outside, then back in the gym. In another segment they have a lesson from an artist in a classroom. They appear in a wooded area briefly to count to six. And a few kids in tuxedos serve as background dancers for Janelle Monae's song "The Power of Yet."

In my introduction I discussed the "islanding" of children's activities, in regulated zones and places, such as playgrounds, care centers, children's gyms, schools, craft centers, museums, and their consequent disappearance from public view. *Sesame Street*, once committed to showing kids in public spaces, now both reflects and enacts this islanding. While geographers describe the physical islanding of children that occurs when parents shuttle them from one place to another, *Sesame Street* islands them *visually* through its selection of shooting locations and through editing. In contemporary *Sesame Street*, rather than a sense of neighborhood, or a street where "everything happens," we get a postmodern assemblage of spaces that show different themes but that do not cohere to produce a sense of place. Instead of an image of inner-city kids in a neighborhood that invokes Harlem, we get a more idealized and generic image of childhood. Thus, kids have been islanded away from the street, away from encounters with adults. Instead of active participants in urban life, instead of playing on the sidewalk or riding bikes in city streets, instead of meeting strangers, children exist largely as an isolated point of address, hailed in direct address as generic child-spectators at home. The new *Sesame Street* produces a frictionless world of branded characters in a place that bears little resemblance to the world any children inhabit.

So, how did we get from a vision of the street as a utopian place, "where the action is," to displacing children entirely from the street and locating them at home on the couch? Over the course of this book I have been referring off and on to "helicopter parenting," as related to children's loss of independent mobility in the latter part of the twentieth century and into the twenty-first. Indeed, the loss of children's mobility and the absence of children in public urban space today largely motivates this book, as I have sought to recover a different way of imagining kids in the city, by examining films, books, and other media that represent the urban child as mobile and free.

The Rise of Helicopter Parenting

Contemporary parenting and childhood have changed dramatically from the 1930s, when we could imagine Shirley Temple or the Dead End Kids walking city streets alone, and from midcentury, when Harriet the Spy could be portrayed roaming New York freely, or we could see the mother in *Little Fugitive* leave her kids overnight without fear of being arrested; and they have changed from when many of us—the children of the 1960s and 1970s, the original audience for *Sesame Street*—grew up. As Hanna Rosin says, "Like most parents my age, I have memories of childhood so different from the way my children are growing up that sometimes I think I might be making them up, or at least exaggerating them" (77). As our parents once told us apocryphal tales of walking five miles to school in the snow, we now tell our kids that once upon a time we used to go outside, by ourselves, and not come home until dinner, with our parents having no idea where we were, and no undue concern, either.

Parenting has shifted from a model of largely benign neglect to one of total supervision. As Rosin says, "Failure to supervise has, in fact, become synonymous with the failure to parent" (82). As parenting has shifted, childhood has also changed from kids having some autonomous mobility to being largely contained. Rosin gives a striking account of this change, describing the work of British geographer Roger Hart. In 1972 Hart went to New England to research his dissertation on the geography of children. After winning the trust of children in the town, and following them on their various routes, Hart came to know the landscape of childhood. He reported that "the children spent immense amounts of time on their own, creating imaginary landscapes their parents sometimes knew nothing about" (Rosin 82). In 2004 Hart returned to the same town to do a follow-up study, to see how the children he studied in 1972 parented their children now. Like Rosin, those parents admitted to a stark contrast between their own childhood and the childhood they grant their own kids. "Roger Hart! Oh my God," one of the women exclaims, "my childhood existed! . . . I'm always telling people what we used to do, and they don't believe me" (Rosin 83). While remembering fondly their own freedom, these parents now nonetheless raise their kids very differently, fencing their yards to "contain" their kids, following the kids around, even in their own backyard, and claiming changes in the community—"transients" and "people coming in and out"—to justify their more anxious and controlling parenting (Rosin 83–84).

When asked why parenting and childhood have changed, most people respond with a litany of reasons why parents have become more fearful for their children and thus more protective. Many locate the turning point in the late 1970s and early 1980s. Rosin cites the Etan Patz case from 1979, when six-year-old Patz went missing from his SoHo neighborhood and was never found. Commentators on the recent mistrial of the Patz case agree that Patz's disappearance "transformed the experience of childhood for many boys and girls his age and set the mold for the sort of fathers and mothers they would become" (Wilson). In addition to citing the Patz case, both Lenore Skenazy and Julia Lythcott-Haims, former dean of freshman and undergraduate advising at Stanford, cite the 1981 kidnapping and brutal decapitation of Adam Walsh, and the subsequent screening of the TV miniseries *Adam* (Michael Tuchner 1983) about his murder, as a turning point. Both the Patz and Walsh cases engendered "stranger danger" and led in 1984 to the creation of the National Center for Missing and Exploited Children and the creation by the National Child Safety Council of the Missing Children Milk Carton program, which put faces of missing kids on breakfast tables across America, asking, "Have You Seen Me?" Further, as Skenazy notes, their cases coincided with the expansion of the burgeoning cable TV industry, which fed off scaremongering and quickly realized that missing kids would attract viewers (*Free-Range Kids* 14–16).

Along with these cases of disappeared children, the "media perpetuated endless cycles of panic" about day-care centers and pedophilia (Matchar 128). In what has come to be viewed as a hysteria akin to the Salem witch trials, numerous day-care providers were accused in the early-to-mid-1980s of child abuse, child sexual abuse, and satanic ritual abuse of preschool children. The sensational McMartin day-care trial that began in Manhattan Beach, California, in 1983 included not only allegations of sodomy and other forms of sexual abuse but also claims that the day-care providers were witches who could fly, that they flushed the children into tunnels beneath the building via the toilets, and that children flew in hot-air balloons and participated in orgies at car washes. The McMartin trial was followed by similarly bizarre cases involving the Fells Acre Day Care Center in Malden, Massachusetts; the Wee Care Nursery School in Maplewood, New Jersey; the Fester home-care trial in Dade County, Florida; and many others, all of whom were accused and tried for satanic and sexual abuse of toddlers and many of whose employees were jailed.

As Skenazy and others have pointed out repeatedly, in reality there is no more "stranger danger" for kids now than in the past, and, in fact, most missing kids either run away or are taken by family members, not strangers; similarly, sexual abuse is more likely to occur with someone the child knows than with a stranger off the street. Yet the anxiety persists. And other anxieties, about vaccinations, food allergies, school success, obesity, and a host of other issues, have also emerged, contributing to a perceived need to constantly supervise and hover over children. These anxieties go beyond the fear of strangers, and their roots extend further than the cases of Etan Patz or Adam Walsh or day-care hysteria.

Helicopter parenting relates to the anxieties I mentioned above, but, more than that, it stems from ideologies of parenting that place full responsibility for the child's well-being and future success on parents. Under what Stephanie Coontz refers to as "the myth of parental omnipotence" (225), and Emily Matchar describes as hyperintensive parenting, child rearing not only encompasses the need to supervise children and escort them from one islanded activity to another but also extends to such activities as home schooling, monitoring the child's diet, preparing homemade baby food, wearing the baby in a sling or Baby Bjorn, cosleeping (sharing the bed with your child), home birthing, breastfeeding, resisting vaccinations, sending the child to tutors, working on the child's homework, writing the child's college applications, and other modes of parental micromanagement.

As I articulated in chapter 3, the pressure on mothers especially has been creeping into ideologies of childhood and parenting from at least the 1950s, when mothers were accused of both overparenting their children (momism) and underparenting them (the rejecting mother). As ideas about childhood focused more on issues of the happy personality and individual identity, and less on large-scale social issues such as poverty or schools, the onus for producing healthy and happy children fell increasingly on mothers. The child's self-actualization, her creativity, and her intellectual abilities are all seen to depend on the parent, who must work to draw out and enhance the child's talents (see also Warner, chap. 2). While moms were often critiqued in the 1950s and 1960s for falling down on the job, 1970s popular discourse explicitly linked feminism to the figure of the rejecting mother; and women were chastised even more in the context of the women's liberation movement for seemingly rejecting their role as mothers.

As Matchar notes, the practice of attachment parenting is the fulfillment of this push to make parents, especially mothers, responsible for the child's healthy development. The guru for this form of parenting is Dr. William Sears, author of *The Baby Book* (1992) and *The Attachment Parenting Book* (2001), among many other best sellers. Attachment theory takes the premise of attachment from developmental psychology, which argues that the infant has a biological instinct to seek comfort and safety by proximity to its caregivers (often fathers) and that successful attachment produces a feeling of trust whereas unsuccessful attachment can lead to anxiety. Sears takes this instinctual behavior on the part of the baby and turns it into an active practice for the parent. Sears claims that to form a proper attachment with her baby, the mother must bond with the baby 24-7 through breastfeeding, baby wearing, and cosleeping. Attachment parenting demands that the mother respond to the baby's cues; let the baby eat and sleep on his or her schedule, not the parents' schedule; and always respond to a child's cries, to never let the baby cry it out (Matchar 129–130). While fathers participate in attachment parenting, too, by wearing the baby, cosleeping, following the baby's sleep schedule, etc., Sears tends to emphasize the role of the mother, claiming that the mother has "natural" instincts she must follow and arguing that a mother's work outside the home can be disruptive to the baby's attachment (Matchar 144). Beyond babies, Sears and his family (his sons are also prominent doctors, authors, and experts on TV) have become influential voices in child care more broadly. In magazines, books, and TV shows the Sears family speaks about child care and nutrition, and one son has been a proponent for delaying or avoiding altogether common vaccines.

This model of parenting and ideal of maternity, especially, needs to be understood in the context of feminism. With so much pressure to attach and stay attached, and to manage every facet of your child's life, it is no wonder, then, that Judith Warner finds American women "burdened by a new set of life-draining pressures, a new kind of soul-draining perfectionism" that she terms the "Mommy Mystique." For Warner, contemporary ideologies of motherhood replay the dynamic of Betty Friedan's "feminine mystique" in a postfeminist arena. Attachment parenting operates much like the suburban housewifery Friedan describes insofar as the intensive requirements of it fill the woman's time (e.g., breastfeeding, pumping milk, never sleeping) in ways that eliminate or complicate her ability to work outside the home.

For Matchar, attachment parenting and related forms of hyperintensive parenting and domesticity stem simultaneously from feminism and challenge second-wave models of feminism. On the one hand, Matchar argues, the feminist movement taught women to "question the paternalism of doctors and child rearing experts" (127)—even Spock, who taught women to trust themselves and initiated some of the changes in ideas about parenting that led to hyperintensive parenting. Thus, women turned to women-authored books such as *Our Bodies, Ourselves* (originally printed as a pamphlet in 1970, then commercially published in 1973 by Simon and Schuster) to talk about women's sexuality, reproduction, and other health issues. This opened the door to contemporary women's confidence that they "know better" than doctors on topics such as vaccination or can self-diagnose their child's food allergies (though, ironically, Dr. Sears and sons are widely trusted on these topics, perhaps owing to their emphasis on the woman's own instincts). In addition, feminism led to more women working and being educated, and thus women having fewer kids later in life, so they had more time and greater resources to invest in their child (Matchar 128). On the other hand, contemporary women often feel that second-wave feminism either held up impossible goals (having it all, breaking through the glass ceiling) or produced undesirable outcomes (rejecting domesticity and child care, forgetting home-crafts). While Anne-Marie Slaughter's widely noted 2012 article "Why Women Can't Have It All" in the *Atlantic* argued that women had been fed a set of false promises and that the realities of the workplace did not allow women to "have it all," other texts, such as the knitting manifesto *Stitch 'n Bitch*, Erin Bried's *How to Sew a Button and Other Nifty Things Your Grandmother Knew*, or Cheryl Mendelson's best-selling *Home Comforts: The Art and Science of Keeping House* politicized housekeeping by reclaiming it as a lost art that had been taken away from women by feminists. Using the language of liberal feminism, but asserting different goals, many contemporary women "choose" to be stay-at-home moms, arguing, in some cases, that those who reject house-work are, as Debbie Stoller, editor of *Bust* magazine and author of *Stitch 'n Bitch* argues, "anti-feminist, since they seemed to think that only those things that men did, or had done, were worthwhile" (qtd. in Matchar 169).

Against the stereotype of the "Dropout Wife" that emerged in the 1970s (discussed in chapter 3), we now have "The Opt-Out Revolution," the title of a famous and influential *New York Times* article by Lisa Belkin. The article profiles a group of women of different generations, all of whom graduated from Princeton and got advanced degrees or went into high-powered jobs and all of whom have "opted out" of the workplace. "Why don't women run the world?" Belkin asks. "Maybe it's because they don't want to." The women use the language of cultural feminism, which views gender equality as "gender difference" and claims that we should "honor women's (and men's) natural, inherent natures" (Matchar 141). "This is what I was meant to do," one woman tells Belkin. "I know that's very un-p.c., but I like life's rhythms when I'm nurturing a child." Another woman, discussing her enjoyment of the role of "female/mother/caregiver" says, "I think we were born with these feelings." For Belkin, these women do not represent "the failure of a revolution, but the start of a new one."

As Matchar emphasizes, Belkin's article and the many copycat articles that followed tended to present women's choice to "opt out" as biological, a natural "pull" toward motherhood. Rather than analyzing the causes of her dissatisfaction at work, or demanding changes to the workplace, such as flexible hours, better day care, better leave policies, days off to care for sick kids, and better pay, writers tend to "enshrine stay-at-home parenting as natural and noble" (Matchar 181). But hyperintensive parenting is not limited to stay-at-home opt-out moms. As Warner notes, working moms share "the same high-level at-home parenting ambitions as the nonwork-ing moms. But they held down out-of-home jobs, too—and if this wasn't enough, they also had to shoulder the burden of Guilt, a media-fed drone that played in their ears every time they sat in the traffic at dinnertime: Had they made the right choices? Were their children well-taken care of? Should they be working less, differently, not at all? Were they really good enough mothers?"

My point here is not to rejuvenate the mommy wars, to castigate stay-at-home moms, or even to mourn the loss of liberal feminist goals (well,

maybe the latter, a little). Rather, I am pointing to these contemporary ideologies about parenting, and especially motherhood, to suggest that helicopter parenting emerges at least partially as a response to feminism. And,
more important, I want to suggest that the loss of mobility and freedom
for children goes hand in hand with these changing ideas about parenting
and motherhood.

As I discussed in my introduction, there are myriad ways in which
hyperintensive parenting and the containment of children have been critiqued: as part of the obesity epidemic and as a loss for children—of spatial
knowledge, of how to handle strangers, and of a role in the public sphere.
Most important, perhaps, children lose the autonomy to make choices and
mistakes that enable them to grow; being micromanaged from birth, they
fail to develop basic life skills and they struggle to become mature adults
(Lythcott-Haims). And when children lose these things, adults lose, too.
We lose our own autonomy; we invest our identities in those of our children rather than in ourselves; we measure our worth by their success; and
we lose the ability to trust our kids and truly foster their growth. Also, we
lose a sense of community: as parenting becomes more of a private job, we
lose the "village" that might help us raise our children (Lythcott-Haims,
chap. 10). This is why movements such as free-range parenting are important and why representations of an alternative form of childhood are
important, too, to remind us of other ways of being.

In this book I have looked to representations of the urban child seeking alternatives that might revamp a different model of childhood, and I
have traced ways in which children's mobility became associated with various kinds of neglect, with the power and value of that mobility varying for
different classes and races and genders. Against the veracity of most kids'
experiences in the 1960s and 1970s, I have suggested that at the level of
representation and discourse, white middle-class children's mobility was
already starting to contract and be contained, while African American
urban kids were seen as overly free and undisciplined.

In contemporary representations, it is not hard to find instances of
mobile urban children, but the circumstances that enable the children's
mobility have come to seem extraordinary, by which I mean both out of
the ordinary, even fantastic, and nonnormative. Some books opt for fantasy in order to send children on urban adventures. In the *Magic Tree House*
series of books, for example, the two child protagonists, siblings Jack and
Annie, discover a tree house in the woods near their home in Frog Creek,

Pennsylvania. Once they go inside and open one of the many books in the tree house, they find themselves traveling through space and time. Morgan Le Fay, of Arthurian legend, sends them on numerous adventures and missions to help free people from spells, solve ancient riddles to become Master Librarians, and save ancient stories from being lost forever. Later, the children solve problems for Merlin, the magician. Over the course of more than fifty books they go to Shakespeare's London, 1910s New Orleans, the 1889 World's Fair in Paris, Depression era New York, the ancient city of Edo (now Tokyo) in the 1600s, Da Vinci's Florence, eighteenth-century Vienna, and other urban settings from the historical past. The children use reason and logic to solve problems; they encounter strangers, they navigate strange landscapes and unfamiliar mores; they master their fears, take risks, and accomplish their goals. And their parents are none the wiser, because, while the children go on their extensive and sometimes dangerous journeys, no time passes in Frog Creek. From their parents' perspective, the kids have just stepped outside for a moment before dinner and come straight inside when called.

Other texts manage to represent the urban child by setting their stories in the past. For example, the film *Hugo* (Martin Scorsese 2011), adapted from Brian Selznick's 2007 graphic novel, *The Invention of Hugo Cabret*, is set in early 1930s Paris. Its tale of an orphan boy secretly living in a Paris train station and maintaining the clocks pays homage not only to early cinema, especially the work of Georges Méliès, but also invokes the 1930s films I have discussed here, with their penchant for waifs and orphans and alternative family structures. Orphaned when his father dies in a museum fire, Hugo lives alone secretly in the tunnels of a Paris train station where he maintains the clocks. Finding a notebook and parts of an automaton that his father was building, Hugo tries to restore it. He meets the toy-store owner who works in the train station. Though they initially have a hostile relationship, Hugo eventually discovers that he is the long-thought-dead filmmaker Georges Méliès, whose films Hugo loves and watched with his father, and who is the inventor of the automaton. Eventually, Hugo restores Méliès's career and reputation and forms a new unconventional family with Méliès, his wife, and their goddaughter.

By situating children's mobility within either fantastic narratives or set in the past—*The Magic Tree House* and *Hugo* each do both—writers and filmmakers can, without challenging the mores of contemporary helicopter parenting, portray children having some autonomy, navigating urban landscapes, having encounters, and attaining mastery over their world. These narratives provide an imaginative escape from the everyday rather than a mirror. The popularity and quantity of such texts indicate that children's autonomy still functions as a powerful fantasy, even if it mainly exists outside the realm of most kids' everyday lives.

In contrast to these escapist modes, some contemporary texts mediate the traumatic effects of contemporary living, related to many of the anxieties that color contemporary parenting, such as issues related to the environment (global warming, food scarcity, drought) but also war, terrorism, poverty, and national and global insecurity. In most cases texts displace the trauma of contemporary living into a dystopic future. The figure of the child serves to mediate the trauma, much as the child worked to mediate the traumatic effects of modernity in 1930s films. At the same time, the trauma, in effect, enables a reimagining of childhood. The traumatic imagination—by which I mean a near fetishistic interest in dystopic landscapes, zombie apocalypses, failed government, war, and environmental disasters—seems, on the one hand, an extension of the many everyday anxieties that shape contemporary parenting and, on the other, a way to work through those anxieties and enable the child to imaginatively achieve mastery.

Catastrophic Neglect

Rather than present-tense world historical events, many recent texts portray imaginary traumatic events in dystopic futures.[1] But the dystopic futures of contemporary comics, young adult novels, and films mediate anxieties about the real world, including fears about health, ecology, terrorism, and war. Texts along this line would include *The Walking Dead* graphic novels by Robert Kirkman and the TV adaptation (2010–), *The Divergent* series of books by Veronica Roth and their film adaptations, and *The Hunger Games* series by Suzanne Collins and the four film adaptations of it. Each of these texts, in different ways, forcibly removes children from the sheltering influence of their parents and forces them to adapt and mature, especially through their experience of—and acculturation into— acts of violence. *The Walking Dead*, for example, situates child protagonists amid a zombie apocalypse and shows children being victimized by zombies, turning into zombies, and brutally killing zombies. *Divergent* presents a coming-of-age tale in which teenagers separate from their biological family to join "factions" that reflect their skills and traits; when one faction seeks to gain control, the teens are both victims of violence and engage in violent acts themselves to stage a revolution.

Here I will examine *The Hunger Games* because, unlike *The Walking Dead*, it focuses primarily on a teen, not the adults, and most clearly stages a conflict between children and the city. But much of what I say will apply to the remarkably similar (even derivative) narrative of *Divergent*. The main characters in *The Hunger Games* range in age from twelve to eighteen, so they skew slightly older than the children I have been discussing in this book. But because the Games loom over childhood, and effectively block futurity for children, I include it here.

The premise of *The Hunger Games* is that there has been a series of ecological global catastrophes followed by war and that the newly risen government shut down the war by destroying one area of rebellion, District 13; in the seventy-five years since, the government has staged an annual event that requires each of the remaining twelve districts in the land to send two children, or "tributes," a boy and girl, to a reality-TV game in which the contestants battle to the death.

The Hunger Games is frequently compared to William Golding's *Lord of the Flies* for its representation of child-on-child violence. More surprisingly, perhaps, many people see parallels to *The Wizard of Oz* insofar as both texts show a girl who travels from a drab space of poverty to a wealthy, colorful, and surreal city (including a "horse of a different color" in a pink Afghan); meets a good witch who aids her (Effie in *The Hunger Games*); encounters three male figures who help her on her journey (Haymitch, Cinna, and Peeta in *The Hunger Games*); gets a full beauty makeover; and unseats a powerful leader (The Wizard/President Snow).[2] Visually, certainly, *The Hunger Games* links to Depression-era Kansas in imagery that echoes Dorothea Lange's documentary photographs for the Farm Security Administration. But Dorothy's relationship to Oz, an unknown land in which she functions as an immigrant stranger, differs from that of *The Hunger Games*, in which Katniss travels to the urban capital of her own nation. And whereas *The Wizard of Oz* was initially inspired by such signifiers of modernity as commodity culture and Frank Baum's visit to the White City at the 1893 World's Fair in Chicago, *The Hunger Games* engages concerns about late modern global warming, revolution, and government run amuck. Collins writes that the country Panem "rose up out of the

FIGURE 17. The "horse of a different color" signifies the decadence of the Capitol in *The Hunger Games*.

FIGURE 18. District 12 photographed to look like Depression era photographs, evoking the deep poverty of the citizenry in *The Hunger Games*.

ashes of a place that was once called North America," after "the disasters, the droughts, the storms, the fires, the encroaching seas that swallowed up so much of the land, the brutal war for what little sustenance remained" (*Hunger Games* 18).

The Hunger Games stages an opposition between the city and the child. Throughout the books and films, characters refer to the "Capitol" and the government as one and the same. As Bill Clemente notes, the name *Panem* links the Capitol to the "gladiatorial slaughters" in ancient Rome, *panem et circenses*, "bread and circuses" (21). The Capitol thus links to the corruption, brutality, and extravagance of classical Rome; its name serves as a warning to a "citizenry that had abdicated its political responsibility for the comforts complacency provided" (Clemente 22). The sense of the Capitol's inauthenticity and corruption is rendered visually by the outrageous hair, makeup, and costumes of its inhabitants. The districts surround the Capitol, but people from the districts only ever visit it as tributes (there is no tourism, no business trips, etc.). When they arrive, after the "reaping" that selects tributes, they are treated as commodity and spectacle (Clemente 25). The Capitol differs dramatically from the districts: in terms of contemporary allegory, the wealth of the Capitol evokes the concentration of wealth among the top 1 percent and contrasts markedly with the districts, which signify the 99 percent who hold much less wealth: it is rich, urban, and colorful, and its people are merely observers of the games, not participants; consumers, not makers; well-fed, not starving; whereas the districts are poor, rural, drab, and their people are starving workers whose children are unprotected and victimized by the Capitol.

Furthermore, the Capitol is a highly technologized society whereas the districts seem premodern. In the Capitol we see high-tech body-modification technologies, holograms, television studios, computer imaging, and visual and aural surveillance equipment that tracks and displays the movements of the tributes and other citizens. The Gamekeepers in the Capitol not only design the arena for the yearly Games but can manipulate them at will, controlling fire, water, and wind; sending supplies via parachute drones; and even creating vicious creatures that attack the tributes with a mere swipe of the hand over a remote computer. In contrast, the districts seem to exist in an early or even premodern world. They are each assigned a specific industry. Although the industries include solar power and computers, the districts themselves do not have access to these technologies: they are manufactured for the Capitol. Most districts are linked to more traditional products and modes of life, such as knitwear, textiles, farming, mining, masonry, and fishing. Rather than guns, citizens hunt using bows and arrows, knives, and traps. While the Capitol exists as a consumerist culture of spectacle, the districts barely survive. In part, the imagining of a premodern world fits into contemporary artisan and DIY culture and efforts to get back to nature, traditional crafts, and natural food. And, in part, having the children of Panem live in a premodern world produces a fantasy of disengaging kids from screens and technology. But instead of skipping rope, the children of Panem are imagined as primitives engaged in murder and basic survival skills.

The Hunger Games posits the city—and all attendant manifestations of urbanism—as dangerous for children. If we often think of countries as parental—the motherland, fatherland, or *patris* (from which the notion of patriotism comes)—the Capitol functions as a bad parent. Rather than fostering its children's creativity and intellect, the Capitol denies them their future. The Capitol twists the logic of helicopter parenting into a surveillance state. As Susan Shau Ming Tan suggests, "To be tribute is to be the object of constant surveillance, control and punishment" (89).

The Games depend on a number of contradictory views of children and childhood. As Tan argues, the Games rely, on the one hand, on a romantic or Rousseauian notion of childhood innocence—the child as vulnerable— and, on the other, the child as potentially dangerous, even lethal (85–87). The Games instill fear for children and the desire for their destruction. Against the notion that children are the future, the Games force children to embody the past (Koenig 41): the Games serve as reminder and punishment for the Dark Days of rebellion and are meant to ensure that those days will never happen again. As Katniss glosses the Capitol's message in the novel, "Look how we take your children and sacrifice them and there's nothing you can do. If you lift a finger we will destroy every last one of you. Just as we did in District Thirteen" (Collins, *Hunger Games* 19).

The Games not only complicate views of childhood but also undermine adulthood. Tan argues that they produce "a carnivalesque reversal of family hierarchy" (87). Children can save their family not only by serving as tributes but also by buying "tesserae," getting additional grain and provisions for their family for each extra time their name is added to the reaping lottery. (At sixteen, Katniss's name is in the reaping twenty times; her best friend, Gale, who is eighteen, has his name listed forty-two times [Collins, *Hunger Games* 13].) Adults are "infantilized and disempowered" (Tan 97) and children forced to act as adults.

In *The Hunger Games*, within this global system of disempowering adults, Katniss's mother is viewed as an especial maternal failure. In both the novel and film we learn that when Katniss's father died in a mining accident, her mother, "locked in some dark world of sadness" (Collins, *Hunger Games* 26), became unable to care for Katniss and her sister. Her mother is ineffectual and does not get a job, so at age eleven Katniss has to become mother and father to herself and her sister, Prim. Katniss is helped once by Peeta, now the male tribute, who throws her a loaf of bread when she is starving, and then she learns to gather food and hunt, making her the literal and metaphoric breadwinner. When Katniss (Jennifer Lawrence) volunteers for the Games, to save her sister Prim, whose name is called as tribute, Katniss scolds her mother (Paula Malcomson): "You can't tune out again. . . . No matter what you feel, you have to be there for her." In the novel Katniss says she cannot forgive "the woman who sat by, blank and unreachable, while her children turned to skin and bones" and refers to "all the anger, all the fear I felt at her abandonment" (Collins, *Hunger Games* 9, 35).

Because children have no future, Katniss says repeatedly, "I'm never having kids." She succeeds in the Games, however, by becoming maternal.[3] First, Katniss sacrifices herself for the good of her sister, Prim, and volunteers to be tribute in her place. Then she takes care of Rue (Amandla Stenberg), a competitor at the Games who reminds her of Prim. She feeds her, sleeps with her, and, when Rue is fatally wounded, sings her a lullaby and then covers her corpse with flowers. Katniss's care for Rue and her use of "an old and rarely used gesture of our district, occasionally seen at funerals" (Collins, *Hunger Games* 24), touching three fingers to one's lips and then holding them out, asserts Rue's humanity and initiates the rebellion in Rue's home district. Finally, Katniss cares for Peeta (Josh Hutcherson), the male tribute from her district. Told that two tributes from the same district will be allowed to win if they survive, Katniss nurses a wounded and weak Peeta back to health, feeds him, and protects him, as she is a much better warrior than he.

Of course, these maternal acts, while seemingly sincere, are also part of Katniss's performance for the viewing audience—including potential sponsors who will help her succeed. As Haymitch (Woody Harrelson) advises Katniss to pretend to be likable and to play up the star-crossed lover theme with Peeta; as Cinna (Lenny Kravitz) dresses her to make an impact as the "girl on fire"; as we see her waxed and buffed and made up by her "team"; and as we see her learn that kissing Peeta wins her sponsors and aid, we understand that Katniss is performing a role. She is not lying, but she is engaged in a masquerade. If, as Joan Riviere has famously suggested, "genuine womanliness" and the masquerade or "mask of womanliness" are "the same thing" (38), then perhaps Katniss's performance of maternity and her performance of childhood are both "genuine" and a mask.

Ultimately, when the "arenas have been completely destroyed, the memorials built," Katniss, reluctantly, after fifteen years, becomes a mother. She and Peeta have two children and ponder how to "tell them about the world without frightening them to death" (Collins, *Mockingjay*, epilogue). The children of Panem, no longer punished for the past, will nonetheless have to confront the past and face the trauma of knowing. Although machines from the Capitol break new ground to construct a factory for medicine in their district, Katniss still lives an agrarian life: "Peeta bakes. I hunt.... The Meadow turns green again" (Collins, *Mockingjay*, pt. 2, chap. 27).

Extremely Close

While most contemporary texts displace trauma into a dystopic future, Jonathan Safran Foer's 2005 novel *Extremely Loud and Incredibly Close* and its 2011 film adaptation, directed by Stephen Daldry, represent directly traumatic world historical events and their aftereffects. *Extremely Loud and Incredibly Close* addresses the traumatic effects of 9/11 by focusing on the experience of a young boy, Oskar Schell, whose father dies in the World Trade Center collapse. The boy experiences both the collective trauma of 9/11, as one who lives in New York City and sees the events unfolding around him and on TV, and the personal trauma of losing his father. The novel links the events and traumatic effects of 9/11 to the Allied fire-bombing of Dresden at the end of World War II by interweaving Oskar's narrative with the stories of his grandmother and grandfather, both of whom survived Dresden and came to America (see Bardizbanian) and both of whom lost loved ones in the bombings. The story links the personal traumas of each individual to the collective national and global trauma of the two moments of urban devastation.

The novel uses experimental techniques, inserting blank pages, photographs, typescript marked up in red, x'd out type, and other elements that variously represent not only Oskar's subjectivity and memories, including a scrapbook of "things that have happened to me" and letters he has written to famous people and their replies (Stephen Hawking, Jane Goodall, et al.), but also his grandparents' subjectivity. The inclusion of his grandparents' story illuminates the problematic of articulating traumatic experience, and the experience of alienation and melancholia attendant on trauma, as Oskar's grandmother attempts to type an autobiography on a typewriter with no ribbon, his grandfather writes but never delivers letters to the son he abandoned, the grandfather writes notes that substitute for speech (as he lost the ability to speak after Dresden), and the grandparents attempt to create Nothing spaces that are spaces of safety (Bardizbanian 302–305).

The film intercuts flashbacks to fill out Oskar's story, and especially to showcase his father, but streamlines the grandparents' narrative and places all of Oskar's images in a book he compiles near film's end. The film barely references Dresden and significantly cuts the role of Oskar's grandmother; it focuses more on the boy's efforts to cope with his trauma from "the worst day." It is a more conventional narrative than the book, more confident in the ability to speak trauma and work through it, and offers a much stronger sense of closure. The film shifts attention from the difficulty of speaking or writing trauma and the sense of connectedness among historical events and collective traumas to more narrowly focus on the affective dimension of trauma, its impact on the individual personality. The film is also more confident in the "cure" and in the ability to work through trauma and achieve closure.

In addition to linking Dresden and 9/11, both the novel and film further intertwine a fantastic story of loss that serves an allegorical function: the story of the Sixth Borough of New York. This story is one that Oskar's father tells him the night before he is killed. The Sixth Borough was once "an island, separated from Manhattan by a thin body of water whose narrowest crossing happened to equal the world's long jump record" (Foer 217). Its existence was celebrated each year when the world-record holder would jump from Manhattan to the Sixth Borough, and "every New Yorker felt capable of flight" (Foer 218). The island starts to drift away, making the jump harder and harder, until eventually the jumper can't make the distance and falls. Eventually, the borough floats away, leaving behind only Central Park, which is forcibly pulled into Manhattan from the floating borough. The story of the Sixth Borough functions as a displacement of the story of 9/11, as a story of a disappeared population, severed phone lines, and, above all, a falling man. As Oskar (Thomas Horn) notes near the end of the film, making clear the link between the borough and both the Twin Towers and his father, "They tried to save it, but they couldn't. It's never coming back."

The story of the Sixth Borough is also a rehearsal for Oskar's quest in the novel, as he seeks clues to his father. His father tells him the story to generate what he and Oskar call a Reconnaissance Expedition, a Sunday game in which Oskar is sent on a scavenger hunt in Central Park. The unfinished Reconnaissance Expedition for the Sixth Borough sends Oskar into Central Park to find evidence of the lost borough. When his father dies, Oskar is left with a note his father had written: a newspaper clipping with a typo circled in red that that says, "notstop looking." Oskar creates his own Reconnaissance Expedition as a means of dealing with his traumatic loss and takes "notstop looking" as his mantra. A year after his father's death, Oskar finds a blue vase at the top of his father's closet and, inside it, a manila envelope with the word "Black" written on it and a key inside. Convinced that this key is, materially, the key to his father—to somehow bring him closer to his father so that he can more fully say good-bye—Oskar sets out an elaborate plan to meet every person in the five boroughs of New York named Black to find out what the key fits and what it means.

The Reconnaissance Expedition designed by Oskar's father, Thomas (Tom Hanks), is a sort of free-range parenting exercise intended to help Oskar overcome his fears, which are many and increase after 9/11. Pre-9/11, his fears include talking to strangers, swings, elevators, and public transportation; after 9/11 they expand to include old people, running people, airplanes, tall things, "things you can get stuck in," bags without owners, children without parents, towers, tunnels, and especially bridges. Thomas Schell designs the expedition to force Oskar to address his fear of talking to strangers, especially. "I'm gonna send him all over the park," Thomas tells his wife, Linda (Sandra Bullock) (never called anything but Mom in the film), "and he'll have to talk to every person he meets." When his wife questions whether the expedition might be "too hard," Thomas answers with a rhetorical question, "What kind of adult is he going to be?"

On the surface the expedition Oskar designs for himself fulfills his father's goal of helping the boy to become more independent and less fearful. Oskar's quest forces him to talk to hundreds of strangers named Black and to travel all over the city by himself. Many of the people Oskar meets are grappling with their own loss, and each has a story to tell, just like Oskar. He meets lonely people and people with large families. He meets a couple who each maintain a museum of the other person, treasuring each artifact as a souvenir of the one they love. He meets a woman who moved to the top of the Empire State Building when her husband died and has not left since.

In the novel Oskar quickly gets a partner to travel with him. When he goes to see the fifth person named Black, ordered alphabetically by first name, he finds him just one floor above him in the same building (Foer 151–168). This Mr. Black has his own unfinished mourning: he lost his wife twenty-four years ago, has not left the apartment since, and hammers a nail into his bed every day that she is gone. (He has had to reinforce the

FIGURE 19. Oskar faces his fear and runs across the Brooklyn Bridge in *Extremely Loud and Incredibly Close*.

FIGURE 20. Oskar introduces himself to Abby Black, showing his "business card" in *Extremely Loud and Incredibly Close*.

apartment's structure to prevent collapse under the weight of the bed.) When Oskar asks why, he says he does not know but that it "keeps me going!" (Foer 162). Oskar invites him to join the quest and he agrees, leaving the house for the first time and traveling with Oskar all over the city for weeks. Mr. Black helps Oskar confront some of his fears—he forces him to take the Staten Island Ferry, for example—but he also provides company and security for Oskar's travels for six and a half months.

The film emphasizes Oskar's independence much more strongly. He does not meet the Mr. Black in his building, and he performs the quest alone for months. We see Oskar confront his fear of crossing the Brooklyn Bridge alone. Gathering his courage, he runs across the bridge, shaking a tambourine he uses for comfort, and yelling his destination, "Fort Greene!" A montage of his expeditions shows him walking alone on city streets, knocking on strangers' doors, telling strangers his story, and listening to theirs. We see him with people of different ages, races, and genders. He accepts beverages from the various Blacks, participates in a religious ceremony at one house, visits a horse stable in another, meets kids, and receives hugs.

In addition to the mobility shown when Oskar is on his expedition, the film also shows him sneaking out of his apartment building twice in the middle of the night. Both incidents are scenes that occur during the day in the book. The film's choice to set them in nighttime makes Oskar's daring walks seem more surprising and risky. In one we see Oskar sneak out and run to a convenience store to buy a new answering machine. At home he switches it with the one his family owns because he is trying to hide the fact that his father called six times on 9/11, including one last time just before the World Trade Center fell, when Oskar was home but froze without picking up the phone. The other time, Oskar goes to see his grandmother, who lives across the street. Accustomed to waking her in the middle of the night to talk via a walkie-talkie, Oskar becomes concerned when one night she does not answer. He goes to her apartment and meets "the renter," a mysterious figure his grandmother keeps hidden. It turns out that the renter is Oskar's grandfather who had abandoned Thomas Schell before he was born and has returned on learning of his son's death. Viewing him as a safe stranger, Oskar tells him his secret about the answering machine.

Eventually, in both book and film, the grandfather accompanies Oskar on his quest. In the book the grandfather tells Mr. Black who he is, so Mr. Black leaves Oskar, to enable the grandfather to take over; and Mr. Black goes to live with the woman named Black who lives on top of the Empire State Building. In the film the grandfather (Max von Sydow) offers to help Oskar after their midnight meeting, without revealing his identity. In the film Oskar's grandfather pushes him to confront his fears. He forces him to take public transportation. At a houseboat he makes Oskar cross a rickety wooden footbridge and then ducks into a bar so that Oskar has to cross back on his own and find him.

In the end Oskar miraculously solves the mystery of the key. Oskar finds out that his father went to an estate sale at the phone number of one of the first Blacks he met, a woman named Abby (Viola Davis). Abby, now divorced, brings Oskar to the office of her husband, William. Oskar learns from William (Jeffrey Wright) that the key opens a safe deposit box that belonged to *his* father and that he has been searching for Oskar's father to get it back. Although finding the key does not reveal anything about Oskar's father—aside from the fact that he had purchased a blue vase for his wife and planned an anniversary dinner—Oskar is able to move on. He reworks a series of photos of a man falling from the World Trade Center—an image he had imagined might be his father—and, in a flip book, shows the man falling up, to arrive safely back in the building. In the film he writes a letter to all the Blacks he met, thanking them and letting them know the end result, and tells them that he now knows he cannot bring his father back. Oskar also writes to his grandfather, who had left again, and invites him back home, reuniting him with his grandmother.[4] In the film's final shots Oskar braves the swings and is caught in a buoyant freeze-frame in midair, another positive reworking of the falling-man image.

Extremely Loud and Incredibly Close shows a boy overcoming his fears to achieve some mastery over the world by leaving home and connecting with the world on his own. Instead of a celebration of Oskar's autonomy and mastery, however, the text reveals a deception that undermines Oskar's autonomy by showing his mother to have been micromanaging his quest all along.

Earlier, we learn that Oskar has a distant relationship with his mother. In the book he thinks it would be nice if an ambulance could flash the names of people the injured person knew, ranking them according to who "the person loved the most, or the person who loved *him* the most" (Foer 72; emphasis mine). Oskar ranks the people in his life and places his mother third, after his dad and grandma, signaling either that he loves her less than he loves them or perceives her as loving him less than they do. In the book, resentful that his mother seems to be moving on because she has a male friend, Ron, with whom she laughs, Oskar tells her, "If I could have chosen, I would have chosen you" (Foer 171). The film eliminates Ron—whom the mother has met in a grief recovery support group—and any sign that the mother is moving on. Until the end of the film we mainly see her in the apartment, except a flashback scene that shows her getting a call from Thomas at her office before the Towers fall. Nonetheless, Oskar still cruelly accuses her of bad mothering. When she asks him why he can't talk to her about things, he answers, "In case you haven't noticed, half the time you

FIGURE 21. Oskar's mother explores his secret plans and documents.

are asleep and the other half the time you forget about the first half. You're what they call in the law *in absentia*. An absent parent." In both novel and film, then, the child views the mother as neglectful: in the book because she claims her own needs (for a friend, for release, for her own therapy) and in the film because she doesn't, because she is too lost in her grief to care for her son. When Oskar yells in the film, "I wish it were you. I wish it were you in the building instead of him," she answers, "So do I."

The mother is redeemed in a sleight of hand at the end of the text that reveals that she has not been neglectful but secretly micromanaging Oskar's expedition. "I know how proud your dad would have been that you didn't stop looking," she says. In the book a call from Abby Black alerts her to Oskar's quest. In the film she figures it out on her own when she learns that he has borrowed phone books from the doorman. She goes into Oskar's bedroom, rummages through his belongings, and figures out his plan; she makes her own maps of his trips and her own list of Blacks. She calls the ones he met so far on his first day, and then she visits in advance each of the rest. She meets each one, explains Oskar's story, and asks them to be nice to him. At a construction site, for example, she tells the workers to let him play on the equipment; and they do. Rather than dismiss parental anxiety, the film commends it. Oskar asks, "You were never worried that I was going to be raped or killed or strangled or stabbed or something?" His mother answers, "Every minute of every day. I couldn't breathe until the door closed." But instead of copping to anxiety because he is independent of her, she asserts her presence. "Sweetie," she says, "do you think I would

FIGURE 22. Mother and son finally achieve closeness in *Extremely Loud and Incredibly Close*.

ever let you out of my sight? Do you think I would let anything happen to you? I always knew where you were, always." Rather than resentful that his mother meddled and that his hard-won autonomy was false, Oskar seems pleased to learn that his mother could think like him and know him well. This, as much or more than solving the mystery of the key, enables him to move on, because he now has a closeness to his mother that was lacking. *Extremely Loud and Incredibly Close*, then, reasserts the primacy of attachment parenting to enable the child to feel secure in the face of trauma. Despite the fact that Oskar's father promoted some form of free-range parenting, the text suggests that parenting "in absentia" is unacceptable.

The Hunger Games presents a story of female empowerment as a disobedient or defiant girl leads a revolution against an unjust government.[5] *Extremely Loud and Incredibly Close* shows a boy overcoming his fears to achieve mastery over his world, leaving home to encounter others. Both these texts imagine children who are competent, mobile, and somewhat autonomous in an urban context. But they can only imagine the child's empowerment in the context of catastrophe and the breakdown of the social order. And both imagine the child's mother as, in some way, an absent or rejecting mother. These texts conjoin a fantasy of maternal neglect with one of societal failure.

Each of these texts needs to be read not only in the context of contemporary trauma and catastrophe—as reflections and refractions of contemporary concerns over war, terrorism, global warming, and more—but also in the context of changing ideas of childhood and parenting. As I have argued, ideas of childhood, neglect, and the child's relation to the city have changed dramatically in the last century. Our collective nostalgia tells us that children were more innocent in the early twentieth century than they are now, but the discourse on children and representations of them, in films, comics, and popular fiction, tell a different story. Texts from the 1930s tell us that kids were once perceived as knowing, available to encounter, as streetwise, as agents of change, as inhabitants of the streets—as available to influence, sure, but also as influential. Midcentury, kids were still imagined as mobile agents in the city, but ideas about parenting and motherhood began to shift, to contain kids somewhat more and view mothers, especially, as responsible for the child's happiness. African American kids were viewed differently from white kids—their future much less certain, their happiness less secure. Now we imagine our kids as less innocent but keep them more protected, more contained. Yet in films and fictions we place them in extreme jeopardy and scenes of catastrophe.

Imagining disaster—abductions, evil day-care providers, strangers as danger, evil doctors, food allergies—we have imagined our children as helpless victims and sought to contain them. I am not suggesting that we abandon our children or that we give up efforts to protect them. But we need to reconsider what we are protecting them from, and how. What would it look like to imagine an urban child who is mobile and free without imagining such a scenario as our failure? And what if we stopped blaming mothers for abandoning children and viewed parenting as something other than constant supervision and self-abnegation? What if we thought of parenting as shepherding rather than micromanaging? Rather than project our fantasies of empowerment into a dystopic future, what if we imagined children in the present as empowered, capable citizens? Throughout this book I have examined representations of the urban child in order to provide a different vantage on both childhood and the urban; to recover and revive different models, different ways of imagining childhood, parenting, and children's place in the city; and to begin to map a different future.

Notes

Introduction: Mapping the Urban Child

1 In more insidious cases than Skenazy's, in recent years, numerous parents have been arrested for letting their children go "free range." Parents in Maryland were found guilty of neglect for letting their eight- and ten-year-old walk home from the park without parents (Wergin); a Florida mom was arrested for letting her seven-year-old son walk alone to the park, a half mile from home (Caulfield); and a South Carolina mother was arrested for letting her nine-year-old go to a park while she worked at McDonald's nearby (Friedersdorf).

2 The *Oxford English Dictionary* dates the term *helicopter parent* back to the 1980s, "from the notion of the parent 'hovering like a helicopter' over the child or children" (www.oxforddictionaries.com/us/definition/american_english/helicopter-parent). Julia Lythcott-Haims dates it to 1990 and claims that child development researchers Foster Cline and Jim Fay coined the term. The metaphor may have earlier origins. In the 1969 book *Between Parent and Teenager*, by Haim G. Ginott, a teenager complains, "Mother hovers over me like a helicopter and I'm fed up with her noise and hot air. I think I'm entitled to sneeze without an explanation" (18).

3 Robin Wood claims that "in American film the Child has his full meaning only in relation to" the family (201).

4 Galia Benziman views neglect as a key trope of nineteenth-century literature. Rather than urbanism or questions of the child's mobility, she focuses on ways in which narratives of neglect serve to shape "the interiority of the literary child" (16) as "the oppressed and/or abandoned child serves as a major site for exploring the development of one's interiority as valuable, vulnerable, and in constant need of protection" (17). In this sense neglect comes to be seen as "formative for the adult-to-be," a "shaping ordeal" (143).

5 James Kincaid views neglect narratives, as well as narratives of abuse and molestation, as going hand in hand with the alignment of childhood with happiness and innocence. In this sense neglect is the denial of happiness: "we are obsessed with its denial, with the outrageous withholding of happiness" (*Erotic Innocence* 282).

6 The original program, Aid to Dependent Children (ADC), was created as part of the Social Security Act of 1935 to dispense relief to single mothers. In 1962 the program name changed to Aid to Families with Dependent Children (AFDC) to reflect changes to the law that allowed aid to children with two parents "if unemployment forced the family income below what the state deemed essential" (Ashby 129).

7 Over time, in much discourse, the phrase "urban child" has come to signify poor, nonwhite children in ghettos; whereas "city kid" tends to be reserved for predominantly white, middle- to upper-class children in gentrified areas. My analysis links them but acknowledges that the reformist view tends to be used for the urban poor.

8 Imagination Playground website, www.imaginationplayground.com/images/content/3/4/3492/Mission-Brochure.pdf.

9 In *Precocious Children and Childish Adults* Claudia Nelson discusses the dominance of the "old-fashioned" child, or children who seem like "pocket versions of adults" (12) in Victorian literature beyond Dickens. She argues that such children "draw attention to the dark as well as the brilliant side of progress" (13).

10 Benziman claims that Dickens's concerns about the institutional neglect of children only extend to those children, like Oliver, who are granted a known biography, history, and interiority. She claims that this "narrative preoccupation with the interiority of the privately neglected child-as-self obscures the concern for working class children and their social neglect. The latter are either marginalized to the degree of narrative disappearance, or undergo a massive process of othering by being represented as repellent or threatening figures" (151).

11 Gornick, for example, describes her first childhood encounters with Manhattan from her home in the Bronx as one of indeterminate class: "These people I could see weren't working class, but what class *were* they?" (12). She notes broad differences in affect and behavior: "It was the boldness of gesture and expression everywhere that so captivated us: the stylish flirtation, the savvy exchange, people sparking witty, exuberant responses in one another, in themselves" (13). For Gornick these differences are aspirational and identity forming: she becomes a Manhattanite.

12 Joe Sutliff Sanders argues that in the nineteenth-century Golden Age of children's literature, the lines between adult and children's reading, and indeed between men's and women's, or boys' and girls', had yet to form (181–183). This related not only to shared public reading practices, and adults reading with children, but also to independent reading of children's books by both male and female adults. The blurriness between readerships at the dawn of marketing to children suggests that perhaps the boundaries between age-based readers have always been more imagined than real.

13 Blurring the lines between child and adult texts from a different vantage point, Marah Gubar makes a case for understanding popular nineteenth-century theater as children's theater. Arguing against the notion that children's theater was a niche specialty or only began with the arrival of the play *Peter Pan* in New York in 1905, Gubar claims that children were active participants as performers, subjects, and audience in popular theater as a whole ("Entertaining Children").

Chapter 1   Boys, Movies, and City Streets; or, The Dead End Kids as Modernists

1   In Lowry's reading Hines bridges the gap between late Victorian humanitarianism and modernist "straight" photography, thus producing a form of sentimental modernism (188).

2   Ben Highmore similarly calls for "hopscotch modernism," an "expanded understanding of modernism, an understanding that would include sociology, anthropology, and psychoanalysis, not as intellectual materials *informing* modernism, but as modernist practices themselves" (71).

3   My analysis of the Dead End Kids' performance of urbanism is indebted to Erving Goffman.

4   For the sake of simplicity I will call this the Lower East Side. The Kids' particular neighborhood is never named. *Dead End* situates the kids at Sutton Place and East Fifty-Third Street, but the particularities of this address—its juxtaposition of rich and poor—are not typical of the cycle. The Kids could be in East Harlem, another white ethnic ghetto. However, as they later become the East Side Kids and Bowery Boys, and since the Bowery was initially part of what was then referred to as the Lower East Side, assuming the Lower East Side seems apt. In at least one film after *Dead End*, they live near what is labeled Dock Street, so proximity to the East River can be assumed. Gorcey speaks in a Brooklyn accent, which further confuses the setting.

5   In *The Roaring Twenties* (Raoul Walsh 1939), similarly—not a Dead End Kids film but another in the series of Warner Bros. crime films starring Cagney and Bogart that buttress the cycle—the rather strange image of two girls dancing on the sidewalk also establishes the milieu of the Lower East Side.

6   After *Dead End*, Samuel Goldwyn sold the Kids' contracts to Warner Bros., supposedly because they were so troublesome on set. After the early cycle of films I discuss, the Little Tough Guys move to Universal, and the East Side Kids head to Monogram Pictures. See Klein (62) and Getz.

7   In a lovely description of Nigel Henderson's photographs of children playing in the street, Ben Highmore writes: "Spontaneity and play mark this mystic urban writing pad" (70).

8   Getz (52) notes that in *On Dress Parade* (William Clemens 1939) Gorcey is given a female name, Shirley, that is shortened to *Slip*. The name *Slip* stays with Gorcey throughout the Bowery Boy films. In the East Side Kids, also, his character has a female-sounding given name, Ethelbert, though his character goes by Muggs.

9   Cressey's manuscript is, perhaps, an instance of the "hopscotch modernism" Highmore describes in its sociological and anthropologic attention to all aspects of everyday life (see note 2).

10   Cressey's attention to traffic opens up an arena that the Dead End Kids films elide. Traffic accidents are not a dominant trope of child films in the 1930s—though a car accident kills one boy in Jackie Coogan's *Boy of the Streets*, and who can forget the cruel car accident that kills the daughter in *The Crowd* (King Vidor 1928)? But traffic is an important component in the discourse on urban children and neglect. Zelizer discusses the rise of vehicular accidents as a key component of the playground movement. Between 1910 and 1914 and as late as 1927, 40 percent of traffic accidents involved kids getting hit, and mortality rates were very high. By the 1930s,

despite the increase in car accidents overall, the rate of accidents involving children decreased (Zelizer 33–35). Even so, poor immigrant kids were still more vulnerable than middle-class kids to traffic accidents, and their parents were often blamed as being "neglectful" (Zelizer 47).

Chapter 2   Shirley Temple as Streetwalker: Girls, Streets, and Encounters with Men

1   Gaylyn Studlar argues in *Precocious Charms* that the juvenation of girls is a long-term process that occurs from the silent era to the 1960s.

2   Male child-loving is certainly not unique to the context of the American Depression but has antecedents across the nineteenth century. Joe Sutliff Sanders considers the girl's "disciplining" of the adult male a key trope of American orphan girl narratives of the nineteenth century linked to earlier sentimental novels. Catherine Robson identifies "the idealization and idolization of little girls" as a dominant aspect of the Victorian era. For Robson the "intimate relationship between middle-class men and little girls in nineteenth-century British culture . . . cannot be thought of without reference to a pervasive fantasy of male development in which men become masculine only after an initial feminine stage. In this light, little girls represent not just the true essence of childhood, but an adult male's best opportunity of reconnecting with his own lost self" (3). James Kincaid situates the imagined eroticized relationship between adult males and young girls as central to Victorian culture and beyond (*Child Loving*). In a different vein Leslie Elaine Frost reads Temple's relation to her father in *The Little Princess* as redeeming masculine service to mobilize British home-front patriotism under the threat of fascism (122–125). Each of these readings points to a pervasive but variable trope of adult male relationships with girls. Along with Hatch and Studlar, I argue that this trope registers differently in the context of the American Depression and its discourses on masculinity and childhood.

3   IMDb and most references to this film title it *Kid in Hollywood* or *Kid 'n Hollywood*, but the film's title card clearly reads *Kiddin' Hollywood*.

4   Laura Mulvey describes the male gaze as central to classical Hollywood's gendering of the image. The male gaze relates most specifically to eyeline matches that show a male character's point-of-view shot of a woman, but it also encompasses ways in which women are costumed, framed, and made-up to appear sexually available or "to-be-looked-at."

5   In Vered's reading a similar process of erasure occurs in Temple's star text, as the role of Bill Robinson in her career is elided in promotional materials.

6   The recent film *Annie* (Will Gluck 2014), starring Quvenzhané Wallis, situates the action in the present, creating a parallel between our contemporary recessionary period of austerity and the Depression. Whereas, in the 1976 musical and its film adaptation, Annie meets Franklin Delano Roosevelt, in the 2014 version Annie gives a school report on the New Deal president, claiming that the Depression was "pretty much like now, but without the Internet."

7   Many people assume that Gray took the name from the 1885 poem. "Little Orphan Annie" (called "Little Orphant Annie" until a typo switched the word to "Orphan"), by James Whitcomb Riley. Riley's poem was based on an orphan taken in by his family in Indianapolis:

Little Orphant Annie's come to our house to stay,
An' wash the cups an' saucers up, an' brush the crumbs away,
An' shoo the chickens off the porch, an' dust the hearth, an' sweep,
An' make the fire, an' bake the bread, an' earn her board-an'-keep;
An' all us other children, when the supper-things is done,
We set around the kitchen fire an' has the mostest fun
A-list'nin' to the witch-tales 'at Annie tells about . . .

8 Joanne Hall reads Annie as a female hobo (42–44) and cites a 1926 sequence in the strip in which Annie literally becomes a hobo, crossdressing as "Dannie." See Gray 1:309–319. While the term "female hobo" captures Annie's mobility, it does not fully account for her movement in and out of homes or her constantly changing familial and economic status.

9 The word or name *Daddy* is always in quotation marks in the comic strip. For Joanne Hall this signifies "the lack of blood ties between Annie and her adopted father" (42).

10 The arrival of Annie's Indian protector Punjab in 1935 adds diversity but removes the strip somewhat from its realist form; rather than represent aspects of the melting pot, it moves the strip into a world of fantasy. See Heer, "Punjab and Politics" 5.

11 This plotline echoes Little Orphan Annie's hobo episode in which she also disguises herself as a boy and travels with an older male hobo. See note 8.

12 In an earlier essay I read *The Wizard of Oz* as a queer road movie. See Robertson, "Home and Away."

13 Against this view Ina Rae Hark argues that the film contains Dorothy's "home-leaving" fantasy in a gendered project of containment.

Chapter 3 Neglect at Home: Rejecting Mothers and Middle-Class Kids

1 In England, similarly, postwar child advocates shifted their attention to children's happiness. The 1948 Children Act "endowed children with subjective rights, such as the right to happiness and a loving, supportive family environment" (Kozlovsky 176).

2 In England Katie Nana's leaving would likely have resonated with readers for whom being "servantless" had been a cause for anxiety, parody, feminist critique, and more from the early twentieth century forward. As Lucy Delap explains, the nanny represents a transitional figure of sorts between the taken-for-granted dominance of domestic servants and being servantless. Delap writes, "The 'nanny' had been an upper class institution, but became more widely employed in twentieth-century middle-class households, while retaining a social distance from 'servantdom.' Nannies hovered on the cusp of being servants, or being social equals with a professional status" (108).

3 The film *Saving Mr. Banks* (John Lee Hancock 2013) egregiously renders the narrative as reflecting P. J. Travers's own neglect, linking the need to "save" Mr. Banks to her feelings of abandonment by her father—a failed banker, a drunk, and a gambler—and her feelings of guilt that she was unable to save him. This film cares little for the mother and instead makes Walt Disney a substitute savior father-figure

for Travers. Travers is seen overcoming her animosity to the film only when Mr. Banks is "saved" by the screenplay to become a better father at film's end; and Travers embraces Disney to the point of sleeping with a giant Mickey Mouse cuddly toy in her London home.

4 These scenes are eerily echoed a decade later in *Baby Boom* (Charles Shyer 1987), a film about a career-driven woman—one who has rejected the role of mother altogether—who suddenly becomes caretaker for an infant and has to discover the joys of motherhood in opposition to careerism.

5 For Sonya Sawyer Fritz, Harriet's mobility depends on economic privilege. Fritz notes that Sport does not have the same luxury of mobility because he is tied to the apartment, where he serves as his father's caretaker. I would argue, however, that Janie is also wealthy and less mobile than Harriet because her passions lead her to stay home and work in her "lab." Rather than economics determining mobility in the book, it may be that economics determines the child's labor. Where Sport must perform housework for his single father, Harriet and Janie are free to engage in imaginative play versions of "work," being a detective and a scientist, respectively. The "work" of each of the three kids challenges gender stereotypes.

Chapter 4 "The Odds Are against Him": Archives of Unhappiness among Black Urban Boys

1 My chapter is indebted to Massood's book, *Making a Promised Land*, not only for her claims about representations of black urban youth but also because her discussion led me to consider *The Quiet One*, *The Street*, and *The Cool World* here. I hope that the different emphasis of my work complements rather than duplicates her important analyses of Harlem representations.

2 The film's credits list Agee as writing "commentary and dialogue." The Internet Movie Database claims that it was written by Agee and Levitt, and, uncredited, Meyers and Loeb. According to Massood, Levitt and Agee wrote the screenplay, but Agee wrote the dialogue and voice-over. Two contemporary newspaper accounts do not mention Agee at all and instead attribute the screenplay to Loeb and Levitt and highlight the role of Meyers and Levitt's brother, William, who served as associate producer (Adams, Pryor). According to Pryor, Wiltwyck's female psychiatric consultant, Dr. Viola Bernard, also worked with the writers.

3 Opened in 1936 as a school for African American delinquent boys under the leadership of the Episcopal City Mission Society, Wiltwyck nearly closed in 1942 because of a lack of funding. At that time, with Eleanor Roosevelt's help, Wiltwyck was reorganized, secularized, and opened to boys of all races.

4 Massood claims that Thompson is a resident of Wiltwyck (107), but, according to Pryor, he is a "gifted child," "the complete opposite of the maladjusted child he portrays," and he goes to a school in the city (see also Adams). Donald's father allowed him to shoot only on weekends and holidays to avoid missing classes (Pryor).

5 Levitt and Loeb are both credited with documentary segments, whereas Bagley is credited as the film's cinematographer. These scenes seem to combine documentary footage with scenes that may be shot by Bagley. I am attributing these shots to Levitt because they resemble her still photography.

6 My analysis will be limited to the novel and film as I do not have access to any detailed information about the play.

Chapter 5   Helicopters and Catastrophes:
The Failure to Neglect and Neglect as Failure

1   Exceptions that do represent present-tense world historical events would be child soldier films such as *Blood Diamond* (Edward Zwick 2006) and *War Witch* (Kim Nguyen 2012), but these are set in Africa, not the United States, and are outside my purview here.

2   On the links between *The Hunger Games* and *The Wizard of Oz* see, for example, www.redfeatherjournal.org/uploads/Hunger_Games_Review4.pdf; www.reddit. com/r/WritingPrompts/comments/2mv510/ff_hunger_games_vs_wizard_of_oz_ parallels/; http://bblitandmediastudies.blogspot.com/2013/08/wizard-of-oz-vs-hunger-games.html; http://artdomannie.blogspot.com/2013/11/hunger-games-meets-oz.html.

3   Katie Arosteguy refers to Katniss's maternal acts as "othermothering," or mothering outside the bounds of biological mothering (155).

4   The film diverges significantly from the book in relation to Oskar's grandparents. In the novel the grandmother and grandfather have a complicated relationship, related to their experience in the war and also the grandfather's love for the grandmother's sister, who died in Dresden. Before he abandons the family, the grandfather spends time sitting in the international terminal at the airport. When he leaves a second time in the novel, after meeting Oskar, the grandmother finds him there and joins him. Their permanent liminal space matches that of the woman who lives atop the Empire State Building and Mr. Black's apartment, signaling an inability to find closure but a way of coping.

5   In "The Lady or the Tiger?" Claudia Nelson links Katniss to a long tradition of principled nonconformist girl citizens in literature.

Bibliography

Adams, Marjory. "Four Who Made 'The Quiet One' Are New Toasts of Film World." *Daily Boston Globe* 10 May 1949: 8. *ProQuest*.

Ahmed. Sara. *The Promise of Happiness*. Durham, NC: Duke UP, 2010.

Alexander, Ruth M. *The "Girl Problem": Female Sexual Delinquency in New York, 1900–1930*. Ithaca, NY: Cornell UP, 1995.

"All Dolled Up! Childhood Star Jane Withers Tours the Nation with Her Dolls … One Last Time." *PR Newswire* 9 June 2004: www.prnewswire.com/news-releases/all-dolled-up-74906212.html.

Alt, Herschel. "In Defense of Mothers." *Parents Magazine* Feb. 1950: 26.

Anthony, E. James, and Therese Benedek, eds. *Parenthood: Its Psychology and Psychopathology*. Boston: Little, Brown, 1970.

Arosteguy, Katie. "'I have a kind of power I never knew I possessed': Transformative Motherhood and Maternal Influence." Garriott, Jones, and Tyler 146–159.

Ashby, LeRoy. *Endangered Children: Dependency, Neglect, and Abuse in American History*. New York: Twayne, 1997.

Atkinson, Michael. "Our Man in London: The Nuanced and Endlessly Suggestive Film Criticism of Graham Greene." *Moving Image Source*. Astoria, NY: Museum of the Moving Image. 21 August 2009. www.movingimagesource.us/articles/our-man-in-london-20090821.

Baldwin, James. "Fifth Avenue, Uptown." *Esquire* July 1960: 70–76.

Bardizbanian, Audrey. "Writing Post-Traumatic Memories, Writing the City: Jonathan Safran Foer's *Extremely Loud and Incredibly Close*." *Mapping Generations of Traumatic Memory in American Narratives*. Ed. Dana Mihailescu, Roxana Oltean, and Mihaela Precup. Cambridge: Cambridge Scholars, 2014. 300–319.

Barrie, J. M. *Peter Pan: "Peter and Wendy" and "Peter Pan in Kensington Gardens."* New York: Penguin, 2004.

Basinger, Jeanine. *Shirley Temple*. New York: Pyramid, 1975.

Beekman, Daniel. *The Mechanical Baby: A Popular History of Writings on the Theory and Practice of Child Raising*. New York: New American Library, 1977.

Belkin, Lisa. "The Opt-Out Revolution." *New York Times* 26 Oct. 2003: www.nytimes.com/2003/10/26/magazine/26WOMEN.html.

Benjamin, Walter. *Selected Writings.* Vol. 3. Ed. Howard Eiland and Michael W. Jennings. Cambridge, MA: Harvard UP, 2002.

———. *The Work of Art in the Age of Its Technological Reproducibility and Other Writings on Media.* Ed. Michael W. Jennings, Brigid Doherty, and Thomas Y. Levin. Cambridge, MA: Belknap P of Harvard UP, 2008.

Benziman, Galia. *Narratives of Child Neglect in Romantic and Victorian Culture.* New York: Palgrave Macmillan, 2012.

Bernstein, Robin. *Racial Innocence: Performing American Childhood from Slavery to Civil Rights.* New York: New York UP, 2011.

Bersani, Leo. *No Future: Queer Theory and the Death Drive.* Durham, NC: Duke UP, 2004.

Billingsley, Andrew, and Jeanne M. Giovannoni. *Children of the Storm: Black Children and American Child Welfare.* New York: Harcourt Brace Jovanovich, 1972.

Boas, George. *The Cult of Childhood.* London: Warburg Institute, 1966.

Booker, M. Keith. *The Post-Utopian Imagination: American Culture in the Long 1950s.* Westport, CT: Greenwood P, 2002.

Brace, Charles Loring. *The Dangerous Classes of New York.* New York: Wynkoop and Hallenbeck, 1872.

Breckinridge, Sophonisba, ed. *The Child in the City: A Series of Papers Presented at the Conferences Held during the Chicago Child Welfare Exhibit, May 11–25, 1911.* Chicago: Department of Social Investigation, Chicago School of Civics and Philanthropy, 1912.

Brown, Noel. "A New Movie-Going Public: 1930s Hollywood and the Emergence of the 'Family' Film." *Historical Journal of Film, Radio, and Television* 33.1 (April 2013): 1–23. http://dx.doi.org/10.1080/01439685.2013.764720.

Carter, Michael. "244,000 Native Sons." *Look* 29 May 1940: 8–13.

Caulfield, Philip. "Florida Mom Arrested for Letting Son, 7, Play Alone in the Park." *New York Daily News* 31 July 2014. www.nydailynews.com/news/national/florida-mom-arrested-letting-son-7-play-park-article-1.1887049.

Certeau, Michel de. *The Practice of Everyday Life.* Trans. Steven Rendall. Berkeley: U of California P, 1984.

Child Welfare League of America (CWLA). "The History of White House Conferences on Children and Youth." http://66.227.70.18/advocacy/whitehouseconfhistory.pdf.

Christensen, Pia. "Place, Space and Knowledge: Children in the Village and the City." Christensen and O'Brien 13–28.

Christensen, Pia, and Margaret O'Brien, eds. *Children in the City: Home, Neighborhood, and Community.* New York: Routledge Falmer, 2003.

"City Kids: A Survival Guide for New York Parents." *New York Magazine* 28 April 1997. Spec. issue.

Clark, Kenneth B. *Dark Ghetto: Dilemmas of Social Power.* 2nd ed. Middletown, CT: Wesleyan UP, 1989.

Clemente, Bill. "Panem in America: Crisis Economics and a Call for Political Engagement." Pharr and Clark 20–29.

Coles, Robert. "What Poor Children Know about Buildings." *Connection* (Summer 1966): 48–50.

Collins, Suzanne. *Catching Fire.* New York: Scholastic, 2009. Kindle ed.

———. *The Hunger Games.* New York: Scholastic, 2008.

———. *Mockingjay.* New York: Scholastic, 2010. Kindle ed.

Comer, James P., and Alvin F. Poussaint. *Black Child Care: How to Bring Up a Healthy Black Child in America.* New York: Pocket Books, 1975.

Coontz, Stephanie. *The Way We Never Were: American Families and the Nostalgia Trap*. New York: Basic Books, 1992.

Creekmur, Corey, and Alexander Doty. Introduction to *Out in Culture: Gay, Lesbian, and Queer Essays on Popular Culture*. Ed. Corey Creekmur and Alexander Doty. Durham, NC: Duke UP, 1995. 1–11.

Cressey, Paul. "The Community: A Social Setting for the Motion Picture." *Children and the Movies: Media Influence and the Payne Fund Controversy*. Ed. Garth S. Jowett, Ian C. Jarvie, and Kathryn H. Fuller. New York: Cambridge UP, 1996. 133–216.

Crowther, Bosley. "Boy's Coney Island Adventures Recorded in 'Little Fugitive,' Feature at Normandie." *New York Times* 7 Oct. 1953: 35.

Cunningham, Hugh. *Children and Childhood in Western Society since 1500*. 2nd ed. Edinburgh Gate, UK: Pearson Education, 2005.

Davis, Michael. *Street Gang: The Complete History of Sesame Street*. New York: Viking Adult, 2008.

Delap, Lucy. *Knowing Their Place: Domestic Service in Twentieth-Century Britain*. Oxford: Oxford UP, 2011.

Derry, Mark. "Black to the Future: Interviews with Samuel R. Delaney, Greg Tate, and Tricia Rose." *Flame Wars: The Discourse of Cyberculture*. Ed. Mark Derry. Durham, NC: Duke UP, 1994. 179–222.

Dickens, Charles. *Oliver Twist*. New York: Vintage Classics, 2012.

Dillard, Annie. *An American Childhood*. New York: Harper Perennial, 1988.

Donald, James. *Imagining the Modern City*. Minneapolis: U of Minnesota P, 1999.

Drake, St. Clair, and Horace R. Cayton. *Black Metropolis: A Study of Negro Life in a Northern City*. 1945. Revised and enlarged ed. Chicago: U of Chicago P, 1993.

"Dropout Wife: A Seattle Woman Who Walked Out on Her Family Is Part of a New Class." *Life* 17 March 1972: 34B–44.

Dube, Rebecca. "Sending Your Nine-Year-Old on the Subway Alone: Child Abuse?" *Globe and Mail* 8 April 2008. www.theglobeandmail.com/life/parenting/sending-your-nine-year-old-on-the-subway-alone-child-abuse/article570509/.

duCille, Anne. "The Shirley Temple of My Familiar." *Transition* 73 (1997): 10–32. www.jstor.org/stable/2935441.

Dudek, Mark, ed. *Children's Spaces*. Burlington, MA: Architectural Press, 2005.

Durgnat, Raymond, and Scott Simmon. *King Vidor, American*. Berkeley: U of California P, 1988.

Dyer, Richard. "Entertainment and Utopia." *Only Entertainment*. New York: Routledge, 1992. 19–35.

Eckert, Charles. "Shirley Temple and the House of Rockefeller." *Jump Cut* 2 (1974): 1, 17–20. www.ejumpcut.org/archive/onlinessays/JC02folder/shirleytemple.html.

Eisenstein, Sergei. "Dickens, Griffith, and the Film Form Today." *Sergei Eisenstein—Film Form: Essays in Film Theory*. Ed. Jay Leyda. New York: Harcourt, 1949. 195–255.

Eleftheriotis, Dimitris. "Early Cinema as Child: Historical Metaphor and European Cinephilia in *Lumiere and Company*." *Screen* 46.3 (2005): 315–328.

Ellis, Effie O. "The Quality of Life." *The Black Child*. Spec. issue of *Ebony* August 1974: 37–41.

Fischer, Lucy. *Cinematernity: Film, Motherhood, Genre*. Princeton, NJ: Princeton UP, 1996.

Fitzhugh, Louise. *Harriet the Spy*. New York: Harper and Row, 1964.

Foer, Jonathan Safran. *Extremely Loud and Incredibly Close*. New York: Houghton Mifflin, 2005.

Forbush, William Byron. *The Boy Problem*. Boston: Pilgrim Press, 1901, 1903, 1907, 1913.

Forman, Henry James. *Our Movie Made Children*. New York: Macmillan, 1934.

Freed, Leonard. *Black and White in America*. 1967/1968. Los Angeles: J. Paul Getty Museum, 2010.

Freud, Anna. "The Concept of the Rejecting Mother." Anthony and Benedek 376–386.

Freud, Sigmund. *Beyond the Pleasure Principle*. Trans. James Strachey. New York: Norton, 1961.

Friedersdorf, Conor. "Working Mom Arrested for Letting Her 9-Year Old Play Alone at Park." *Atlantic* 15 July 2014. www.theatlantic.com/national/archive/2014/07/arrested-for-letting-a-9-year-old-play-at-the-park-alone/374436/.

Fritz, Sonya Sawyer. "'New York Is a Great Place': Urban Mobility in Twentieth-Century Children's Literature." Whyte and O'Sullivan 85–96.

Frost, Leslie Anne. *Dreaming America: Popular Front Ideals and Aesthetics in Children's Plays of the Federal Theatre Project*. Columbus: Ohio State UP, 2013.

Fuller-Seeley, Kathryn. "Shirley Temple: Making Dreams Come True." *Glamour in a Golden Age: Movie Stars of the 1930s*. Ed. Adrienne McLean. New Brunswick, NJ: Rutgers UP, 2011. 44–64.

Garber, Marjorie. *Vested Interests: Cross Dressing and Cultural Anxiety*. New York: Routledge, 1997.

Garriott, Deidre Anne Evans, Whitney Elaine Jones, and Julie Elizabeth Tyler, eds. *Space and Place in "The Hunger Games": New Readings of the Novels*. Jefferson, NC: McFarland, 2014.

Gaudin, James M., Jr. *Child Neglect: A Guide for Intervention*. Washington, DC: U.S. Department of Health and Human Services, 1993. www.childwelfare.gov/pubPDFs/neglect_1993.pdf.

Gesell, Arnold. *The Guidance of Mental Growth in Infant and Child*. New York: Macmillan, 1930.

Getz, Leonard. *From Broadway to the Bowery: A History and Filmography of the Dead End Kids, Little Tough Guys, East Side Kids, and Bowery Boys Films with Cast Biographies*. Jefferson, NC: McFarland, 2006.

Gillis, John R. "Epilogue: The Islanding of Children—Reshaping the Mythical Landscapes of Childhood." Gutman and Coninck-Smith 316–330.

Ginott, Haim G. *Between Parent and Teenager*. New York: Macmillan, 1969.

Goffman, Erving. *The Presentation of Self in Everyday Life*. New York: Anchor, 1959.

Gornick, Vivian. *The Odd Woman and the City: A Memoir*. New York: Farrar, Straus and Giroux, 2015.

Gray, Harold. *The Complete Little Orphan Annie*. Vol. 1, *Will Tomorrow Ever Come? Daily Comic Strips, 1924–1927*. Library of American Comics. Ed. Dean Mullaney. San Diego, CA: IDW, 2008.

———. *The Complete Little Orphan Annie*. Vol. 2, *The Darkest Hour Is Just before the Dawn. Daily and Sunday Comics, 1927–1929*. Library of American Comics. Ed. Dean Mullaney. San Diego, CA: IDW, 2009.

———. *The Complete Little Orphan Annie*. Vol. 3, *And a Blind Man Shall Lead Them. Daily and Sunday Comics, 1929–1931*. Library of American Comics. Ed. Dean Mullaney. San Diego, CA: IDW, 2009.

———. *The Complete Little Orphan Annie*. Vol. 5, *The One-Way Road to Justice. Daily and Sunday Comics, 1933–1935*. Library of American Comics. Ed. Dean Mullaney. San Diego, CA: IDW, 2010.

———. *The Complete Little Orphan Annie.* Vol. 6, *Punjab the Wizard. Daily and Sunday Comics, 1935–1936.* Library of American Comics. Ed. Dean Mullaney. San Diego, CA: IDW, 2010.

———. *The Complete Little Orphan Annie.* Vol. 7, *The Omnipotent Mr. Am! Daily and Sunday Comics, 1936–1938.* Library of American Comics. Ed. Dean Mullaney. San Diego, CA: IDW, 2011.

———. *The Complete Little Orphan Annie.* Vol. 8, *The Last Port of Call. Daily and Sunday Comics, 1938–1940.* Library of American Comics. Ed. Dean Mullaney. San Diego, CA: IDW, 2012.

Greene, Graham. *The Graham Greene Film Reader: Reviews, Essays, Interviews and Film Stories.* Ed. David Parkinson. New York: Applause Theatre Book Publishers, 1995.

Grindon, Leger. "*The Champ* (1931/1979): Parenting and Gender." *Knockout: The Boxer and Boxing in Cinema.* Jackson: UP of Mississippi, 2011. 130–139.

Griswold, Jerry. *The Classic American Children's Story: Novels of the Golden Age.* New York: Penguin, 1996.

———. "There's No Place but Home: *The Wizard of Oz.*" *Antioch Review* 45.4 (1987): 462–475. www.jstor.org/stable/4611799.

Gubar, Marah. *Artful Dodgers: Reconceiving the Golden Age of Children's Literature.* New York: Oxford UP, 2009.

———. "Entertaining Children of All Ages: Nineteenth-Century Popular Theater as Children's Theater." *American Quarterly* 66.1 (2014): 1–34.

———. "Who Watched *The Children's Pinafore*? Age Transvestism on the Nineteenth-Century Stage." *Victorian Studies* 54.3 (2012): 410–426.

Gunning, Tom. "The Cinema of Attractions: Early Film, Its Spectator, and the Avant-Garde." *Wide Angle* 8.3–4 (1986): 63–70.

Gutman, Marta, and Ning de Coninck-Smith, eds. *Designing Modern Childhoods: History, Space, and the Material Culture of Children.* New Brunswick, NJ: Rutgers UP, 2008.

Hains, Rebecca. "The Origins of the Girl Hero: Shirley Temple, Child Star and Commodity." *Girlhood Studies* 1.1 (2008): 60–80. http://dx.doi:10.3167/ghs.2008.010105.

Hall, Joanne. "The Wanderer Contained: Issues of 'Inside' and 'Outside' in Relation to Harold Gray's 'Little Orphan Annie' and Marilynne Robinson's *Housekeeping.*" *Critical Survey* 18.3 (2006): 37–50.

Hamilton, Virginia. *The Planet of Junior Brown.* 1971. New York: Aladdin Paperbacks, 2006.

Hampton, Gregory Jerome, and Wanda M. Brooks. "Octavia Butler and Virginia Hamilton: Black Women Writers and Science Fiction." *English Journal* 92.6 (2003): 70–74.

Hampton, Jane. "Robbing the Cradle for Stars." *Photoplay* Nov. 1934: 34–35, 98.

Hansen, Miriam Bratu. *Cinema and Experience: Siegfried Kracauer, Walter Benjamin, and Theodor W. Adorno.* Berkeley: U of California P, 2012.

———. "Fallen Women, Rising Stars, New Horizons: Shanghai Silent Film as Vernacular Modernism." *Film Quarterly* 54.1 (2000): 10–22.

———. "The Mass Production of the Senses: Classical Cinema as Vernacular Modernism." *Modernism/Modernity* 6.2 (1999): 59–77. Reprinted in *Reinventing Film Studies.* Ed. Christine Gledhill and Linda Williams. New York: Oxford UP, 2000. 332–350. Citations refer to the reprint.

———. "Room-for-Play: Benjamin's Gamble with Cinema." *October* 109 (Summer 2004): 3–46.

———. "Tracking Cinema on a Global Scale." *The Oxford Handbook of Global Modernisms.* Ed. Mark Wollaeger and Matt Eatough. New York: Oxford UP, 2012. 601–626.

Hardyment, Christina. *Dream Babies: Child Care from Locke to Spock*. New York: Oxford UP, 1984.

Hark, Ina Rae. "Moviegoing, 'Home-Leaving,' and the Problematic Girl Protagonist of *The Wizard of Oz*." *Sugar, Spice, and Everything Nice: Cinemas of Girlhood*. Ed. Frances Gateward and Murray Pomerance. Detroit: Wayne State UP, 2002. 25–38.

Hatch, Kristin. "Discipline and Pleasure: Shirley Temple and the Spectacle of Child Loving." *Camera Obscura* 79, 27.1 (2012): 127–155.

———. *Shirley Temple and the Performance of Girlhood*. New Brunswick, NJ: Rutgers UP, 2015.

A Healthy Personality for Every Child: A Digest of the Fact Finding Report to the Midcentury White House Conference on Children and Youth. Raleigh, NC: Health Publications Institute, 1951.

Heer, Jeet. "A Dickens of a World: Annie's Literary Ancestors." Gray 2:11–21.

———. "Dream Big and Work Hard." Gray 1:11–27.

———. "The Economy of Little Orphan Annie." Gray 3:9–18.

———. "Punjab and Politics." Gray 6:5–12.

Hesford, Victoria. *Feeling Women's Liberation*. Durham, NC: Duke UP, 2013.

Heynen, Hilde. "Modernity and Domesticity: Tensions and Contradictions." *Negotiating Domesticity: Spatial Productions of Gender in Modern Architecture*. Ed. Hilde Heynen and Gülsüm Baydar. London: Routledge, 2005. 1–29.

Highmore, Ben. "Hopscotch Modernism: On Everyday Life and the Blurring of Art and Social Science." *Modernist Culture* 2.1 (2006): 70–79.

Hillman, Mayer, John Adams, and John Whitelegg. *One False Move . . . A Study of Children's Independent Mobility*. London: Policy Institute, 1990.

Hoben, Allen. "The Child in the City." Breckinridge 451–460.

Holloway, Sarah L., and Gill Valentine, eds. *Children's Geographies: Playing, Living, Learning*. New York: Routledge, 2000.

Horning, Kathleen T. "On Spies and Purple Socks and Such." *Horn Book Magazine* Jan.-Feb. 2005: 49–55.

Hörschelmann, Kathrin, and Lorraine van Blerk. *Children, Youth, and the City*. New York: Routledge, 2012.

Hugo, Victor. *Les Misérables*. N.p.: Ignacio Hills Press, 2008. Kindle ed.

Hulbert, Ann. *Raising America: Experts, Parents, and a Century of Advice about Children*. New York: Vintage, 2003.

Hutcheon, Linda. *A Theory of Parody: The Teaching of Twentieth-Century Art Forms*. New York: Methuen, 1985.

Illick, Joseph. *American Childhoods*. Philadelphia: U of Pennsylvania P, 2002.

Jacobs, Jane. *The Death and Life of Great American Cities*. New York: Random House, 1961.

Jackson, Kathy Merlock. *Images of Children in American Film: A Sociocultural Analysis*. Metuchen, NJ: Scarecrow, 1986.

Jenkins, Henry. "Introduction: Childhood Innocence and Other Modern Myths." *The Children's Culture Reader*. Ed. Henry Jenkins. New York: New York UP, 1998. 1–37.

Jones, Owain. "Little Figures, Big Shadows: Country Childhood Stories." *Contested Countryside Cultures: Otherness, Marginalisation, and Rurality*. Ed. Paul Cloke and Jo Little. New York: Routledge, 1997. 158–179.

———. "'True Geography [ ] Quickly Forgotten, Giving Away to an Adult-Imagined Universe.' Approaching the Otherness of Childhood." *Children's Geographies* 6.2 (2008): 195–208.

Jowett, Garth S., Ian C. Jarvie, and Kathryn H. Fuller. *Children and the Movies: Media Influence and the Payne Fund Controversy*. New York: Cambridge UP, 1996.

Key, Ellen. *The Century of the Child*. Originally published G. P. Putnam and Sons, 1909. Reprint, New York: Arno Press and the New York Times, 1972.

———. *The Renaissance of Motherhood*. Trans. from Swedish by Anna E. B. Fried. New York: Knickerbocker Press, 1914.

Kincaid, James. *Child Loving: The Erotic Child and Victorian Literature*. New York: Routledge, 1994.

———. *Erotic Innocence: The Culture of Child Molesting*. Durham, NC: Duke UP, 1998.

Kinchin, Juliet, and Aidan O'Connor, eds. *Century of the Child: Growing by Design, 1900–2000*. New York: Museum of Modern Art, 2012.

King, Rob. "The Kid from *The Kid*: Jackie Coogan and the Consolidation of Child Consumerism." *Velvet Light Trap* 48 (Fall 2001): 4–19.

Kingsley, Sidney. *Dead End: A Play in Three Acts*. New York: Random House, 1936.

Klein, Amanda Ann. *American Film Cycles: Reframing Genres, Screening Social Problems, and Defining Subcultures*. Austin: U of Texas P, 2011.

Koenig, Gretchen. "Communal Spectacle: Reshaping History and Memory through Violence." Pharr and Clark 39–48.

Kozlovsky, Roy. "Adventure Playgrounds and Postwar Reconstruction." Gutman and Coninck-Smith 171–190.

Kracauer, Siegfried. *Theory of Film*. Princeton, NJ: Princeton UP, 1997.

Lawrence, Michael. "Juvenile Performance and International Cooperation in *The Pied Piper* (1942) and *Heavenly Days* (1944): Hollywood Cinema and the Children of the Nations during World War II." Paper presented at the Society for Cinema and Media Studies Conference, Boston, 23 March 2012.

Lebeau, Vicky. *Childhood and Cinema*. London: Reaktion, 2008.

Lefebvre, Henri. *The Production of Space*. Trans. Donald Nicholson-Smith. 1974. Oxford: Blackwell, 1991.

———. *Right to the City*. In *Writings on Cities*. Trans. and ed. Eleonore Kofman and Elizabeth Lebas. 1968. Oxford: Blackwell, 2003. 63–181.

Levander, Caroline F., and Carol J. Singley, eds. *The American Child: A Cultural Studies Reader*. New Brunswick, NJ: Rutgers UP, 2003.

Levy, David M. "The Concept of Maternal Overprotection." Anthony and Benedek 387–409.

Lewis, Oscar. "The Culture of Poverty." *Scientific American* Oct. 1966: 19–25.

Lindenmeyer, Kriste. *The Greatest Generation Grows Up: American Childhood in the 1930s*. Chicago: Ivan R. Dee, 2005.

Logan, John R., and Harvey L. Molotoch. *Urban Fortunes: The Political Economy of Place*. 20th anniversary ed. Berkeley: U of California P, 2007.

Lowry, Richard S. "Lewis Hines's Family Romance." Levander and Singley 184–207.

Lukashok, Alvin K., and Kevin Lynch. "Some Childhood Memories of the City." *Journal of the American Institute of Planners* 22.3 (1956): 142–152.

Lury, Karen. *The Child in Film: Tears, Fears, and Fairytales*. New Brunswick, NJ: Rutgers UP, 2010.

Lynch, Kevin, ed. *Growing Up in Cities: Studies of the Spatial Environment of Adolescence in Cracow, Melbourne, Mexico City, Salta, Toluca, and Warszawa*. Cambridge, MA: MIT Press, 1977.

Lythcott-Haims, Julie. *How to Raise an Adult: Break Free of the Overparenting Trap and Prepare Your Kids for Success*. New York: Henry Holt, 2015. Kindle ed.

Marcus, Sharon. *Apartment Stories: City and Home in Nineteenth-Century Paris and London*. Berkeley: U of California P, 1999.

Massood, Paula J. *Black City Cinema: African American Urban Experiences in Film*. Philadelphia: Temple UP, 2003.

———. *Making a Promised Land: Harlem in 20th-Century Photography and Film*. New Brunswick, NJ: Rutgers UP, 2013.

Matchar, Emily. *Homeward Bound: Why Women Are Embracing the New Domesticity*. New York: Simon and Schuster, 2013.

Matthews, Hugh. "The Street as Liminal Space: The Barbed Spaces of Childhood." Christensen and O'Brien 101–117.

Matthews, Hugh, Melanie Limb, and Mark Taylor. "The 'Street as Third Space.'" *Children's Geographies: Playing, Living, Learning*. Ed. Sarah L. Holloway and Gill Valentine. New York: Routledge, 2000. 63–79.

May, Elaine Tyler. *Homeward Bound: American Families in the Cold War Era*. New York: Basic Books, 1988.

Merish, Lori. "Cuteness and Commodity Aesthetics: Tom Thumb and Shirley Temple." *Freakery: Cultural Spectacles of the Extraordinary Body*. Ed. Rosemarie Garland Thomson. New York: New York UP, 1996. 185–203.

Michael, Jennifer, and Madeleine Goldstein. "Reviving the White House Conference on Children." Child Welfare League of America. www.cwla.org/reviving-the-white-house-conference-on-children/.

Miller, Warren. *The Cool World*. Boston: Little, Brown, 1959.

Mintz, Steven. *Huck's Raft: A History of American Childhood*. Cambridge, MA: Belknap P of Harvard UP, 2004.

Mitchell, Claudia, and Jacqueline Reid-Walsh. *Researching Children's Popular Culture: Spaces of Childhood*. New York: Routledge, 2002.

Mitchell, Sally. *The New Girl: Girls' Culture in England, 1880–1915*. New York: Columbia UP, 1995.

Moynihan, Daniel P. *The Negro Family: The Case for National Action*. Washington, DC: U.S. Government Printing Office, 1965.

Mulvey, Laura. "Visual Pleasure and Narrative Cinema." *Issues in Feminist Film Criticism*. Ed. Patricia Erens. Bloomington: Indiana UP, 1990. 28–40.

Nasaw, David. *Children of the City: At Work and at Play*. New York: Oxford UP, 1985.

Nelson, Alondra. "'Making Possible the Impossible': An Interview with Nalo Hopkinson." *Afrofuturism*. Spec. issue of *Social Text* 71 (Summer 2002): 97–114.

Nelson, Claudia. "Drying the Orphan's Tear: Changing Representations of the Dependent Child in America, 1870–1930." *Children's Literature* 29 (2001): 52–72.

———. "The Lady or the Tiger? The Shifting Gender of the Girl Citizen." Keynote address delivered at "Fun with Dick and Jane: Gender and Childhood," University of Notre Dame, 5 Dec. 2014.

———. *Little Strangers: Portrayals of Adoption and Foster Care in America, 1850–1929*. Bloomington: Indiana UP, 2003.

———. *Precocious Children and Childish Adults: Age Inversion in Victorian Literature*. Baltimore: Johns Hopkins UP, 2012.

Nodelman, Perry. *The Hidden Adult: Defining Children's Literature*. Baltimore: Johns Hopkins UP, 2008.

O'Brien, Margaret, Deborah Jones, David Sloan, and Michael Rustin. "Children's Independent Spatial Mobility in the Urban Public Realm." *Childhood* 7.3 (2000): 257–277.

Ogata, Amy. *Designing the Creative Child: Playthings and Places in Midcentury America.* Minneapolis: U of Minnesota P, 2013.

Olsen, Liesl. *Modernism and the Ordinary.* New York: Oxford UP, 2009.

Parr, Albert Eide. "The Child in the City: Urbanity and the Urban Scene." *Landscape* 16.3 (1967): 3–5.

Paul, Lissa. "Enigma Variations: What Feminist Theory Knows about Children's Literature." *Children's Literature: The Development of Criticism.* Ed. Peter Hunt. New York: Routledge, 1990. 148–165.

Penn, Helen. "Spaces without Children." *Children's Spaces.* Ed. Mark Dudek. Burlington, MA: Architectural Press, 2005. 178–194.

Petry, Ann. *The Street.* 1946. New York: Houghton Mifflin, 1998.

Pharr, Mary F., and Leisa A. Clark, eds. *Of Bread, Blood, and "The Hunger Games": Critical Essays on the Suzanne Collins Trilogy.* Jefferson, NC: McFarland, 2012.

Pike, David L. "Buried Pleasure: Doctor Doolittle, Walter Benjamin, and the Nineteenth-Century Child." *Modernism/Modernity* 17.4 (2010): 857–875.

Pogrebin, Lettie Cottin. "Do Americans Hate Children?" *Ms. Magazine* Nov. 1983: 47–50, 126–127.

Pryor, Thomas M. "Prelude to 'The Quiet One,' or the Story of How Four Determined Young People Developed an Experimental Idea into an Unusual Theatrical Film." *New York Times* 9 Jan. 1949: *ProQuest.*

Rainwater, Lee. *Behind Ghetto Walls: Black Families in a Federal Slum.* Piscataway, NJ: Aldine Transaction, 2006.

Relph, E. *Place and Placelessness.* London: Pion, 1976.

Ress, Stella. "Bridging the Generation Gap: Little Orphan Annie in the Great Depression." *Journal of Popular Culture* 43.4 (2010): 782–800.

Riesman, David. *The Lonely Crowd: A Study of the Changing American Character.* New Haven, CT: Yale UP, 1950.

Riis, Jacob. *How the Other Half Lives: Studies among the Tenements of New York.* 1890. New York: Dover, 1971.

Riviere, Joan. "Womanliness as a Masquerade." 1929. *Formations of Fantasy.* Ed. Victor Burgin, James Donald, and Cora Kaplan. London: Methuen, 1986.

Robertson, Pamela. "Home and Away: Friends of Dorothy on the Road in Oz." *The Road Movie Book.* Ed. Steven Cohan and Ina Rae Hark. New York: Routledge, 1997. 271–286.

Robson, Catherine. *Men in Wonderland: The Lost Girlhood of Victorian Gentlemen.* Princeton, NJ: Princeton UP, 2001.

Rose, Jacqueline. *The Case of Peter Pan, or the Impossibility of Children's Fiction.* Philadelphia: U of Pennsylvania P, 1984.

Rosin, Hanna. "Hey! Parents, Leave Those Kids Alone." *Atlantic* April 2014: 75–86.

Rousseau, Jean-Jacques. *Emile; or, On Education.* New York: Basic Books, 1979.

Rushdie, Salman. "A Short Text about Magic." *The Wizard of Oz.* London: British Film Institute, 1992. 9–57.

Sammond, Nicholas. *Babes in Tomorrowland: Walt Disney and the Making of the American Child, 1930 to 1960.* Durham, NC: Duke UP, 2005.

Sanchez-Eppler, Karen. "Playing at Class." Levander and Singley 40–62.

Sanders, James. *Celluloid Skyline: New York and the Movies.* New York: Alfred A. Knopf, 2002.

Sanders, Joe Sutliff. *Disciplining Girls: Understanding the Origins of the Classic Orphan Girl Story.* Baltimore: Johns Hopkins UP, 2011.

Sedgwick, Eve Kosofsky. "Tales of the Avunculate: *The Importance of Being Earnest*." *Tendencies*. Durham, NC: Duke UP, 1993. 52–72.

Seldes, Gilbert. "Two Great Women: Intimations of the Mae West of Tomorrow on Seeing the Shirley Temple of Today." *Esquire* July 1935: 86, 143.

Shaffer, George. "Shirley Temple Is Bowery Kid in New Movie: Reporter Visits Studio Set of Child Star." *Chicago Daily Tribune* 18 June 1936: 18. *ProQuest*.

Sieving, Christopher. *Soul Searching: Black-Themed Cinema from the March on Washington to the Rise of Blaxploitation*. Middletown, CT: Wesleyan UP, 2011.

Simmel, Georg. "The Stranger." *The Sociology of Georg Simmel*. Trans. and ed. Kurt H. Wolff. New York: Free Press, 1950. 402–403.

Skenazy, Lenore. *Free-Range Kids: How to Raise Safe, Self-Reliant Children (without Going Nuts with Worry)*. New York: Jossey-Bass, 2010.

———. "Why I Let My 9 Year Old Ride the Subway Alone." *New York Sun* 1 April 2008. www.nysun.com/news/why-i-let-my-9-year-old-ride-subway-alone.

Sklar, Robert. *City Boys: Cagney, Bogart, Garfield*. Princeton, NJ: Princeton UP, 1992.

Slaughter, Anne Marie. "Why Women Can't Have It All." *Atlantic* July-August 2012: 84–100.

Smith, Betty. *A Tree Grows in Brooklyn*. 1943. New York: Harper Perennial, 2001.

Stahl, J. D. "Louise Fitzhugh, Marisol, and the Realm of Art." *Children's Literature Association Quarterly* 24.4 (1999): 159–165.

———. "Satire and the Evolution of Perspective in Children's Literature: Mark Twain, E. B. White, and Louise Fitzhugh." *Children's Literature Association Quarterly* 15.3 (1990): 119–122.

Steedman, Caroline. *Strange Dislocations: Childhood and the Idea of Human Interiority, 1780–1930*. Cambridge, MA: Harvard UP, 1995.

Stewart, Susan Louise. "In the Ellison Tradition: In/Visible Bodies of Adolescent and YA Fiction." *Children's Literature in Education* 40.3 (2009): 180–196.

Stockton, Kathryn Bond. *The Queer Child; or, Growing Sideways in the Twentieth Century*. Durham, NC: Duke UP, 2009.

"The Strange Case of Jackie Coogan's $4,000,000." *Life* April 1938: 50.

Studlar, Gaylyn. *Precocious Charms: Stars Performing Girlhood in Classical Hollywood Cinema*. Berkeley: U of Californian P, 2013.

Tan, Susan Shau Ming. "The Making of the Citizen and the Politics of Maturation." Garriott, Jones, and Tyler 83–101.

Thompson, Kay. *Eloise*. 1955. New York: Simon and Schuster, 2005.

Travers, P. L. *Mary Poppins*. 1934. New York: Harcourt Brace Jovanovich, 1962.

Tribunella, Eric L. "Children's Literature and the Child Flâneur." *Children's Literature* 38 (2010): 64–91.

Trites, Roberta Seelinger. "'I double never ever lie to my chil'ren': Inside People in Virginia Hamilton's Narratives." *African American Review* 32.1 (1998): 147–156.

Turner, Jeffrey. "On Boyhood and Public Swimming: Sidney Kingsley's *Dead End* and Representations of Underclass Street Kids in American Cultural Production." Levander and Singley 208–225.

Urwick, Edward Johns, ed. *Studies of Boy Life in Our Cities*. London: J. M. Dent, 1904.

U.S. Department of Health and Human Services (DHHS). *Study of National Incidence and Prevalence of Child Abuse and Neglect*. Washington, DC: DHHS, 1988.

Valentine, Gill. *Public Space and the Culture of Childhood*. Burlington, VT: Ashgate, 2004.

Varty, Ann. *Children and Theatre in Victorian Britain: "All Work, No Play."* London: Palgrave Macmillan, 2008.

Vered, Karen Orr. "White and Black in Black and White: Management of Race and Sexuality in the Coupling of Shirley Temple and Bill Robinson." *Velvet Light Trap* 39 (Spring 1997): 52–65.

Vogel, Amos. *How Little Lori Visited Times Square*. Pictures by Maurice Sendak. 1963. New York: HarperCollins, 1991.

Ward, Colin. *The Child in the City*. New York: Pantheon, 1978.

Warner, Judith. *Perfect Madness: Motherhood in the Age of Anxiety*. New York: Riverhead Books, 2006. Kindle ed.

Watson, John B. "Against the Threat of Mother Love." *The Children's Culture Reader*. Ed. Henry Jenkins. New York: New York UP, 1998. 470–475.

———. *The Psychological Care of Infant and Child*. New York: Norton, 1928.

Wergin, Clemens. "The Case for Free-Range Parenting." *New York Times* 20 March 2015: A7.

Whyte, Pàdraic, and Keith O'Sullivan, eds. *Children's Literature and New York City*. New York: Routledge, 2014.

Whyte, William H. *The Organization Man*. Garden City, NY: Doubleday, 1957.

Williams, Raymond. *The Country and the City*. New York: Oxford UP, 1973.

———. *Marxism and Literature*. New York: Oxford UP, 1978.

Wilson, Michael. "The Legacy of Etan Patz: Wary Children Who Became Watchful Parents." *New York Times* 8 May 2015: www.nytimes.com/2015/05/10/nyregion/etan-patzs-disappearance-has-a-lasting-impact-on-parenting.html.

Windeler, Robert. *The Films of Shirley Temple*. Secaucus, NJ: Citadel P, 1978.

Witmer, Helen Leland, and Ruth Kotinsky, eds. *Personality in the Making: The Fact Finding Report of the Midcentury White House Conference on Children and Youth*. New York: Harper and Brothers, 1952.

Wojcik, Pamela Robertson. *The Apartment Plot: Urban Living in American Film and Popular Culture, 1945 to 1975*. Durham, NC: Duke UP, 2010.

Wojcik-Andrews, Ian. *Children's Films: History, Ideology, Pedagogy, Theory*. New York: Routledge, 2000.

Wolff, Janet. "The Invisible *Flâneuse*: Women and the Literature of Modernity." *Feminine Sentences: Essays on Women and Culture*. Berkeley: U of California P, 1990. 34–50.

Womack, Ytasha L. *Afrofuturism: The World of Black Sci-Fi and Fantasy Culture*. Chicago: Lawrence Hill, 2013.

Wood, Robin. "Images of Childhood." *Explorations in Film: Personal Views*. Revised ed. Detroit: Wayne State UP, 2006. 189–212.

Wright, Richard. *Native Son*. 1940. New York: Harper Perennial Modern Classics, 2005.

———. *12 Million Black Voices*. 1941. New York: Basic Books, 2008.

Wylie, Philip. *Generation of Vipers*. New York: Rinehart, 1942.

Yamin, Priscilla. "The Search for Marital Order: Civic Membership and the Politics of Marriage in the Progressive Era." *Polity* 41.1 (2009): 86–112.

Zeiher, Helga. "Children's Islands in Space and Time." *Childhood in Europe: Approaches, Trends, Findings*. Ed. Manuela du Bois-Reymond, Heinz Sünker, and Heinz Hermann Krüger. New York: Peter Lang, 2001. 139–160.

———. "Shaping Daily Life in Urban Environments." Christensen and O'Brien 66–81.

Zelizer, Viviana A. *Pricing the Priceless Child: The Changing Social Value of Children*. Princeton, NJ: Princeton UP, 1985.

Zhang Zhen. *An Amorous History of the Silver Screen: Shanghai Cinema, 1896–1937*. Chicago: U of Chicago P, 2006.

Zierold, Norman J. *The Child Stars*. New York: Coward-McCann, 1965.

Index

About the Author

PAMELA ROBERTSON WOJCIK is a professor in the Department of Film, TV, and Theatre at the University of Notre Dame. She is author of *The Apartment Plot: Urban Living in American Film and Popular Culture, 1945 to 1975* and *Guilty Pleasures: Feminist Camp from Mae West to Madonna*; and editor of *New Constellations: Movie Stars of the 1960s, Movie Acting: The Film Reader*, and, with Arthur Knight, *Soundtrack Available: Essays on Film and Popular Music.* She lives in Chicago and, with her husband, is raising two urban children.